From Adam to Christ

FROM ADAM TO CHRIST

Essays on Paul

MORNA D. HOOKER

*Lady Margaret's Professor of Divinity, University of Cambridge
and Fellow of Robinson College, Cambridge*

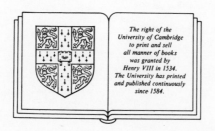

The right of the
University of Cambridge
to print and sell
all manner of books
was granted by
Henry VIII in 1534.
The University has printed
and published continuously
since 1584.

CAMBRIDGE UNIVERSITY PRESS

CAMBRIDGE

NEW YORK   PORT CHESTER

MELBOURNE   SYDNEY

Published by the Press Syndicate of the University of Cambridge
The Pitt Building, Trumpington Street, Cambridge CB2 1RP
40 West 20th Street, New York, NY 10011, USA
10 Stamford Road, Oakleigh, Melbourne 3166, Australia

First published 1990

Printed in Great Britain at the University Press, Cambridge

British Library cataloguing in publication data
Hooker, Morna D. (Morna Dorothy), *1931–*
From Adam to Christ
1. Bible N.T. Epistles of Paul. Special
subjects: Christian doctrine. Atonement
1. Title
232'.3

Library of Congress cataloguing in publication data
Hooker, Morna Dorothy.
From Adam to Christ: essays on Paul / Morna D. Hooker.
p.   cm.
ISBN 0-521-34317-8
1. Bible. N.T. Epistles of Paul – Theology. 2. Bible. N.T.
Epistles of Paul – Criticism, interpretation, etc. 1. Title.
BS2651.H63   1990
227'.06 – dc20
89-33199 CIP

ISBN 0 521 34317 8

CONTENTS

ACKNOWLEDGEMENTS

The following chapters originally appeared in the publications indicated:

1 'Interchange in Christ', *Journal of Theological Studies*, NS 22 (1971).
2 'Interchange and atonement', *Bulletin of the John Rylands University Library of Manchester*, 60 (1978).
3 'Interchange and suffering' in W. Horbury and B. McNeil (eds.), *Suffering and Martyrdom in the New Testament, Studies presented to G. M. Styler by the Cambridge New Testament Seminar* (Cambridge, 1981).
4 'Interchange in Christ and ethics', *Journal of the Study of the New Testament*, 25 (1985).
5 'Adam in Romans 1', *New Testament Studies*, 6 (1960).
6 'A further note on Romans 1', *New Testament Studies*, 13 (1967).
7 'Philippians 2.6–11' in E. E. Ellis and E. Grasser (eds.), *Jesus und Paulus, Festschrift für W. G. Kümmel* (Göttingen, 1975).
8 'Hard sayings: 1 Corinthians 3.2', *Theology*, 69 (1966).
9 '"Beyond the things which are written": an examination of 1 Corinthians 4.6', *New Testament Studies*, 10 (1964).
10 'Authority on her head: an examination of 1 Corinthians 11.10', *New Testament Studies*, 10 (1964).
11 'Were there false teachers in Colossae?' in B. Lindars and S. S. Smalley (eds.), *Christ and Spirit in the New Testament, Studies in Honour of Charles Francis Digby Moule* (Cambridge, 1973).
12 'Beyond the things that are written? St Paul's use of scripture', *New Testament Studies*, 27 (1981).
13 'Paul and "covenantal nomism"' in M. D. Hooker and S. G. Wilson (eds.), *Paul and Paulinism, essays in honour of C. K. Barrett* (London, 1982).
14. 'Πίστις Χριστοῦ', *New Testament Studies*, 35 (1989).

ABBREVIATIONS

ASNU	*Acta Seminarii Neotestamentici Upsaliensis*
Bibl	*Biblica*
BJRL	*Bulletin of the John Rylands Library*
CBQ	*Catholic Biblical Quarterly*
Exp.Tim.	*Expository Times*
FRLANT	*Forschungen zur Religion and Literatur des Alten und Neuen Testaments*
HTR	*Harvard Theological Review*
ICC	*International Critical Commentary*
JBL	*Journal of Biblical Literature*
JSOT	*Journal of the Study of the Old Testament*
JThCh	*Journal for Theology and Church*
JTS	*Journal of Theological Studies*
NT	*Novum Testamentum*
NTD	*Das Neue Testament Deutsch*
NTS	*New Testament Studies*
SNTS	Studiorum Novi Testamenti Societas
TDNT	*Theological Dictionary of the New Testament*
TWNT	*Theologisches Wörterbuch zum Neuen Testament*
ZNTW	*Zeitschrift für die neutestamentliche Wissenschaft*
ZThK	*Zeitschrift für Theologie und Kirche*

AV	Authorized Version
NEB	New English Bible
RSV	Revised Standard Version
RV	Revised Version

Babylonian Talmud tractates

Ab.Zar	Abodah Zarah
Erub.	Erubin
Sab.	Sabbath

Sanh.	Sanhedrin
Yeb.	Yebamoth

Pseudepigrapha

Apoc.Abr.	Apocalypse of Abraham
Apoc.Moses	Apocalypse of Moses

Further abbreviations

Eccles. Rab.	Ecclesiastes Rabbah
Exod.Rab.	Exodus Rabbah
Gen.Rab.	Genesis Rabbah
Num.Rab.	Numbers Rabbah
P.R.E.	Pirqei deRabbi Eliezer

Introduction

The essays in this volume were written over a period of thirty years, and attempt to deal with diverse problems in Paul's writings. No doubt my understanding of Paul's thinking has changed and developed in the course of that time: I hope I am closer to comprehending him than when I began, though I frequently find myself baffled by him. Whenever I imagine I have grasped the true significance of his arguments, I find myself stumbling over a passage which apparently undermines my interpretation. It is well to remember that Paul's own thinking also changed and developed over the course of the years. I do not share the belief of those who suppose that his views shifted so radically that no reconciliation between his earlier and later views is possible, but certainly his understanding of the Christian gospel changed and deepened, as he sought to understand its implications in different contexts. Moreover, those different contexts influenced the way in which he expressed the gospel, since in applying it to a particular situation he used terms which were appropriate to that situation. Paul was a pragmatic theologian, not a systematic one, and any attempt to reduce his thinking to a system runs the danger of distorting him. What he gave us is a series of documents, written in response to different situations, dating from different periods of his life. Taken together, the letters which are discussed here offer more agreements than disparities. Apparent contradictions may be due to Paul handling topics in somewhat different ways in different circumstances; they may also be the result of our misunderstanding of the context in which Paul's statements were intended to be heard.

Because Paul writes for particular situations, his teaching is shaped by the particular circumstances which he is addressing; if we are to understand any of his letters, we must attempt to discover its original context. But Paul himself must also be seen in context. What manner of man was he, and what was his basic understanding of the gospel? In recent years we have become aware of the danger of reading Paul in the light of later situations: we have learned to be wary of imposing the doctrinal problems of later centuries on his words. But it is easier to strip away the false interpretations than to uncover the true Paul. One conclusion has emerged, however, and that is the thoroughgoing Jewishness of Paul's thinking. The consensus of scholarly opinion now recognizes that most (if not all) our New Testament documents were written by men who were soaked in Jewish thought. In modern, sociological terms, New Testament Christianity is seen as a Jewish sect; in Paul's eyes, it was the fulfilment of Judaism: both interpretations stress the continuity between the old faith and the new, which is at least as important as the discontinuity. To be sure, Paul says some very harsh things about his fellow-Jews, and some very negative things about the Law. But the former result from the failure of Jews to respond to the gospel – a failure which entails, in Paul's eyes, their own condemnation – while the latter are caused by the attempts by some Christians to put themselves under the Law, not realizing that the Law, having been brought to fulfilment in Christ, now belonged to a former age. The subsequent break between Judaism and Christianity was inevitable, but this break led to an emphasis on everything that was new in Christianity, and a downplaying of everything that linked the two religions together: as tensions increased, it meant that Paul's statements about the Law were now interpreted as anti-Jewish. By the time of the Reformers, the apostle to the Gentiles had come to be treated as an honorary Gentile, so that his use of the word 'we' was naturally understood as a reference to 'we Christians', never as meaning 'we Jews'; Luther's antithesis between Law and Grace sharpened the division between old and new; and Paul's concern for the people of God sank into the background, as preachers emphasized the doctrine of the justification of the individual believer by grace alone. Certainly we shall understand Paul himself better if we remember that even in Galatians, his most bitter and strident letter, he dismisses the suggestion that the Law is contrary to the promises of God as absurd (Gal. 3.21); the Law is the authority he uses to back all his arguments, and it is superseded only because the one to whom it points has come. Paul is truly a 'Hebrew of Hebrews', and if he now regards his birthright as dross, it is only because Christ is the fulfilment of all the Law's promises. Every argument that Paul uses for the gospel is based on Jewish premises. His faith is an amalgam of Jewish hopes and Christian experience, seen in terms of promise and fulfilment; of course the experience goes beyond the expectation, but its interpretation and expression are primarily Jewish.

One important corollary of this understanding is the realization that

Paul saw redemption primarily in corporate terms. His concern is with the whole people of God. True, individuals become members of that community by personal faith; but in doing so they are incorporated into 'the Israel of God' (Gal. 6.16). An interesting practical example of the difference which our overall understanding of Paul makes on our interpretation of an epistle can be seen in Romans. Older exegetes were puzzled by Paul's discussion of the fate of Israel in chapters 9–11; this section of the letter tended to be seen as an irrelevance to his main theme, attached only loosely to the exposition of justification by grace in chapters 1–8. The realization that Paul interprets the gospel primarily in corporate, rather than individualistic, terms allows us to see Romans 9–11 as the climax of his argument, rather than as an afterthought. His concern is with God's dealings with those whom he regards as his people – a group once limited to the physical descendants of Abraham, but now embracing the whole of humanity, since both 'the fulness of the Gentiles' and 'all Israel' are included (Rom. 11.25f).

As a Jew, Paul had seen God's dealings with mankind in terms of his covenant relationship with Israel. Gentiles were outsiders to that covenant, and had no share in the promises of God. As a Christian, he continued to think in corporate terms. But now he understood God's salvation as embracing the whole of mankind. No longer did he believe that God's purpose was confined to Israel: the gospel was 'the power of God to salvation for all who believe – the Jew first, and the Gentile' (Rom. 1.16). This is why the only figure who is truly comparable to Christ is Adam, the father of the whole human race: in Christ a new creation comes into being, in which there is no distinction between Jew and Gentile. God's purpose of redemption is now understood to include men and women of every race. But this in no way undermines the past – rather it confirms it; even the Law is established, not destroyed, by the gospel (Rom. 3.31). Thus Abraham is a model for Christian faith: he believed in God, who brought life out of dead bodies; all who believe are 'sons' of Abraham, inheritors of God's covenant promises, whether Jew of Gentile, male or female, slave or free. This is effected through incorporation into Christ, who is described in Galatians as the true seed of Abraham. But the 'seed' is greater than Abraham, for by incorporation into Christ, believers become not only 'sons of Abraham' but 'sons of God': the glory lost by Adam is restored to mankind.

This glory was glimpsed by Moses on Sinai. One might have expected Paul to regard Moses – the greatest figure in Jewish history – as parallel to Christ. But Paul now views Moses as a temporary figure who points forward to Christ, 'minister' of the covenant between God and Israel, whereas Christ is the very embodiment of God's glory. Thus Paul boldly compares himself, as minister of the new covenant, with Moses, God's earlier spokesman, and maintains the superiority of his own ministry to that of Moses (2 Cor. 3). Once again, Moses is not a great enough figure to stand in comparison with Christ. Adam is the only figure with universal significance, and in contrast to Adam, Christ is the true εἰκὼν Θεοῦ, who embodies the light of God's creation (2 Cor. 4.4,6).

The true model for understanding Paul's interpretation of the relationship between the old and the new is not antithesis but fulfilment. Paul does not abandon his belief in the God who called Abraham and who revealed himself to Moses. But he has to adapt his understanding of the past to his experience of the present. Why, then, the antithetical statements? Why the apparent denigration of the Law? It is because the fulfilment is eschatological; by their incorporation into Christ, believers have become incorporated into redeemed humanity, and have entered a new existence. Anything belonging to the old existence thus belongs to the sphere of σάρξ, not πνεῦμα. Even God's greatest gift to Israel, the Law, belongs to the sphere of flesh, and is thus temporary. This is why Paul views the Galatians' attempt to subject themselves to the authority of the Law with such horror: to accept circumcision and put themselves under the Law is to abandon life in the Spirit for life in the flesh, to reject the joys of the New Age for the frustrations of the Old. As a Jew, Paul rejoiced in God's gifts to Israel – 'sonship, glory, covenants, law, service, promises' (Rom. 9.4); he was proud of his background and achievements (Phil. 3.5f). But by comparison with life in the New Age, which he enjoys through union with Christ, he considers his former privileges to be rubbish. He does not deny that these gifts are from God, or that they are good, but they belong to the realm of flesh, and as such they are obsolete.

It is no accident that several of the essays in this book (chs. 2–4, and 14) discuss the theme of 'interchange in Christ'. It has long been my belief that Paul's notion of participation in Christ (conveyed in such phrases as 'in Christ' and 'with Christ') is the key to understanding his Christology, and these essays explore various aspects of that relationship. To be sure, the word 'interchange' is not a wholly satisfactory word to express this idea: it suggests an exchange, whereas what we have in mind is a mutual participation. But it has become a convenient term for conveying the idea which was so aptly summed up later by Irenaeus: 'factus est quod sumus nos, uti nos perficeret esse quod est ipse' (*Adv. Haer.V praef.*). It is *not* that Christ and the believer change places, but rather that Christ, by his involvement in the human situation, is able to transfer believers from one mode of existence to another. Underlying this understanding of redemption is the belief that Christ is 'the last Adam' (I Cor. 15.45), the true 'image of God', who by sharing fully in humanity's condition – i.e. by being 'in Adam' – opens up the way for men and women to share in his condition, by being 'in Christ'. Not surprisingly, several other essays (ch. 2, in addition to chs. 5–7) examine the role of Adam in Paul's theology. Humanity's problems begin with Adam (whose sin brought death into the world and subjected everything to futility, Rom. 5.12; 8.20). Not only humanity but the universe itself is restored through the righteous obedience of Christ (Rom. 5.15–21; 8).

In contrast to Adam, who was created in the image of God, but who lost God's glory (Rom. 1.23; 3.23), Christ is the true image of God and the embodiment of his glory. But this means that 'by sending his Son in the likeness of sinful flesh, God has achieved what the Law could not do' (Rom. 8.2f). Though the Law expressed the purpose of God and reflected his glory, its power was incomplete. Not surprisingly, the attributes of the Law came to be applied to Christ, who is now identified, as was the Law (e.g. Ecclus. 24.23; Baruch 4.1), with wisdom (1 Cor. 1.24, 30). It was probably Paul himself who drew the logical conclusion that what had hitherto been said of the Law (and wisdom) in relation to creation could now be said of Christ. This theme is dealt with specifically in the essay on Colossians (ch. 11), but chapters 8 and 9 are also concerned with the theme of wisdom; another essay in this section (ch. 10) deals with a specific problem which again links with the themes of 'image' and 'glory'.

The theme which links the majority of the essays in this book is thus the relationship between old and new. This theme is expressly dealt with in chapters 12 and 13, and is basic to 14. Paul's upbringing and training were thoroughly Jewish, and it is my conviction that he remained Jewish in many of his attitudes and beliefs. To be sure, the realization that Jesus was the Messiah shattered many of his assumptions, but much of his Jewish framework remains. For Paul the Christian, as for Paul the Jew, God was the creator of heaven and earth, who had created mankind in his image and had brought Abraham into the land of Canaan and established his covenant with him; who had called Israel to be his chosen people, and had revealed himself to her in various ways, more specifically at Sinai and in the words of the prophets. This God was utterly trustworthy, faithful to his promises and true to his word: there was no question of his covenant with his people being abrogated, nor of the word of God failing; the Law was holy and good. The belief that the crucified and risen Jesus was the Messiah had to be slotted into this framework: the belief caused problems and raised tensions, but however new, startling and disruptive his new-found faith, the continuity between God's purposes in the past and his actions in the present is essential for Paul.

No attempt has been made to update these essays. No doubt if I were to deal afresh with some of the topics treated in the earlier ones I should approach them differently now, because so much has been written since I first tackled them. The basic argument of the earliest essays (ch. 5, supplemented by ch. 6) has been accepted and found illuminating by many subsequent commentators. It is true that A. J. M. Wedderburn questioned some of its conclusions (in 'Adam in Paul's Letter to the Romans', *Studia Biblica 1978*, 3, ed. E. A. Livingstone, Sheffield, 1980, 413–30), but even he conceded that 'the ideas of Gen. 3 have played a part' in Rom. 1.18ff (p. 419). N.T. Wright's recent article on the meaning of ἁρπαγμός (*JTS*, NS 37, 1986, 321–52) might lead me to modify the grammatical analysis of Phil. 2.6ff, but not the fundamental theological exposition. As for my analysis of the structure of this passage, put forward almost light-heartedly, this received surprising support when the 26th edition of Nestle-Aland's *Novum Testamentum Graece* was published a few years later, and its layout of the passage agreed almost exactly with my own!

The essay on 1 Cor. 11.10 (ch. 10) has been much quoted, largely because of the explosion of interest in 'feminist' issues. If I were to examine the passage again, it would have to be in the light of recent suggestions: many exegetes now hold that Paul was not talking about head-coverings at all, but about hair-styles (e.g. J. Murphy-O'Connor, in *CBQ* 42, 1980, 482–500); others solve the problem (in my view unconvincingly) by attributing the whole passage to an interpolator (e.g. G. W. Trompf, *ibid.*, 196–215). It seems better to leave the essay as it stands, as a record of an earlier contribution to the debate. The essay on the Colossian 'heresy' (ch. 11), by contrast, has rarely received whole-hearted support: most commentators continue to believe that Paul (if he was the author of Colossians) was dealing here with a particular aberrant teaching. Nevertheless, I remain persuaded that Paul's warnings are addressed to a situation in which misunderstandings and misinterpretations of the gospel are possible, rather than that he was attacking a particular 'heretical' version of it.

Various commentators have found the essays on 'interchange' (chs.

1–4) helpful. Linking with this theme is the final essay in this collection (ch. 14) on πίστις Χριστοῦ. This supports an interpretation of that phrase (first advocated by J. Haussleiter, in *Der Glaube Jesu Christi und der christliche Glaube*, Erlangen and Leipzig, 1891) which has until recently been dismissed by almost all exegetes, but which has been receiving growing support in recent years. It is only recently that I myself have been persuaded that the view that the genitive must be interpreted as subjective contains – if not the whole truth – a large element of the truth. As will be seen, this interpretation ties in well with the notion of interchange, as well as with the recognition of the importance of the figure of Adam for Paul's Christology.

There is scope to explore this notion of interchange further: I should like, for example, to consider Paul's understanding of his own ministry in the light of this interpretation of Christ's redemptive action. It is my belief that the notion of imitation is much more significant in Pauline thought than has often been allowed. Commentators have tended to shy away from it, but I suspect that this is largely due to a 'Lutheran' suspicion of salvation by works. The idea of imitating Christ has been thought to be contrary to the belief that the Christian depended on the grace of God alone. But for Paul (Gal. 4.19), the 'imitation' of Christ depends on union with him, and is a question of believers being conformed to his image, not of copying an external pattern: what Paul desires for his converts is that 'Christ be formed' in them (Gal. 4.19); it is 'Christ in you' who is 'the hope of glory' (Col. 1.27).

In the third essay in this collection, I have attempted to show how Paul sees the pattern of interchange (Christ's *kenosis* in sharing humanity's condition, which leads to mankind's consequent participation in his exaltation) as forming – paradoxically – a model for Christian life: thus Paul shares in the *kenosis* of Christ, identifying himself with his self-emptying, in order that he might be found in Christ; by sharing his suffering, becoming 'like him' in death, he hopes to share his resurrection (Phil. 3.7–11). Moreover he appeals to the Philippians, also, to make this pattern the basis for their own life-style (Phil. 1.27–2.13). This pattern, I have argued, is the basis of Paul's understanding of atonement, since the believer shares the death and resurrection of Christ in baptism (ch. 2); it is the basis of his interpretation of suffering as a sharing in the sufferings of Christ (ch. 3); it is also the basis for Paul's ethical appeals to his converts, and the standard for his own life-style (ch. 4). In these last two areas, we see how sharing in Christ's self-humiliation and obedience to death benefit not only the individual believer (as in Phil. 3) but the community of the faithful: there is a sense in which those who suffer with Christ bring comfort and salvation to others (2 Cor. 1.3–7; 4.7–15), and those who accept his way of life make others rich (2 Cor. 6.10). Thus those who are conformed to Christ's image, who are part of the new humanity 'in Christ', share in his redemptive work (cf. Col. 1.24).

But there are other passages which suggest that Paul saw this pattern as a model for his own missionary strategy: he is willing (as Christ was) to become what men and women are for their sake. He identifies with their situation. Thus in Gal. 4.12 he declares that he has become what the Galatians are – that is, outside the Law; it is worth noting that this passage follows immediately after the statement that God sent his Son, 'born under the Law, to redeem those who were under the Law'. A similar, but more enigmatic, statement is found in 1 Cor. 9.19-23, where Paul, describing his missionary strategy, declares that though free from all, he has made himself slave to all, in order to win the more; to Jews he became a Jew – in order to win Jews; to those under the Law he became 'as one under the Law' (though not himself under the Law) – in order to win those under the Law. To those outside the Law he became as one outside the Law (though not without law, because under the law of Christ), in order to win those outside the Law. To the weak he became weak – in order to win the weak. He has become all things to all men, in order to save some. Here we have exactly the pattern of the interchange statements (Christ became what we are, in order that we might become what he is). We have also the element of 'detachment' which sometimes characterizes them: Christ is made sin, yet knew no sin (2 Cor. 5.21); he came 'in the likeness of sinful flesh (Rom. 8.3). Whatever Christ becomes, the *kenosis* does not destroy what he *is*: he remains 'in the form of God' (Phil. 2.6) and Son of God (Gal. 4.4). So Paul becomes once again 'as one under the Law', though he is in fact no longer enslaved by it. Commentators have long struggled to make sense of the paradoxical nature of Paul's claims. Perhaps the realization that he sees himself as in some sense sharing in what we today would call the paradox of the incarnation may provide us with a clue to understanding this passage.

Similar ideas are found in 1 Cor. 10.33. Paul tries to please all men, in order that they may be saved. Moreover, this is the basis of his appeal to the Corinthians not to give offence to others. His 'missionary strategy' must be theirs also. Again, in 1 Cor. 8, he argues that the strong should put themselves in the position of the weak, lest they cause the weak to stumble, and declares that he himself is willing so to do (v. 13). The argument is repeated in Rom. 14.13–21. And in Rom. 15

it is clinched with the appeal to the example of Christ, who did not please himself (v. 3): Christians should welcome one another as Christ welcomed them, for he became a servant to the circumcised, for the sake of both Jews and Greeks.

Finally, we have in Rom. 9.3 a remarkable statement by Paul. Speaking of his own kinsmen, he declares that he could wish himself to be 'anathema from Christ' for their sake. Here is paradox indeed! Because of his own experience of restoration in Christ he longs for others to share it: he is willing to become what they are – anathema from Christ – for the sake of his brethren. Paul's words echo those found in Exod. 32.32, when Moses identifies himself with sinful Israel, but they also remind us of his 'interchange' formulae: his longing for the redemption of his people is such that he wishes he could be fully identified with their alienation. But in his case, the longing is fruitless: whereas Christ, by being made sin, was the source of righteousness for many, and by becoming a curse brought blessing to others, Paul cannot help his brethren by becoming anathema from Christ, since it is only *in* Christ that the interchange, the participation in blessing, can take place.

I am persuaded, then, that Paul's idea of participation in Christ is fundamental, not only for his Christology, but for his understanding of salvation, of the nature of the redeemed community, of God's plan for humanity and the world, and of the way of life appropriate for restored humanity. Those who live 'in Christ' depend on him. Being changed into his likeness, they reflect his glory; but the glory of the new humanity is the glory of God's children, who are obedient to him, responding to him in faith, who share the obedience and faith of Christ himself. These essays are an attempt to comprehend something of Paul's understanding of the new creation which takes place 'in Christ', which depends on him and reflects all that he is.

It is the first duty of an exegete to grapple with an author's own intentions and try to unravel his situation and concerns; we need to discover what he was trying to say – and what led him to say it in this particular way. But what of the meaning of Paul for today? Paul himself warns us against the view that scripture has a static meaning (2 Cor. 3), and though he was not thinking of his own writings as 'scripture', his warnings must certainly apply to them. It is an irony of history that Paul's own words came to be treated by the Christian Church as though they were 'Law'; Paul's somewhat muddled metaphor in 2 Cor. 3 may serve to remind us that those who claim to live according to the Spirit should not be chained by words written with ink, any more than by words carved on tablets of stone. We have referred several times in the course of this introduction to Luther's interpretation of Paul's teaching, and suggested that it was in many ways different from Paul's own understanding of his words. But was Luther wrong to interpret Paul in the way he did, given the situation at the time? We may surely claim that Luther's interpretation of Romans (like Paul's interpretation of Exod. 34 in 2 Cor. 3) was an interpretation of the Spirit; the gospel has to be reapplied to the situation of the day if it is to give life; otherwise it becomes merely a written code, bringing condemnation and death. The Spirit takes the words of scripture and reapplies them to new circumstances.

The corollary is this: though Luther's interpretation of Paul's words may have brought the gospel to medieval Europe, it may itself become a 'veil' which conceals the meaning of the gospel in the twentieth century. Paul seen through Luther's eyes may be as much an anomaly in the modern world as is a twentieth-century church built in Gothic style, using a layout which was suitable for a monastic community, but which is inappropriate for twentieth-century needs. This is not to suggest that Luther may not still have much to teach us, both about Paul and about interpretation: certain periods are particularly sensitive to certain ideas, and the Reformation period is undoubtedly one of them. We may certainly learn a great deal from reading Luther – just as we may receive great benefit from worshipping in a medieval church, or perhaps gain new insights into Shakespeare by seeing his plays performed in Victorian dress. But if we want to interpret Paul for today, we must dig back behind Luther's understanding of his words. To those who protest, 'but the gospel does not change', we answer, 'No, but the situation in which it is heard does'. Interpretation of the Bible is always a conversation: what was spoken in one set of circumstances is heard in another; interpretation and application must be allowed a part.

But it is only a part. 'Reader response' must not be allowed to take over. The first task of the exegete remains that of grappling with the text in its original context. It is that which I have attempted to do in these essays.

I

Interchange in Christ

I

Interchange in Christ

Whatever other virtues Paul may or may not have possessed, nobody would be likely to commend him for his lucidity of style. Commentators have a habit of writing in varying degrees of despair: 'this is perhaps the most difficult verse of the epistle.' But if a prize were to be awarded for the most difficult of all Paul's statements, it would surely be divided between Gal. 3.13 and 2 Cor. 5.21 – passages whose difficulty arises not so much from their obscurity as from the impossibility of what they so clearly seem to say: 'Christ became a curse'; 'Christ was made sin.' The two passages are linked together not only by the difficulty of their startling language, but also by the similarity of their theme and of their form: Christ became a curse *in order that* a blessing might come to others; he was made sin *in order that* we might become the righteousness of God.

Does Paul intend us to take his language literally, or has he used the terms 'sin' and 'curse' simply for effect? Are they meant only to startle us, and drive home the truth of what he is saying? Most commentators seem to feel that the terms are to be understood figuratively. Burton, for example, writing on Gal. 3.13, describes Paul's language as a figure of speech: Paul *cannot* mean: 'Christ became a curse'; the noun must be taken as an adjective, and the statement means 'Christ came under a curse', as the LXX quotation suggests.[1]

But to replace the noun with an adjective will certainly not help us when we turn to 2 Cor. 5.21. For here we cannot change 'Christ was made sin' into 'Christ was made sinful' without making nonsense of the argument – and, indeed, of Paul's theology. Here the noun must be retained, and so the attempt to tone the statement down has been made by the suggestion that ἁμαρτία here means not 'sin' but 'sin-offering'. In support of this, it is possible to point to two places in Leviticus where the term does have this sense.[2] But this suggestion is a blind alley. Nowhere else in the New Testament is the word ἁμαρτία

[1] E. D. Burton, *The Epistle to the Galatians* (*ICC*, Edinburgh, 1920), *in loc.*
[2] Lev. 4.25; 5.12.

used in this sense, and one wonders whether even Paul would have played on the meaning of one word by using it with two different meanings in adjacent phrases. Moreover, the words 'he made him to be sin' stand clearly in parallelism and contrast to 'we become the righteousness of God'. We must therefore agree with Plummer when he writes:[3] 'We must face the plain meaning of the apostle's strong words.' This being so, perhaps we ought also to take seriously the parallel statement in Gal. 3.13.

These two verses cannot, of course, be considered in isolation. We must examine them against the background of their contexts. Gal. 3 gives us the hub of Paul's argument against the circumcisers who have failed to comprehend the significance of the Cross. Paul, contrasting the works of the Law and the message of faith, as also flesh and spirit, insists that the true sons of Abraham, inheritors of the promises made to him, are not, as the circumcisers maintain, those who accept circumcision of the flesh and the duty of keeping the works of the Law, but those who share Abraham's faith and who have received the Spirit of God. This he demonstrates by quoting from scripture first a promise that the nations would be blessed through Abraham, and then a statement that those Jews who fail to keep the Law in its entirety are under a curse. At this stage in the argument he introduces his statement that Christ has been made a curse for us, backed up by yet another quotation, to the effect that everyone who is hanged on a tree is cursed. The result is the fulfilment and annulment – respectively – of the previous two quotations: the promised blessing has come to the Gentiles; and we (i.e. the Jews) have been set free from the curse which rested upon us.

In quoting Deut. 21.23 at this point Paul follows the LXX rendering which describes the malefactor as cursed – though significantly he omits the phrase ὑπὸ τοῦ θεοῦ. But in his actual statement that Christ is a curse he follows the Hebrew, which refers to the man's body as קִלְלַת אֱלֹהִים 'a curse of God'. Although later Jewish exegesis tended to interpret this as 'an insult to God',[4] the natural meaning of the phrase is 'a curse *of* God': because the man is a transgressor he has received the curse of God, and in keeping with the very concrete understanding of the curse and blessing, he is regarded as himself a curse;[5] it is because he is a source of infection to the land that his body must be removed before sunset.

[3] A. Plummer, *The Second Epistle of St. Paul to the Corinthians* (*ICC*, Edinburgh, 1915), *in loc.*

[4] S. R. Driver, *Deuteronomy* (*ICC*, Edinburgh, 1895), *in loc.* Num. Rab. 8.4 understands the exposure of a criminal's body overnight as a profanation of the divine name.

[5] Cf. the stories of Achan (Josh. 7) and Jonathan (1 Sam. 14.24–45).

These are the ideas which lie behind Paul's description of Christ as a curse: the Cross demonstrates that he has himself come under the curse from which he sets the Jews free. But what is the logic of Paul's thought? How does Christ come under the curse? – and how, having done so, does he set others free from it and, even beyond that, bring blessing to those outside the borders of Israel? There are several stages in the argument which are only hinted at in these verses. We may note, first, that Christ sets men free from the curse of the Law by coming under the same curse. Since the curse rests on all under the Law, it is possible that Paul understands this as happening at the incarnation rather than the crucifixion.[6] True, the whole argument depends upon a specific reference to the Cross, but the exposure of the criminal's body on a stake in Deuteronomy was the public display of one on whom the curse of God *already* rested. This point should perhaps not be pressed, but it serves to remind us that we ought not to drive a wedge between the incarnation and the crucifixion in Paul's thought. But if Christ is identified with man's condition, how do the conclusions follow? How are the Jews set free from the curse of the Law, and how does the blessing come to the Gentiles? The answer, as the succeeding argument shows, lies in the characteristic Pauline formula 'in Christ': in him old distinctions are done away, and all are one. It is because men and women are in Christ that they are the true seed of Abraham and so receive the blessing promised to him. But underlying this there is an important assumption – the assumption that though Christ became a curse, this curse has in some way been annulled, and been turned into a source of blessing. This idea is not expressed here – perhaps because it is so obvious – but is nevertheless vital to Paul's argument. Christ has set men free from the curse because the judgement of the Law has been overruled; he has brought blessing to the Gentiles because he himself has become a blessing. Blessing has thus proved more powerful than the curse.[7] We may perhaps here compare 1 Cor. 1.18ff, another passage in which Paul is arguing with those whose understanding of

---

[6] Strictly, the curse rests on πᾶς ὃς οὐκ ἐμμένει πᾶσιν τοῖς γεγραμμένοις ἐν τῷ βιβλίῳ τοῦ νόμου τοῦ ποιῆσαι αὐτά, and Paul may have thought of Jesus as the one exception to the Jewish failure to keep the Law. But the reference in Gal. 4.4 to Christ being born ὑπὸ νόμον, suggests that it is his oneness with the human condition which is uppermost in Paul's mind. Cf. D. E. H. Whiteley, 'St. Paul's thought on the atonement', *JTS*, ns 8 (1957), 240–55 (especially 246f).

[7] There is an interesting parallel to this idea in certain of the miracle stories in the gospels, where Jesus touches (or is touched by) those who, according to the Jewish Law, are unclean, which should make him unclean also. Instead of becoming unclean, however, or perhaps in spite of it, he is able to overcome the power of defilement, and to make those with whom he comes in contact clean. See especially Num. 5.1–4; Mark 1.40–5; 5.1–43.

the gospel is, in his view, emptying the Cross of significance. Paul speaks here of the crucified Christ as folly which is wiser than human wisdom, and weakness which is stronger than human strength, and describes Christ as our wisdom and righteousness. So, in Galatians, we might say that Christ has become a curse more powerful to bless than any human blessing. In both cases Paul goes out of his way to emphasize the offence of the Cross to his readers – 'a stumbling-block to Jews and folly to Gentiles'. It is to be noted that in 1 Corinthians, as in Galatians, Paul omits to mention the resurrection: it was apparently unnecessary to remind even the Corinthians at this point how folly and weakness were changed into wisdom and strength.

The results of Christ becoming a curse, then, can be expressed in terms of a sharing in the life of Christ, the idea which Paul has already expounded in Gal. 2, and which he elaborates further at the end of 3. It is by being baptized into Christ, by putting on Christ, by being one man in Christ, that we are able to inherit the promise made to Abraham. In other words, the experience of Gal. 3.13 is not a simple exchange. It is not that Christ is cursed and we are blessed. Rather he enters into our experience, and we then enter into his, by sharing in his resurrection.

This is not, of course, an isolated concept of Paul's thought. Indeed, we find another expression of it, in similar terms, in Gal. 4. Here, although Paul has developed his argument somewhat, and moved from the idea of being heirs of Abraham to that of being heirs of God, the idea is similar, and the language echoes 3.13. This time we are told that God sent his Son, 'born of woman, born under the Law', in order that he might 'redeem those who were under the Law, so that we might receive adoption as sons'. The structure of the statement is parallel to that in Gal. 3.13, with a double ἵνα introducing the purpose of God's act. The language is in part the same – γενόμενον, ἐξαγοράσῃ, ὑπὸ νόμον. And the idea is the same, expressed in similar terms. Christ shares our experience, in order that we might share his; he came under Law, to set free those under Law, and the result is sonship – not of Abraham but of God himself. He who is Son of God was born of a woman in order that those who are born of woman might become sons of God. As proof that his work was effective, we find that the Spirit of God enters our hearts, and we cry, 'Abba, Father', using the prayer of Jesus himself. This time, certainly, we must interpret Paul's statement in terms of the incarnation: Christ became what we are, in order that we might become what he is. But once again, it is not a straightforward exchange. Christ does not cease to be Son of God, and we receive the Spirit of the Son.

The statement in 2 Cor. 5.21 also takes place within a discussion of the significance of the Cross, but this time what the Corinthians have failed to understand is its relevance to their own behaviour and the status of the apostles. They are perhaps somewhat ashamed of Paul, who embarrasses them by his unconventional behaviour and lack of dignity. But for Paul the only basis of his life is the dying and rising of Christ: one has died for all, therefore all have died, and he died for all so that those who live should not live to themselves, but to him who died and rose again. This is effected in Christ, in whom there is a new creation. The ministry of this reconciliation is entrusted to Paul and others, who show by their lives that they are true ministers, for they make many rich. The basis of this reconciliation is the fact that the one who knew no sin was made sin on our behalf, in order that we might become the righteousness of God in him. As Paul is dealing here with reconciliation, it is natural that he should write in terms of 'sin' and 'righteousness'. In some unfathomable way Christ is identified with what is opposed to God, in order that man should be reconciled to him. Once again we notice that a step in the argument has been assumed: for it is 'in him' that we become the righteousness of God. Once again the evil force has been annulled and transformed into the opposing, positive force, and the basis of this reversal is the death and resurrection of Christ. And once again its results for the believer come through incorporation into Christ. The interchange of experience is not a straightforward exchange, for we become the righteousness of God *in him*. If Christ has been made sin, he has also been made our righteousness.

But do the words in verse 21, 'He made him to be sin', refer to the crucifixion or to the incarnation? Commentators are divided in their answer to this question.[8] Perhaps, however, it is an artificial question. For though the context might suggest that the death of Jesus is in mind, and though 'reconciliation' elsewhere in Paul is always linked with the Cross,[9] we should again be wary of driving a wedge between incarnation and crucifixion.[10] This is supported by two other passages which refer quite clearly to the incarnation.

[8] J. Héring, *The Second Epistle of St. Paul to the Corinthians* (ET, London, 1967), *in loc.*; Plummer, *Second Epistle of St. Paul*, *in loc.*; Whiteley, 'St. Paul's thought on the atonement', 245f.

[9] καταλλάσσω (twice) in Rom. 5.10; ἀποκαταλλάσσω in Col. 1.20, 22 and Eph. 2.16. If these last passages are not admitted as evidence, however, we have only Rom. 5.10.

[10] Cf. H. Windisch, *Der zweite Korintherbrief*, 9th edn (Göttingen, 1924). E. Stauffer, *New Testament Theology* (London, 1955), p. 343, describes 2 Cor. 5.21, together with 8.9, Gal. 3.13, 4.5 and Rom. 8.3f as 'Paradoxical Incarnation Formulae' (cf. also p. 117). By this, however, he means expressions of Paul's understanding of the 'word of the Cross' (p. 246). Cf. also Phil. 2.5–11 (discussed below) where the Cross is the supreme act of obedience in that series of events which describe Christ's 'incarnation'.

The first is found in 2 Cor. 8.9, where, in the midst of a mundane catalogue of reasons why the Corinthians should contribute to the collection for Christians in Jerusalem, Paul mentions the real basis for such generous action – the grace of the Lord Jesus Christ, who, though he was rich, became poor for their sake, in order that, through his poverty, they might become rich. Attempts to make this apply to the death of Christ are forced: the wealth and poverty are parallel to the pattern found in Phil. 2, where the pre-existent one accepts the limitations of an earthly existence. But we notice the form of the sentence, which is parallel to the others we have examined: Christ became poor, in order that others might become rich. This time, no explanation is offered as to how this happens – Paul simply introduces the statement with an introductory 'you know'. But we must assume that the basis is the fact that Christians have been incorporated into Christ. Once again, it is not a matter of a simple exchange: if Christians become rich it is presumably because riches have been restored to Christ.

The other passage is found in Rom. 8. So far we have looked briefly at four passages, in Galatians and 2 Corinthians, all of which are in the same general form – Christ became what we are, in order that (in him) we might become what he is. Rom. 8 contains the same underlying idea. Once again, it is a passage full of obscurity: God, sending his own Son in the likeness of sinful flesh and for sin, condemned sin in the flesh, *in order that* the righteous decree of the Law might be fulfilled in us, who live, not according to flesh but according to spirit. In this chapter Paul argues that what the Law could not do, because of the weakness of the flesh, God has done in Christ – namely given us life: this has been achieved by the sending of God's Son in the likeness of sinful flesh, and however we interpret these words, they are surely a reference to the incarnation, and an attempt to affirm that Christ shared fully in human experience.[11] The purpose this time is said to be that the requirement of the Law might be fulfilled in us, and though this happens because we are in him, this is not quite the same kind of interchange that we have met in the other passages. However, if we read a little further in the chapter, we discover what it means to live according to spirit instead of according to flesh. Those who are led by the Spirit of God are sons of God, for they have received a spirit of adoption, and cry 'Abba, Father'. We notice immediately the parallel with Gal. 4.4–7, where the same proof is used of our sonship. But if we

[11] Cf. M.-J. Lagrange, *Epître aux Romains* (Paris, 1950).

take Rom. 8.3 and 14f together, there is an even clearer parallel with the Galatians passage. God has sent his Son in our likeness ('of sinful flesh'/'born of woman'), so setting us free from bondage to the Law: and the result is that we, too, are now sons of God, having received the Spirit of the Son. The language of verse 3 is also reminiscent of 2 Cor. 5.21 – another support for the view that the passage may refer to the incarnation as well as or rather than the crucifixion.

But we have not yet finished with Rom. 8. For in the rest of the chapter Paul elaborates what it means for us to be sons of God. Once again this is done in terms of a new creation – though this time the idea is carried to its logical conclusion, and it is creation as a whole which is renewed. As for the children of God, they are described as being conformed to the image of God's Son, who is the first-born among many brethren: once again, they are said to become like him.

The ideas used by Paul in this chapter are clearly linked with his understanding of Christ as the second Adam. Indeed, the argument leads on naturally from chapter 5, and chapters 6 and 7 are somewhat of a digression. It is therefore permissible to ask whether in fact the discussion of the two Adams in 5.12–21 does not give us the basis for the kind of statement that we have been examining. It is because the second Adam took the form of the first Adam that men can be conformed to *his* likeness in a new creation; it is because of his obedience and his δικαίωμα, that the δικαίωμα is fulfilled in us. Christ became what we are – '*adam* – in order that we might share in what he is – namely the true image of God.

The idea of man's conformity to the image of the second Adam is found widely in the Pauline epistles. Sometimes it is expressed directly in terms of being transformed into Christ's image. In 2 Cor. 3.18, we find that we are changed into his image, through various stages of glory – and a few verses later, in 4.4, we are told that Christ himself is the image of God. In Col. 3.10 we are urged to put on the new man which is being renewed according to the image of the one who created him; we know from 1.15 that Christ himself is the image of God. In these passages, the ideas of a new Adam and a new creation are important. We may classify them as expansions of the second half of our original statements: they describe what we become – in Christ. But since they refer to Christ as the image of God – a phrase which echoes Gen. 1.26f, the idea of Christ's 'manhood' is fundamental.

But there is one passage, Phil 2, which takes up the other part of the pattern, and which describes in detail what Christ became without, apparently, referring to what we become in him. Here we have an account of what Christ became through the incarnation, but instead of leading to a statement that there has been an interchange of experience with the believer, it is followed by a description of what happened to Christ at his exaltation. The interchange of experience takes place within Christ himself. We might perhaps describe this as the missing link behind our interchange passages: it is, of course, only an extended form of the simplest Christian creed that Jesus died and was raised again, that he was humbled and exalted, but here, clearly, it is expressed in terms of incarnation, and not simply of crucifixion. But once again, incarnation and crucifixion are held together, for the climax of the first half of this hymn is the death of Christ. His self-humiliation and self-emptying, seen in his action of becoming man, and taking the likeness of man, lead to this ultimate point – his obedience to death (even the death of the Cross). But in the second half of the hymn it is Christ alone who is exalted, Christ alone who is made Lord.

Many scholars regard the Philippian hymn as non-Pauline,[12] and the pattern which we have traced in it may perhaps support this view. Nevertheless, we might expect Paul to use his material in a Pauline way. And we find, when we examine the context, that this is in fact what he has done. We shall have to read on a long way, however, before we find the other half of the typically Pauline pattern – it does not emerge until the end of chapter 3. Now here immediately is a difficulty: do chapters 2 and 3 both belong to the same letter? Or does 3.1 perhaps introduce an insertion from another letter? It may be that the link between 2.1-10 and the end of 3 will be regarded as an argument in support of the integrity of the letter,[13] for it is difficult to believe that the linguistic echoes and the development of Paul's pattern of interchange are accidental.

The argument in Phil. 3 is once more with those who advocate circumcision, who rely upon the flesh. Paul points, by contrast, to his own example: he, who had so much of which to boast in 'fleshly' terms, has counted all these things loss for the sake of gaining Christ and being found in him. Already we notice that Paul is following, on a lower level, the example of Christ in renouncing all that he held dear, and that the vocabulary – κέρδη, ἡγοῦμαι, κερδήσω, and εὑρεθῶ – echoes the earlier chapters.[14] To be found in Christ is to have the righteousness of

[12] See R. P. Martin, *Carmen Christi* (Cambridge, 1961), pp. 42–62, for a recent summary of opinions and a discussion of the subject.
[13] A similar argument was put forward recently by T. E. Pollard, 'The integrity of Philippians', *NTS*, 13 (1967), 57–66.   [14] Phil. 3.7–9; cf. 1.2 and 2.3, 6, 7.

God, instead of the so-called righteousness of the Law; it is to know the power of his resurrection and the communion of his sufferings, and to be conformed to his death, in hope of the resurrection from the dead.[15]

In verses 17f, the Philippians are urged to follow the example of Paul, and not that of those who are enemies of the Cross of Christ, i.e. those who refuse to be conformed to the pattern of his death; they glory in their shame – an obscure statement that leaves all the commentators guessing, but whatever it means, it is perhaps a wry reference to the shame of Christ in which true glory is to be found. They mind earthly things, instead of having the mind of Christ. So far, the language has been that of Christ-mysticism, though with echoes of chapter 2, such as the reference to the Cross.[16] But in verses 20f the end of the process is envisaged: our citizenship is in heaven, from which we expect a saviour, Jesus Christ the Lord, who will change the body of our humiliation, conform it to his body of glory, according to the power whereby he is able to subject all things to himself. At this point there is a whole cluster of words which occurred in the hymn and its immediate context: πολίτευμα, 'citizenship', echoes the cognate verb used in 1.27; we have also ὑπάρχει, κύριος, compounds of σχῆμα and μορφή, ταπείνωσις, δόξα, τὰ πάντα. But more important even than the language is the theme. Our body of humiliation is to be fashioned anew by Christ, who in chapter 2 humbled himself, becoming man, and was found in fashion as a man; we are to be conformed to the body of his glory, who in chapter 2 took the form of a slave and became man. This is to be done by the Lord Jesus Christ, whom we expect from heaven, through the power with which he can subject all things to himself; and we remember that in chapter 2 he was exalted to heaven, given the name 'Lord', and with it supremacy over all things. In these verses, then, the meaning of Christ's exaltation for the believer is worked out: in Christ the Christian shares in the reversal of status which took place when God raised him. Christ now works our transformation through the power given to him in his ascension. It cannot be accidental that this is stated in terms which so clearly echo the language of the hymn. It is almost as though Paul wrote: Christ humbled himself, becoming man, in order that by his humiliation we might become glorious in him.

This, then, would seem to be Paul's distinctive interpretation of the

---

[15] The language of the hymn (cf. 2.6–8) is echoed in 3.10 in the phrase συμμορφιζόμενος τῷ θανάτῳ αὐτοῦ.

[16] Note also, in 3.19, the words ἀπώλεια (1.28), δόξα (2.2), ἐπίγεια (2.10), and φρονοῦντες (2.2, 5).

meaning of Christ's humiliation and exaltation for those in Christ. And if in Philippians he *has* used a non-Pauline hymn, then perhaps we have an insight into the way in which he took over material and gave it his own characteristic twist: for we seem to see him taking the theme and language of the hymn and working out its application.

In conclusion, we may perhaps list seven possible corollaries which are worthy of consideration:

1 In the sphere of Christology, the statements which we have examined underline the true humanity of Christ. In spite of some slight hesitation in 2 Cor. 5.21 and Rom. 8.3 (due probably to the conviction that Christ did not succumb to sin), he is fully identified with what man is. At the same time, Paul emphasizes both the personal pre-existence of Christ, and what Christ is in relation to God – Son of God, in the form of God, etc. In their Jewish background, these terms express what *man* was intended to be, so that Christ's sonship perhaps means basically being truly human.[17] Certainly it consists of a relationship with God, rather than indicating metaphysical truths. Paul might well have said, with Irenaeus,[18] that Christ became what we are, in order that we might become what he is: but his understanding of this statement would have remained Hebraic; he would not have interpreted it, as happened later, in terms of Greek philosophy.

2 The statements of 'interchange' offer the real clue to Paul's understanding of the atonement. This is much more closely linked with the incarnation than some traditional statements have suggested. The Cross is of course vital, but it is the completion of the obedience which characterizes the whole of Christ's life. It is as man's *representative*, rather than as his substitute, that Christ suffers,[19] and it is only as one who is fully human that he is able to do anything effective for mankind, by lifting man, as it were, into an obedient relationship with God. The work of reconciliation between God and man is not achieved by the work of an outside Saviour (though, of course, it originates in the purpose of God), but is the working-out of utter love and obedience in human nature. The result is that *in Christ* men become what they were intended to be from the creation. In Christ there is a new creation, so that men now bear his image, as they have borne the image of Adam.

[17] Cf. G. B. Caird, 'The development of the doctrine of Christ in the New Testament' in N. Pittenger (ed.), *Christ for Us Today* (London, 1968), pp. 70–5.
[18] *Adv. Haer. V praef.*: 'factus est quod sumus nos, uti nos perficeret esse quod est ipse'.
[19] *Contra* the views of, e.g. L. Morris, *The Apostolic Preaching of the Cross*, 3rd edn (London, 1965), pp. 55–9, and *The Cross in the New Testament* (London, 1965), pp. 220–4.

They share his relationship with God by themselves becoming sons of God, and so finding blessing, righteousness, and glory. In other words, they become truly human.[20]

3 If Christ has become what we are in order that we might become what he is, then those things which governed and characterized the old life of alienation from God in Adam no longer apply. It is the *old man*, i.e. the Adamic existence, which is crucified with Christ, Rom. 6.6, i.e. Christ sums up the old man and the old aeon, because he shares in them fully, and in his death and resurrection their power is annulled. He – and we with him – have died to sin, Rom. 6–10, and to Law, Rom. 7.4,[21] and this means that neither of these powers now has dominion over us. These terms – sin and Law – therefore belong to the old existence, i.e. life in Adam, which Christ shared with us, but which is no longer relevant to those who have died and risen with Christ. The conclusion must be that these words no longer have a place within the Christian vocabulary. It is of course unrealistic to suppose that sin has been abolished even in the believer's life. But it is interesting to note that Paul deals with this situation in a very positive way. He writes continually to his converts – Be what you are! Man has been recreated, called to be 'holy' – he should believe it and behave accordingly. Sin belongs to the old, Adamic existence.[22] Paul was much more positive in his approach than much later Christian liturgy and piety, with their continual emphasis on sin and guilt.

4 Some details of Adamic life, however, continue, and their existence cannot be denied – namely suffering and death. It is notable that the great majority of references to suffering and death in Paul speak of them in terms of our life 'in Christ', not 'in Adam'.[23] This is very strange: it is surely part of our Adamic existence that we are subject to suffering and death – by contrast with the glory and life which we share with Christ. We find this balance in Rom. 8.18: 'I consider that the sufferings of this present time are not worth comparing with the glory that is to be revealed to us.' But in the preceding verse the suffering has been pulled over, as it were, on to the wrong side of the balance sheet, because Paul speaks there of suffering *with* Christ, 'in order that we may also be glorified with him'. Why, then, does Paul

---

[20] A similar view is maintained by G. W. H. Lampe, *Reconciliation in Christ* (London, 1956), especially pp. 61–6, and by Whiteley, 'St. Paul's thought on the atonement'.

[21] Cf. R. Tannehill, *Dying and Rising with Christ* (Berlin, 1967), pp. 27f, on Rom. 6.6.

[22] However Rom. 7 is interpreted, the 'sin' which wars against man does so through the flesh: it is a part of being 'in Adam'.

[23] Cf. E. Ellis, 'II Corinthians v. 1–10 in Pauline eschatology', *NTS*, 6 (1960), 215f.

speak of suffering with Christ and of dying with him? The answer is no doubt to be found in Paul's experience. As far as death is concerned, dying with Christ is precisely the dying to sin and the Law which we have already mentioned. As regards suffering, it is no doubt true that most of Paul's sufferings were literally 'for the sake of Christ': his imprisonments, beatings, hunger, ship-wrecks, were all the direct result of his apostolic mission. Yet it is very doubtful whether Paul would have distinguished between one type of suffering and another, or would have separated 'apostolic' suffering and persecution from ordinary everyday suffering. The 'thorn in the flesh' of 2 Cor. 12.8–10 and the wearing away of physical strength were probably what we would consider as a part of being in Adam. Yet Paul treats them as though they were in Christ. Can it be that these Adamic sufferings have been pulled over (or baptized) into Christ? Man is created again in Christ, but he is not yet free from physical limitations: yet precisely because Christ is fully one with man in all his experiences, these can now be understood in terms of life in Christ.

5 What this means for the individual is seen in some of the passages to which we have already referred. The Christian experiences the same exchange which characterized Christ's life and death. Paul speaks of himself and his fellow apostles as 'dying, and behold we live; . . . as sorrowful, yet always rejoicing; . . . as having nothing, and yet possessing everything'.[24] He refers to the power of Christ which is made perfect in weakness, and declares: 'When I am weak, then I am strong.[25] This is to know the power of Christ's resurrection, through sharing in his sufferings.[26] It is a part of what being 'in Christ' means.

6 But even more significant is the fact that this exchange is something which overflows into the lives of others. So Paul also speaks of himself as 'always carrying in the body the death of Jesus, so that the life of Jesus may also be manifested in our bodies. . . . So death is at work in us, but life in you'.[27] He describes himself as 'poor, yet making many rich'[28] – the very words which he later uses of Christ. He is glad when he himself is weak, and the Corinthians strong.[29] He refers to Christ, crucified through weakness, yet living through the power of God, and to himself as weak in him; but, he declares, though weak, he will live through the power of God toward the Corinthians.[30] As with the interchange between Christ and the believer, these exchanges of experience are

---

[24] 2 Cor. 6.10.   [25] 2 Cor. 12.10.   [26] Phil. 3.10.
[27] 2 Cor. 4.10–12.   [28] 2 Cor. 6.10.   [29] 2 Cor. 13.9.
[30] 2 Cor. 13.4. The words are a promise that he will deal with the Corinthians firmly.

really a sharing of Paul's own experience. This is best seen in 2 Cor. 1. 4–6, where Paul writes: God 'comforts us in all our affliction, so that we may be able to comfort those who are in any affliction, with the comfort with which we ourselves are comforted by God. . . . If we are afflicted, it is for your comfort and salvation; and if we are comforted, it is for your comfort.' Significantly, Paul bases this upon his union with Christ: 'For as we share abundantly in Christ's sufferings, so through Christ we share abundantly in comfort too.' Paul shares in the experience of interchange, and in turn shares his experience with others. But is this simply an experience which belongs to apostles? Can we go on from the comparison between the relationship of Christ with the believer and that of Paul with the Corinthians, to deduce that the same interchange of experience ought to take place between all those who are 'in Christ'? This is, of course, part of the larger problem of the meaning of 'we' in 2 Corinthians. The fact that in 1.6f Paul says that the Corinthians share the 'same sufferings' suggests that the experience belongs to all who are in Christ.

7 There may be another pointer to this solution also in the fact that Paul uses Christ's 'exchange' as the basis of appeals to his converts. We have already noted that 2 Cor. 8.9 is used by Paul as an exhortation to generous giving. Phil. 2 is equally practical: the pattern of Christ's self-humiliation is the basis of the Christian's life and of his dealings with his fellow men. This is not simply a question of following a good example: he *must* think and behave like this, because the behaviour of Christ is the ground of his redemption; if he denies the relevance of Christ's actions to his own, then he is denying his very existence in Christ. He must behave like this because he is *in* Christ, and this is the mind of Christ.

But if this pattern of exchange is the basis of the Christian life – both as its foundation and as its guiding principle – this suggests that the 'overflow' of interchange is not confined to a group of apostles: indeed, to suppose that it could be is to make a false distinction within the Christian community. The interchange of experience – with Christ, within his own life, and with others – is something which ought to be known by every believer.

2

Interchange and atonement

There are in several of Paul's letters statements about the relationship between Christ and the believer which have been aptly if not entirely accurately summed up in the word 'interchange'. The most convenient way of explaining what is meant is to quote an expression of it which is not, in fact, Paul's own – namely the famous saying of Irenaeus: 'Christ became what we are, in order that we might become what he is.'[1] The clearest examples in Paul's own writings are found in 2 Corinthians, the first in 5.21, 'he became sin, that we might become the righteousness of God in him', the second in 8.9, 'though he was rich he became poor, in order that many might be made rich'. Here we see the basic pattern of the interchange between Christ and the believer: Christ is identified with the human condition in order that we might be identified with his.

The term 'interchange', though very useful, is not, however, entirely accurate. According to my dictionary, the word means 'a reciprocal exchange' and implies a mutual 'give and take'. It is immediately obvious that as far as the relationship between Christ and the believer is concerned, the give and take are far from being mutual: the giving is all on one side, and the taking on the other. Nor is it a case of Christ and the believer changing places, as has sometimes been suggested in some crude interpretations of the atonement. In 1 Thes. 5.10 – not itself an interchange statement, but one which nevertheless sums up in a similar way the relationship between Christ's death and our life – Paul speaks of Christ dying in order that we might live, but he adds the significant words *with him*: Christ 'died for us so that . . . we might live with him'. If Christ shares our death, it is in order that we might share his resurrection life. Paul's understanding of the process is therefore one of participation, not of substitution; it is a sharing of experience, not an

The Manson Memorial Lecture delivered in the University of Manchester on 27 October 1977. This lecture explores a topic ('The idea of interchange as a clue to Paul's understanding of the atonement') on which the author began work under Professor Manson's guidance in October 1957, and which was put on one side after his death the following year. [1] See above ch. 1, n. 18.

exchange. Christ is identified with us in order that – in him – we might share in what he is.

The words *with him* in 1 Thess. 5.10 emphasize the dependence of the believer upon Christ. So do the words *in Christ* in 2 Cor. 5.21 – and they point also to another way in which this interchange is not a mutual one. When Paul says that Christ came 'in the likeness of sinful flesh' (Rom. 8.3), or that he was 'born of a woman' (Gal. 4.4), he is describing universal human experiences; to borrow Paul's own way of putting it, Christ is sharing fully in the condition of Adam. The process of reversal, however, is – at least at present – by no means universal. It may well be that Paul believed that in the end it would be, that all men would be 'in Christ' and so share in all that this implied; but for the moment, at least, the reciprocal relationship is limited to those who are 'in Christ'.

Paul's understanding of interchange is therefore one of interchange *in Christ*. It is achieved, on the one hand, by Christ's solidarity with mankind, on the other, by our solidarity with Christ. The former idea can be conveniently summed up in the non-Pauline term 'incarnation'; the latter concerns our incorporation into Christ, and is expressed by Paul in terms of faith in Christ, baptism into Christ, and dying and rising with Christ. It is because Christ himself shared in the condition of being 'Adam', man, that man is now offered the possibility of entering a new kind of existence.

In asking how this idea of interchange fits into Paul's understanding of redemption, therefore, it is natural to turn to the contrast which Paul sets out between Adam and Christ in Rom. 5, and I want to begin my investigation there, even though this particular chapter does not contain any formulae of interchange.

It is perhaps a measure of our distance from Paul's way of thinking that many commentators have found themselves puzzled by verses 12–19 of Rom. 5. One scholar described them as 'perhaps the most peculiar verses in all the epistle';[2] another as a 'theological digression';[3] even Luther referred to them as 'a pleasant excursion'.[4] But however pleasant they may be, they are certainly no excursion; I suggest, on the contrary, that they are the key to Romans, summing up the argument of the previous chapters in terms of the contrast between Adam and Christ. Throughout the early part of Romans Paul demonstrates how man lost his relationship with God, how he forfeited the divine glory

---

[2] A. Nygren, *Commentary on Romans* (London, 1952), p. 207.
[3] K. E. Kirk, *The Epistle to the Romans* (Oxford, 1937), p. 195.
[4] Preface to the Epistle to the Romans, 1522, ET, *Works of Martin Luther*, the Philadelphia edn, 6 (Philadelphia, 1932), p. 456.

and came under the wrath of God; in chapter 5, he declares that man is restored to a right relationship with God, and that he can therefore rejoice in hope of the restoration of God's glory, and can be assured of salvation from the wrath to come. Paul reaches his triumphant conclusion in verses 9–11: having been reconciled to God by Christ's death, we shall certainly be saved by his life. The opening 'therefore' of verse 12 introduces the final Q E D of Paul's argument:[5] because man is not only 'justified' and reconciled with God, but has assurance that he will be saved from wrath, *therefore* everything which happened to man in Adam is paralleled, or rather reversed, by what has happened to man in Christ. Therefore, as through one man sin came into the world, and death through sin, so through one man righteousness came, and life through righteousness.

In spite of Paul's somewhat confused syntax, the parallels and contrasts between Adam and Christ in this passage are clear: five times over, first negatively and then positively, everything which happened 'in Adam' is more than counterbalanced by what happens 'in Christ'. If we understand his argument simply in terms of Adam and Christ, however, we shall misunderstand his purpose, for I suggest that there is another even more important contrast here, and that is the contrast between the activity of man and the activity of God himself; it is the results of the latter which are so much greater than the results of the former. This is clearly seen if we analyse the balance sheet which is

---

[5] Commentators tend to give the introductory διὰ τοῦτο of v. 12 less than its full force, suggesting that it indicates only a loose relation with the preceding argument in 5.1–11. The difficulty in understanding the logic at this point is partly the result of Paul's broken construction, since the ὥσπερ of v. 12 has no corresponding οὕτως. Nevertheless, Paul's meaning here is clear from the rest of the paragraph: everything which happened 'in Adam' has been more than balanced by what happened 'in Christ'. Paul is able to introduce this pronouncement at this stage because in the preceding paragraph he has taken an important new step in his argument: he has moved on from the idea of 'justification' or being put right with God to talk about the hope of glory, v. 2, and about salvation, vv. 9f. The wheel of the argument has now come its full circle. Paul has shown how man sinned, how he lost his relationship with God, how he forfeited the divine glory and came under God's wrath. Now he has said that man is restored to a right relationship with God through faith and that his sins have been dealt with – and that, this being so, he can rejoice in hope of the restoration of God's glory and can be assured of salvation from future wrath. The restoration of man is complete – or will be, when the eschatological hope is realized. Romans 5.9–10 are therefore the climax of the whole argument from 1.16 onwards – man's fall into sin and wrath is now reversed by his restoration in Christ. Now at last Paul can sum up all that he has said so far in a triumphant conclusion. Because man is not only 'justified' but has confidence that he will be saved from wrath (v. 9); because man is not only reconciled but has a sure hope of salvation (v. 10); *therefore* everything which happened to man in Adam is paralleled by what has happened to man in Christ (v. 12). Far from being a loose linking phrase, the διὰ τοῦτο of v. 12 provides the vital introduction to this final step in Paul's argument.

drawn up in verses 15–19 and examine the terms which Paul uses. First (5.15), we are told that the παράπτωμα, the 'transgression', is not like the χάρισμα, the 'gracious gift'. It is the gracious gift of *God* which stands in contrast with the sin of Adam, so that it is hardly surprising that Paul declares that the two are not strictly comparable. In what follows, Paul underlines the contrast between Adam's transgression and God's gracious gift. Though many – i.e. all – died as the result of one transgression, the grace of God and his gift (which came in Christ) have proved abundant for many: since one transgression brought death, it is clear that the gift must bring life. The contrast is then (5.16) elaborated in terms of the results of the sin and the gift respectively: the judgement of one transgression led inevitably to condemnation, but the gracious gift of God, coming after many transgressions, led to acquittal. Paul uses here the unusual term δικαίωμα, and it is often argued that he has chosen this, rather than the more usual word for righteousness, δικαιοσύνη, because its form balances that of the word for condemnation, κατάκριμα. Yet the meaning, as well as the form, of δικαίωμα makes it appropriate in this context; for it means not only a regulation or commandment (as often in the LXX) but also the amendment of a wrong, the act of vindication.[6] The emphasis here falls on the action of setting things right. Paul sums up his argument in verse 17 with a contrast between the act of transgression on the one hand and God's abundant grace and gift of righteousness on the other; as the former leads to death, so the latter leads to life; and the two agents of death and life are Adam and Christ.

Paul has argued, then, that whereas Adam's transgression led to death for all, God's gracious act has led to life for all: the terms which fill out the progression are, on the one hand, sinning, judgement and condemnation, and on the other, grace, gift and acquittal. Since the condemnation of the many results from the condemnation of Adam, the logic of the argument suggests that the acquittal of the many depends on the acquittal of Christ. This acquittal, which leads to life for the many, would have taken place at the resurrection, an act of vindication which established his righteousness. Just as men share Adam's condemnation and death, so now they share Christ's vindication and life.

After these three statements in which what happened in Adam and what happened in Christ are contrasted, Paul presents two positive statements of the parallels. Once again we are told that transgression

---

[6] Cf. H. G. Liddell and R. Scott, rev. H. S. Jones, *A Greek-English Lexicon* (Oxford, 1940).

led to condemnation for all men; but this time the parallel to παράπτωμα is δικαίωμα, and the result of this δικαίωμα is righteousness of life for all men. The sentence is most commonly understood to mean: just as *the transgression* of one man led to condemnation for many, so too *the righteous act* of one man led to righteousness of life for many. This, of course, necessitates taking δικαίωμα in a different sense from that which it has in verse 16, and understanding it of Christ's righteous activity. The sentence is then parallel to the final declaration in verse 19: as through *the disobedience* of one man many were made sinners, so through *the obedience* of one man many were made righteous.

This interpretation is not, however, without its problems. For one thing, 'condemnation' and 'righteousness of life' are not true parallels. Moreover, it necessitates understanding δικαίωμα in two different senses in verses 16 and 18 – and though this is possible, δικαίωμα then seems an odd term to use of Christ in verse 18: what does Paul mean by Christ's 'righteous act'? Is it simply another way of referring to his obedience? Is it not more natural to understand it here, as in verse 16, as an act of acquittal or vindication (in contrast to κατάκριμα) – this time, however, with reference to Christ himself?[7] A great deal depends on how we understand the phrase δι' ἑνὸς: does Paul intend to compare one man's transgression and one man's righteous act, or is he referring here to one act of transgression and one act of righteousness?[8] In the former case, the contrast has shifted already to the two representative figures of Adam and Christ; in the latter, the contrast is still between man's transgression and God's activity in setting things right, and δικαίωμα is the equivalent of χάρισμα.

If δικαίωμα does, in fact, have the same meaning in verse 18 as in verse 16, and refers to one act of vindication or acquittal, then Paul's statement here not only sums up the argument of the previous three verses, but explains how the reversal of man's situation has taken place: just as one act of trespass led to condemnation for all men, so one act of setting things right led to righteousness of life for all men. The two statements are not, as we have seen, strictly parallel, for the comparison is between the two different ways in which one act leads to

---

[7] Cf. J. C. O'Neill, *Paul's Letter to the Romans* (Harmondsworth, 1975), *in loc.*

[8] C. E. B. Cranfield, *The Epistle to the Romans (ICC,* Edinburgh, 1975), vol. 1, *in loc.*, argues that since ἑνός is masculine throughout vv. 17 and 19, and since the whole section is concerned with the parallel between Adam and Christ, it is natural to take ἑνός as masculine in v. 18 also. The closest parallel to the statement in v. 18 is, however, v. 16b, where ἑνός clearly refers to παράπτωμα. Moreover, in vv. 15, 16a, 17 and 19, the use of ἄνθρωπος (or an equivalent) makes the personal reference plain.

something of universal significance, and not between the results: but there is also a contrast between the two judicial acts of κατάκριμα and δικαίωμα. God's act of vindication in raising Christ from the dead stands over against the initial transgression, and the contrast in verse 19 between Christ's obedience and Adam's disobedience explains how this act of acquittal was possible. The surprise comes in the fact that it is acquittal which leads to righteousness of life and not vice versa.[9]

However we interpret this passage, it is clear that Paul understands the 'justification' of believers to be dependent upon the death and resurrection of Christ. What I am concerned to argue is that this dependence is for Paul even closer and more logical than is often recognized: Christ's death and resurrection lead to 'justification' for many precisely because he himself is 'justified' by God and acknowledged as righteous. The disobedience of Adam led to condemnation for him and for all men, who share the consequence of condemnation, namely death, because they are 'in Adam';[10] the obedience of Christ led to vindication for him and for all those who are 'in him', and the consequence of his acquittal is life. The symmetry in these verses is not perfect, and the reason for this is, I suggest, that Paul is not only contrasting Adam and Christ as representative figures, but also opposing the transgression of Adam and *God's* act of restoration in Christ.

Although we have no actual formula of interchange in Rom. 5, therefore, it seems that the idea itself underlies Paul's understanding of the way in which man's condition in Adam is reversed in Christ: Christ shares in man's situation, i.e. he comes under condemnation and sentence of death, and men in turn share in his vindication and resurrection.

The clearest expression in Romans of this idea of interchange is found in chapter 8. In this chapter Paul reaches the climax of his exposition of man's redemption. I have already argued that 5.12–19 is a key passage in that it sums up what Paul has said in the previous chapters about man's plight, in the representative figure of Adam; in typically chiastic form, the implications of what he says in those verses about the parallel figure of Christ are drawn out in terms of man's salvation in chapters 6–8. At the beginning of chapter 8, Paul declares

---

[9] Diagrammatically, one would have to set the contrast out in this way:

παράπτωμα → κατάκριμα
δικαίωμα → δικαίωσις.

[10] This solidarity with Adam means that they come under the condemnation of death even when they do not share his transgression, vv. 13–14.

that those who are in Christ are free from condemnation, κατάκριμα: what the Jewish Law had been unable to do, i.e. set men free from the grip of sin and death consequent to Adam's transgression, has now been done by God himself. By sending his own Son in the likeness of sinful flesh and for sin, he has condemned sin in the flesh, in order that the δικαίωμα of the Law might be fulfilled in us. Once again we meet the perplexing word δικαίωμα, and once again there is considerable debate regarding its meaning. Many commentators give to it the meaning which it frequently has in the LXX, as well as in Rom. 1.32 and 2.26, i.e. 'regulation' or 'requirement'.[11] But Paul has just stated that the Christian is dead to the Law, and it would therefore seem very strange if he were now to tell us that by sending his Son God enables us to keep the Law's requirements. Others have understood the Law's requirement to be a verdict of condemnation:[12] but condemnation was something which the Law had shown itself entirely capable of doing! Paul is here referring to something which the Law could *not* do, and which only God could do; moreover this δικαίωμα which is fulfilled in us seems to stand in *contrast* to the condemnation of verse 1: as in Rom. 5.16, κατάκριμα and δικαίωμα are in opposition. It therefore seems best to interpret δικαίωμα as meaning the Law's requirement that we should be found righteous.[13] The meaning is close to that which it has in chapter 5, but not exactly the same, since this time Paul is concerned with the condemnation and declaration of righteousness which are pronounced by the Law rather than by God himself; in both passages Paul is concerned with the declaration of righteousness which reverses our previous condition of being under condemnation.

The connection between Paul's argument in chapter 5 and what he says in chapter 8 is clear: it is by entering the condition of Adam – coming in the likeness of sinful flesh[14] – that Christ has been able to free men from condemnation. The consequences are worked out in the rest of chapter 8. Instead of living according to the flesh, believers now live according to the Spirit; they have exchanged the death which comes through sin for the life which comes through righteousness. The Spirit of God who raised Jesus from the dead lives in them, and so they themselves are given life; the Spirit of the Son lives in them, and so they

[11] So, e.g. Cranfield, *Epistle to the Romans, in loc.*
[12] P. Benoit, 'La Loi et la Croix d'après saint Paul', *Revue Biblique* (1938), 481–509: ET in *Jesus and the Gospel* (London, 1974), pp. 11–39.
[13] So, e.g. C. K. Barrett, *The Epistle to the Romans* (London, 1957), *in loc.*
[14] The notion of interchange gives us the explanation for that puzzling use of the word 'sinful', which serves to stress the idea of Christ's solidarity with mankind.

too become children of God. Here we have the full working out of the idea of 'interchange': God sent his Son in the likeness of sinful flesh, *in order that* the Law's demand for righteousness might be fulfilled in us, who no longer live according to flesh but according to the Spirit – the Spirit by which we share Christ's relationship of sonship to God. The remaining verses of the chapter elaborate what it means to be children of God: we are to be conformed to the image of the Son, so that he becomes the first-born among many brothers; Christians share his glory, and creation itself is restored. The resurrection of Christ means new life for the whole of creation.

The argument in Rom. 8 is very similar to that used in Gal. 3–4, where we have two of Paul's statements of 'interchange'. The clearer of them is in Gal. 4.4f, where Paul writes: 'God sent his Son, born of a woman, born under the Law, *in order that* those under the Law might be redeemed, and *in order that* we might receive sonship'; here, as in Romans, the proof of sonship is the gift of the Spirit. The saying in Gal. 3.13 is more difficult: 'Christ redeemed us from the Law, becoming a curse for us, in order that the blessing of Abraham might come in Christ Jesus to the Gentiles.' Here, too, we have the idea of redemption from the Law; the curse of the Law is contrasted with the blessing promised to Abraham's descendants, who are now identified as those who are in Christ, whether they are Jew or Gentile. Paul does not explain how one who is made a curse becomes a source of blessing; but since it is 'in Christ' that the blessing comes, and since it is by being identified with the one true descendant of Abraham that Jews and Gentiles receive the promise, it is clear that the curse has been annulled – transformed into blessing. This can only be through the resurrection: the judgement of the Law – that Christ was under a curse – has been overthrown; God himself has vindicated his Son as righteous and those who have faith in him are reckoned righteous and live (Gal. 3.11).[15]

Paul does not explain in Rom. 8 how it is that the sending of God's Son in the likeness of sinful flesh frees men from condemnation. There is, however, a significant hint in verse 17 as to how the change in our status is effected. We share Christ's status in relation to God, only if we suffer with him in order that we may be glorified with him. It is not only that Christ shares our death, but that we deliberately share his – and in doing so are enabled to share in his resurrection. This idea has

---

[15] A. T. Hanson, *Studies in Paul's Technique and Theology* (London, 1974), pp. 13–51, argues that the quotation from Hab. 2.4 is understood by Paul as a prophecy of the Messiah himself. Although this seems unlikely, Hanson's stress on Jesus as the vindicated one in Paul's understanding is welcome.

already been spelt out in chapter 6, where Paul speaks of baptism as a burial into the death of Christ: if we are united with his death, we shall also be united with his resurrection; in dying, Christ died to sin, in living, he lives to God, and the Christian who has died with Christ must consider himself, also, to be dead to sin and alive to God *in Christ Jesus*. To be 'in Christ', therefore, to be joined to him in baptism, and so to die with him and rise with him, means to share in his death to sin and in his release from the power of sin; it is to share in his acquittal before the Law, and in the declaration of his righteousness before God. Paul's understanding of redemption here is based on the idea of Christ as Representative Man: we share in his righteousness, just as we once shared in Adam's transgression and condemnation. This is precisely the idea which I suggested was summed up in Rom. 5.18: one act of transgression led to condemnation for all: one act of acquittal led to righteousness for all. It is by union with Christ that men and women share in his experience and are declared righteous by God.

This interpretation of Paul's thought implies that he must have understood the resurrection of Christ as itself a great act of vindication, a declaration of his righteousness by God. The only clear statement of this idea in the Pauline literature occurs in 1 Tim. 3.16, where we read that Christ was 'manifested in the flesh, vindicated (justified) in the spirit'. It would be rash indeed to give undue weight to a passage from the Pastorals, especially to one which is clearly a quotation from an earlier 'creed' unless, of course, we were to argue that this is a 'Pauline fragment' incorporated by the author. Nevertheless, it is interesting to notice that the idea of Christ's vindication at the resurrection occurs in a confession of faith which is quoted as though it were well known in Pauline circles. Moreover, there are significant links between this statement and the one found in Rom. 1.3f, which may or may not be Paul's own formulation, but which is of importance because it presents his introductory summary of the gospel as being about God's Son, 'who was descended from David according to the flesh and has been declared to be Son of God in power according to the Spirit of holiness by the resurrection from the dead'. Here we have the same contrast as in 1 Tim. 3 between flesh and Spirit, between what Christ was by birth and what he was declared to be by the resurrection. These two verses in Rom. 1 have been the centre of much debate, in particular as to whether or not the formula is adoptionist. It is however clear that for Paul himself the resurrection is an acknowledgement of what Christ is, and that the participle ὁρισθέντος should be understood as 'declared' rather than as 'appointed': the resurrection is the acknowledgement of

Jesus by God as his Son.[16] The resurrection in itself implies that Jesus is recognized as righteous before God, and the title 'Son of God' expresses the same idea, since in Jewish thought the term is used for those who are righteous and are acknowledged by God as such.[17] It would seem, then, that Rom. 1.3f expresses ideas which are very close indeed to those found in 1 Tim. 3.16, where the resurrection is spoken of as the 'vindication' or 'justification' of Christ.

Similar ideas are found in Phil. 2, once again in a crucial summary of the saving events, and once again in a passage which may well be common tradition rather than Paul's own composition. Here, too, we have a contrast between the two modes of Christ's existence, expressed this time in terms of humiliation and exaltation. Although the terms are different, the pattern is similar to the one we find in Rom. 1.3f. There, the gospel is about God's Son, who was son of David according to the flesh, and declared to be Son of God by the resurrection. In Philippians, the so-called 'hymn' is about one who was in the form of God, who took the form of a slave in his human life, and who was exalted by God and acknowledged to be Lord. In both cases, God's action in raising or exalting Christ is understood as an act of vindication which, though it gives him a new status, is nevertheless an acknowledgement of what is already true.[18]

We have seen already how the ideas found in Rom. 1.3f – on the one hand, Christ's sharing in our humanity, on the other his unique sonship – form the basis of Paul's argument in later chapters in Romans:[19] it is precisely because he was born 'according to the flesh' and shared *our* death that we can share his; it is because he was acknowledged Son of God 'according to the Spirit of holiness' by the resurrection of the dead that we can share both *his* resurrection and his status of sonship. The christological statement in Rom. 1.3f, when it is brought into relation with man's redemption in the later chapters of

[16] L. C. Allen, 'The Old Testament background of (ΠΡΟ)'ΟΡΙΖΕΙΝ in the New Testament', *NTS*, 17 (1970), 104–8, suggests that the background of the use of the verb here is the enthronement decree in Ps. 2.7.

[17] E.g. Wisd. 2.16, 18; 5.5. The idea of sonship was also linked in Jewish thought with the promise of life; this connection is explored by B. J. Byrne, in *'Sons of God' – 'Seed of Abraham'* (Rome, 1979).

[18] In Rom. 10.9, confession that Jesus is Lord is balanced by the belief that God has raised him from the dead.

[19] Cf. J. D. G. Dunn, 'Jesus – flesh and spirit: an exposition of Romans i. 3–4', *JTS*, NS 24 (1973), 40–68, who argues that the phrases κατὰ σάρκα and κατὰ πνεῦμα have the same connotation in Rom. 1.3f as in the rest of Romans, and that what is said here about Christ's descent from David therefore has a pejorative, not an honorific, significance.

the epistle, is worked out in terms of an interchange of experience between Christ and the believer.

In a very similar way, Paul takes up the ideas expressed in the christological passage in Phil. 2, and applies them, in a pattern of interchange, to the theme of our redemption. This occurs at the end of chapter 3, where we have repeated echoes of the language of chapter 2. Our hope is for the coming of our Lord Jesus Christ – the same Jesus Christ who was acknowledged as 'Lord' in 2.11; the one who was found in the *form* of a slave and the *fashion* of a man, who *humiliated* himself to a shameful death, is going to *refashion* our body of *humiliation, conforming* it to his own body of glory.[20] In these verses, Paul works out the meaning of Christ's exaltation for the believer: those who are in Christ share in the reversal of status which he experienced when God raised him up. If Christ became what we are when he took the form of a slave and was found in the likeness and fashion of a man, we share what he is by virtue of his exaltation.

Once again, however, this idea of interchange is far from being automatic. Christ shares our humiliation, but if we are to share his glory, then we must share *his* humiliation. This refers not simply to the symbolic rite of baptism, but to the Christian's attitude to life, and to the attitude governing the whole Christian community. However paradoxical it may sound, we are to become like Christ in his self-emptying – which for him meant becoming like us: hence we have Paul's appeal to have the mind which is found in Christ Jesus.[21] Just as in Rom. 8.17, Paul declares that we must suffer with Christ if we are to be glorified with him, so in Phil. 3.10, he speaks of experiencing both the power of the resurrection and the fellowship of Christ's sufferings; Paul must be conformed to Christ's death if he is to attain the resurrection from the dead.

But how does this pattern of interchange in Phil. 2–3 work? Why should those who share Christ's sufferings and death share also in his

[20] See above, ch. 1, pp. 20f.

[21] Commentators have given very different interpretations to this appeal, ranging from the traditional 'ethical' interpretation, which understands the words as a command to have the mind seen in Jesus himself, to the more recent interpretation, which takes them as a command to be what one is in Christ. There is no need, however, to make these into exclusive alternatives: Paul's demand is not simply to imitate the historical Jesus, but neither is it to conform to some Christian character which is unrelated to the historical Jesus; rather it is to demonstrate a way of life which has its origin in the life of Jesus himself, and which is possible only because of the saving events of the gospel. Hence the paradox that Christians become like Christ by being identified with an attitude which was expressed in his becoming like us. Cf. below, ch. 7.

resurrection and glory? A clue to Paul's understanding of the process is found in the section in between these two passages, at the beginning of chapter 3, where Paul warns his readers concerning the circumcisers, and opposes two kinds of 'righteousness', the righteousness which is based on the Law and that which is found in Christ. Paul has abandoned everything else in order to gain Christ and be found in him, and the righteousness which he now has is not his own, but the righteousness which proceeds from God and which is given through faith in Christ. One commentator on this passage remarks that 'righteousness has here had forced upon it a meaning which is not really proper to it; in this context, the meaning which is required would be given better by the word "forgiveness".'[22] But Paul is referring here, not simply to something which is received, like forgiveness, but to a status enjoyed by those on whom it is bestowed. God's righteousness is given to those who have none of their own, but who are 'in Christ': it is theirs only because it belongs to Christ and they are in him. To have this righteousness is to know both Christ and the power of his resurrection – the event by which Christ himself was declared to be righteous.

A similar expression of this idea is found in 1 Cor.1.30, another passage which is concerned with the contrast between relying on one's own powers and on the powers of God. In 1 Corinthians, however, this contrast is expressed in terms of wisdom and knowledge, rather than law and righteousness, an interesting example of the 'translation' of the gospel from one culture to another. Nevertheless, the word 'righteous' does occur in the concluding summary of chapter 1, where Paul reminds the Corinthians that God himself is the source of their existence 'in Christ Jesus', who has become for us 'wisdom, righteousness, sanctification and redemption'. Christ is the source of wisdom, and this wisdom turns out to be the self-giving demonstrated on the Cross. The Corinthians, who hanker after wisdom, are therefore wise only when they are 'in Christ' and share this attitude, so contrary to worldly standards. Similarly, it is by being in Christ and by sharing his righteousness that they become righteous.

To be in Christ is to be identified with what he is. It is not surprising, then, if his resurrection and vindication as the righteous one lead both to the acknowledgement of believers as righteous, and to their resurrection. One of the peculiarities of Rom.1.3f is the fact that it refers to the resurrection of the dead in the plural: it seems unlikely that

---

[22] F. W. Beare, *The Epistle to the Philippians* (London, 1959), p. 120.

this was accidental – more probable that it implies that the resurrection of Christ involves the resurrection of those who are united with him. Certainly this link is brought out in the later chapters of Romans. The fullest exploration of this theme is, however, in 1 Cor.15, where Paul uses again the parallel between Adam and Christ: 'for since death came by a man, resurrection of the dead has also come by a man. As in Adam all die, so also in Christ shall all be made alive.' Paul then contrasts what it meant to be 'in Adam' and 'in Christ'. On the one hand, we have a physical body which is corruptible, dishonourable and weak; on the other a spiritual body, characterized by incorruptibility, glory and power. Adam was from the earth, but the last Adam was from heaven, and those who belong to them share in what they are: as we have borne the image of the earthly man, so we shall bear the image of the heavenly – and that means we shall share in his resurrection. Once again, it is because Christ himself was 'Adam', and exchanged corruption for incorruption, shame for glory, weakness for power, that those who are in him are able to exchange the image of the earthly for the image of the heavenly.

In Rom.5 Paul explores the Adam/Christ parallel primarily in terms of sin and righteousness, in 1 Cor.15 in terms of death and resurrection; the two themes are, however, closely intertwined: sin and righteousness lead to death and life respectively in Rom. 5, and the sting of death in 1 Corinthians is sin. If Christ has not been raised, declares Paul in 1 Cor. 15.17, your faith is futile and you are still in your sins. Here we see once again the close link between righteousness and resurrection: it is because Christ has been raised from the dead that we are set free from our sins and accounted righteous.

Christian theology and devotion have both concentrated on the sufferings and death of Christ in attempting to explain the meaning of atonement, often leaving no real place for the resurrection, except as a subsequent event. There are various reasons for this development: one is the fact that the Cross inevitably confronts Christians with the question, 'Why?', a question which many of the New Testament writers were content to answer with a reference to scripture or the purpose of God, but which increasingly was linked with the experience of reconciliation with God; another is the influence played by the epistle to the Hebrews, where the Old Testament sacrificial system is used as a source of imagery in explaining the superiority of Christ to everything which went before. It is natural to read Paul through the spectacles of later theology and to assume that for him, too, his understanding of atonement was concentrated on the death of Jesus.

Nevertheless, however much Paul may insist (in writing to the Corinthians!) that he knows no gospel except Christ crucified, he is equally insistent that if Christ has not been raised from death, Christian faith is vain: 'you are still in your sins', and there is no hope of resurrection life. It would be absurd to deny that Paul does use images which link the death of Christ with the theme of atonement: Christ is sacrificed for us as our Passover (1 Cor. 5.7); he has been put forward by God as an expiation by his blood (Rom. 3.25); we have been justified by his blood (Rom. 5.9). What has often been overlooked, however, is the close link between the resurrection and redemption which we have been exploring: if Chirst's *death* deals with *sin*, it is his *resurrection* which is the basis of our *righteousness*.

This understanding of the atonement is neatly summed up by Paul in Rom. 4.25: 'Jesus our Lord was given up to death because of our trespasses and raised for the sake of our justification.' This antithesis is often assumed by commentators to be merely rhetorical. However, in view of what we have seen elsewhere of Paul's understanding of our justification, it seems more likely that the links between trespasses and death on the one hand and justification and resurrection on the other are deliberate. He shows in Rom. 5 how trespasses led to death for all, and how Christ's resurrection led in turn to justification and life. This is worked out in chapter 6 in terms of our death to sin and resurrection to righteousness, and in chapter 7 in terms of our death to the Law, which means that we can belong to one who has been raised from the dead: in chapter 8 the Spirit of life (i.e. the Spirit who raised Jesus from death, v. 11) sets us free from sin and death. Here in 4.25 we see how it is precisely because Christ shared in the death which results from our transgressions, that he could be raised from the dead and so become the source of our righteousness.[23] This particular summary in Rom. 4.25 comes at the conclusion of an argument demonstrating that Abraham was justified on the basis of his faith – the faith which he displayed when he believed in God 'who gives life to the dead and calls into existence things which do not exist'. Christians share Abraham's faith and show themselves to be his sons, since they believe in one who 'raised Jesus Christ our Lord from the dead'. The faith which is 'reckoned to us for righteousness' is faith in the power of God to raise Christ from the dead. The stress throughout is on faith in the resurrection.

[23] The apparent symmetry of the two clauses disguises the difference in construction; διὰ is used with the accusative in two different senses, since the giving-up of Jesus *follows* human transgression, and his resurrection *leads* to our justification.

The link between justification and resurrection is a natural one. To pronounce a man righteous is to reverse the condemnation which sentenced him to death. It is hardly surprising, then, if Rom. 5.18 apparently identifies righteousness with life; sin and death on the one hand are more than balanced by righteousness and life on the other.

We have seen that the idea of 'interchange' between the believer and Christ is linked with Paul's understanding of the solidarity of mankind with Christ and with Adam. Inevitably, therefore, the relationship cannot be a mutual one, since the believer is always dependent upon Christ. Christ identifies himself with the human situation, and shares human experience, even to the point of death; the Christian, however, is able to share Christ's resurrection (and all that this means) only if he is willing to identify himself with Christ's death. By dying with Christ to sin, the believer is able to share in the verdict of 'not guilty' pronounced on Christ at the resurrection. The process is a paradoxical one: Christ empties himself and humbles himself in identifying himself with mankind and becoming what men are; they in turn must identify themselves with his shame and death if they are to become what he is in his glorious resurrection life. I have argued that the pattern of reversal is based on the resurrection, and that this is understood by Paul in terms of Christ's vindication. It is because Christ is acknowledged as righteous, that believers are 'justified'; because he is declared to be Son of God that we, too, receive sonship; because he is glorified that mankind is restored to glory. This seems to be the logic of Paul's argument, even though it must be admitted that the idea of Christ's resurrection as vindication is very rarely spelt out. The question therefore arises, why is there so little emphasis on this particular idea, if it is the foundation of Paul's understanding of the manner of man's justification?

Twenty-five years ago, Professor Moule presented a paper entitled, 'From defendant to judge – and deliverer',[24] in which he argued that 'the figure of the one who is rejected but is ultimately vindicated is even more widely used in the biblical presentation of the gospel than is sometimes recognized'. He explored this theme primarily in terms of the Son of man, who is (or so some of us believe) a figure who suffers and who looks for vindication, but becomes the one who himself acts as judge of the nations. It is, I believe, possible to trace a shift of emphasis

---

[24] Originally published in the *Bulletin of the Studiorum Novi Testamenti Societas* (Cambridge, 1952), 40–53; reprinted in C. F. D. Moule, *The Phenomenon of the New Testament* (London, 1967), pp. 82–99. See also T. W. Manson, 'The Son of man in Daniel, Enoch, and the Gospels', *BJRL*, 32 (1949–50), 171–95. Reprinted in M. Black (ed.), *Studies in the Gospels and Epistles* (Manchester, 1962).

within the gospel tradition, with the result that sayings which in one context suggest vindication for the Son of man are interpreted in another of his role as deliverer. A similar shift of interpretation has taken place, I suggest, in relation to the resurrection of Jesus in the Pauline epistles. In itself, God's act in raising Jesus from the dead is clearly a vindication of Jesus as righteous, and this interpretation is naturally most clearly to be seen in summaries of the gospel. When Paul explores the theme of redemption, however, and the way in which God has dealt with the plight of mankind, the emphasis shifts somewhat; Christians, rather than Christ himself, are now seen as the recipients of God's deliverance, though it is still those who are 'in Christ' who are justified. Meanwhile Jesus' own role is understood as less passive and more active: he is not only 'given up' by God on our behalf (Rom. 8.32) but 'gives himself up' for our sakes (Gal. 2.20); it is God who justifies (Rom. 8.33), but Jesus, who has been raised from the dead, is now at God's right hand and will intercede for us (Rom. 8.34); having been himself vindicated, he argues the case of those who belong to him.

It is one of the remarkable features of Romans, which sets out the fullest exposition Paul gives us of man's reconciliation to God, that it offers little indication as to how this reconciliation was achieved – except that it was through the death and resurrection of Jesus. The epistle opens with a lengthy declaration of the necessity for dealing with man's sinful condition, and this is followed by a short paragraph at the end of chapter 3 describing how sin has been dealt with; even this is perhaps to be understood as one image among many which could be used of the death of Christ – one way of expressing what has been achieved. Perhaps this lack of explanation is not so strange if we remember that the writers of the New Testament were starting from experience and not from ready-made theories; they used a variety of images, and perhaps never attempted to produce a rational explanation. We distort their meaning when we try to force their metaphors into a consistent pattern.

Yet it is arguable that for Paul the idea of human solidarity is a vitally important factor in the substructure of his thought, more fundamental than all the images he uses; and that for him, man's redemption is seen primarily in terms of moving from the sphere of Adam to the sphere of Christ. The belief that it is possible for the believer to do this is dependent upon the fact that the Son of God came in the likeness of Adam's sinful flesh, and so enabled those in Adam to become children of God. The idea of interchange of experience in Christ is a vital clue to Paul's understanding of atonement.

3
Interchange and suffering

In a book published more than twenty years ago, which he character-istically described as a 'slight essay', Professor Moule[1] discussed what he termed the 'strange paradox' at the heart of Christian faith, arising from 'the finality and yet constantly repetitive nature of salvation – the finished work of God in Christ, over against his continued work in the Body of Christ which is the Church'. It is one aspect of this tension, namely the relationship between the sufferings of Christ and those of Christians, that I wish to explore in this essay.

In the last two essays explaining the theme of 'Interchange', I have argued for the importance of the theme of participation for under-standing the Pauline view of redemption. In various key texts,[2] Paul expresses the belief that – to adapt the words of Irenaeus[3] – Christ became what we are, in order that, *in him*, we might become what he is. Christ identified himself with the human condition, bore the likeness of Adam, in order that men and women might bear his likeness and become children of God. Commentators have at times interpreted some of these passages in substitutionary terms, but a careful analysis shows that this is a misinterpretation. It is not a case of Christ becoming what we are in order that we might become what he once was. If we experience glory and life as a result of Christ's self-humiliation and death, then this is because he himself has been raised in glory; if righteousness comes to us as a result of Christ being made sin, then this is because he himself has been acknowledged as righteous at the resurrection. What happens to us, as a result of what happens to him, happens only because we share in his experience of vindication and reversal. In other words, Christ is so identified with humanity, that he is able to act as our representative. 'Christ died for us so that we might live' (1 Thess. 5.10) may sound like a simple exchange, but in fact our life depends upon the fact that we live 'with him'. Christ died

---

[1] C. F. D. Moule, *The Sacrifice of Christ* (London, 1956).
[2] 2 Cor. 5.21; 8.9; Gal. 3.13; 4.4; Rom. 8.3, 14; Phil. 2.6–10; 3.20f.
[3] See above ch. 1, n. 18.

42

for us, in order that we might share his resurrection. This is no simple exchange, but a sharing of experience, and the phrase 'with him' emphasizes the dependence of the believer upon Christ. The basis of Paul's understanding of the believer's participation in Christ is set out more clearly in Rom. 5.12–19, in his contrast between the representative figures of Adam and Christ. The argument that everything that happened in Adam has been reversed in Christ depends upon the belief that what happens to one man can affect all men. In the case of Adam, he is regarded as a representative and inclusive figure: what he did affects all men because they are all his descendants. In the case of Christ, he too can be understood as a representative figure because he is the Christ/Messiah: what he did affects all who share his experiences because they are 'in Christ'. In the former case, Adam's sin led to condemnation and death for all; in the latter, Christ's righteousness led to acquittal 'for all'. Man's condition in Adam is reversed in Christ because Christ was willing to share in man's condition, i.e. to come under condemnation and sentence of death; the result is that men and women are able, in turn, to share in his vindication and resurrection.

In spite of the problematic πάντες in Rom. 5.18, it is clear that Paul does not think of this interchange taking place automatically. It is necessary, not only for Christ to identify himself with us, but for us to identify ourselves with him. Our union with Adam is involuntary and automatic, but our union with Christ is the result of a deliberate act on our part, and therefore not completely analogous. Christ shares our situation of condemnation and death, but we in turn need to share in his death. It is true that 2 Cor. 5.4 states the representational view of Christ's death in such a way as to suggest that it necessarily involves the whole of humanity; nevertheless, the context makes clear that it is only those who identify themselves with Christ's death, and no longer live to themselves, who share his resurrection life. One obvious way in which this happens is in baptism. 'Do you not know', asks Paul in Rom. 6.3, 'that all of us who have been baptized into Christ Jesus were baptized into his death?' The following verses spell this out: 'We were buried with him in baptism into death *in order that*, as Christ was raised from the dead through the glory of the Father, we too might walk in newness of life' (v. 4). This pattern of death–resurrection is repeated in verses 5 and 8, in parallel conditional sentences: 'If we have been joined to the likeness of his death, we shall also share his resurrection'; 'If we died with Christ, we believe that we shall also live with him.' It is noticeable that in both statements the resurrection is understood as a future event: we have *already* shared Christ's death, and therefore we *expect* to share his resurrection. Verses 6–7 explain the significance of dying with Christ: because we have been crucified with him, we are no longer enslaved to sin, since dying sets us free. Verse 9 explains the significance of Christ's resurrection: he will never die again, for he is no longer subject to death. It should be clear from this why Paul finds it easier to speak of dying with Christ as a past event than to describe rising with Christ in the same way. For while he believes that sin should no longer rule the Christian (v. 14), the 'last enemy', death, is not yet destroyed, and though Christians have died with Christ, it cannot be said of them, as it is of Christ, that they 'will never die again'.[4] Nevertheless the death and resurrection of Christ have set a pattern for the Christian. Christ died to sin once and for all, and lives now to God (v. 10); Christians must therefore reckon themselves to be dead to sin and alive to God in Christ (v. 11). In other words, while the resurrection with Christ lies in the future, there is a sense in which we already share his resurrection life, because we are in him.[5] This is why we can 'walk in newness of life' here and now (v. 4). And this is why Paul can urge the Romans to present themselves to God 'as if' they were dead men brought to life (v. 13).

This particular passage explores the meaning of dying and rising with Christ in two ways: the first is baptism, the dramatic proclamation of Christ's death and resurrection in which the believer identifies himself with the historical event of Christ's crucifixion; the second is the ethical consequence, that one is therefore dead to sin. The two are woven together here because it is the second that Paul is concerned to stress, and he argues it on the basis of the first. Both of them, however, demonstrate that it is not enough for Christ to identify himself with humanity: the believer must also identify himself with Christ. The paradox of Christian salvation is that though Christ shares *our* death in order that we may share his life, the believer can only share that life if he, in turn, is willing to share *Christ's* death. In identifying himself with Christ, the believer makes an act of self-abnegation similar to Christ's own, and trusts himself totally to the God who is able to raise the dead to life. This attitude of total reliance upon God is parallel to that which is expressed elsewhere in the familiar terms of faith that leads to justification: it is because he is content to abandon his own pretensions to righteousness that the Christian is able to share the verdict of

[4] Cf. a similar distinction in 1 Cor. 15. In v. 17, Christ's resurrection means that we *have* been released from sin; in v. 22, it means that we *shall* all be made alive.
[5] Cf. G. M. Styler, 'Obligation in Paul's christology and ethics' in B. Lindars and S. S. Smalley (eds.), *Christ and Spirit in the New Testament: Studies in Honour of C. F. D. Moule*, (Cambridge, 1973), pp. 181–3, where he argues that Paul understands the Christian's union with Christ's resurrection as past and present as well as future.

acquittal pronounced on those who are in Christ (Rom. 8.1). This happens at baptism, but it happens again and again throughout the Christian life, which is a continual process of reckoning oneself dead to sin and alive to God.

These are not the only ways, however, in which the Christian identifies himself with the death of Christ. In Rom. 8.17 we have another form of this idea, expressed in terms that remind us of the statements about death and resurrection with Christ in Rom. 6. This verse forms the climax of a section in which Paul argues that God has set men free from sin and death by sending his Son in the likeness of sinful flesh. Christians, however, are no longer 'in the flesh' (because Christ has died to the flesh) but 'in the Spirit', and this Spirit makes them children of God, and so joint heirs with Christ, who is the Son of God. Paul uses here another form of the idea that Christ participates in the condition of men (coming in the likeness of sinful flesh), in order that they might share in his condition, i.e. be sons of God. Verse 17*b* gives us another hint as to how this change of status takes place. We become God's children and joint heirs with Christ, only if we are prepared to share his sufferings: it is necessary to suffer with him in order to be glorified with him. The verse echoes the structure of the earlier verses in Rom. 6, where dying with Christ was interpreted in terms of baptism and dying to sin:

6.4 συνετάφημεν οὖν αὐτῷ . . . εἰς τὸν θάνατον, ἵνα ὥσπερ ἠγέρθη Χριστὸς ἐκ νεκρῶν . . . οὕτως καὶ ἡμεῖς ἐν καινότητι ζωῆς περιπατήσωμεν.

6.5 εἰ γὰρ σύμφυτοι γεγόναμεν τῷ ὁμοιώματι τοῦ θανάτου αὐτοῦ, ἀλλὰ καὶ τῆς ἀναστάσεως ἐσόμεθα.

6.8 εἰ δὲ ἀπεθάνομεν σὺν Χριστῷ, πιστεύομεν ὅτι καὶ συνζήσομεν αὐτῷ.

8.17 . . . εἴπερ συνπάσχομεν ἵνα καὶ συνδοξασθῶμεν.

It is significant that the theme of 'identification with Christ' is worked out in Rom. 8 in terms of 'suffering with Christ'. Clearly it is not enough for the believer to identify himself with Christ in a once-for-all act, namely baptism. We have seen already that dying with Christ is a continuing process in relation to sin: as long as the believer continues to live 'in the flesh', he must not live 'according to the flesh', but must identify himself with Christ's once-for-all act in dying to sin (Rom. 6.10). Here in Rom. 8 we meet another way in which dying with Christ needs to be worked out in the believer's life. It is only if we suffer with him that we shall be glorified with him. We may become children of God and heirs of glory through Christ's act of self-identification with

45

us, but if we are indeed to share his glory, we must identify ourselves with his suffering. Once again, we find the paradox that though in identifying himself with us Christ made an act of self-abnegation, those who are 'in Christ' must in turn identify themselves with *his* humiliation if they are to share his glory: the pattern of death–resurrection, suffering–glory must be worked out in them.

The theme of suffering leading to glory is found in an earlier section of Romans, in 5.1–5. It is interesting to note that this follows immediately after the summary statement in 5.1, which is similar to 8.1. Both these verses sum up Paul's belief that through Christ's death Christians are free from condemnation in God's sight, and introduce a statement about what it means to live in Christ. In chapter 5, Paul says that we rejoice in hope of sharing the glory of God, and goes on to say that we even rejoice in our sufferings. Why? Because suffering produces endurance, endurance produces tried character, and tried character produces hope. As for this hope – the hope of sharing God's glory – we know that this will not be disappointed, since we have already received a pledge of the future through the work of the Holy Spirit. Support for this confidence is provided by a typically Pauline argument: 'If while we were enemies we were reconciled to God by the death of his Son, much more, now that we are reconciled, shall we be saved [from wrath] by his life' (v. 10; similarly v. 9). Christ's death 'for us' is seen as a supreme demonstration of God's love. It is interesting that in a context that describes how we are justified through the death of *Christ* and will be saved by him from wrath, we find also the theme that *our* sufferings work towards our glorification.

A similar theme is found in Phil. 3. Once again, the idea occurs in the context of a passage that contains the theme of 'interchange'. The form in which this latter theme is expressed is unusual, in that the thought of Christ's participation in our condition is spelt out in chapter 2 (in the famous so-called 'Christ-hymn'), whereas that of our participation in Christ's status does not occur until the very end of chapter 3. Nevertheless, the echoes of chapter 2 are clear: the one who was found in the *form* of a slave and the *fashion* of a man, who *humiliated* himself to a shameful death, is going to *refashion* our body of *humiliation*, con*forming* it to his own body of glory.[6] Paul does not say in Philippians, as he says elsewhere, that Christ became what we are *in order that* we might become what he is. Nevertheless, he works out in 3.21 the meaning of Christ's exaltation for the believer: because Christ took the form of a

---

[6] The details are given above, ch. 1, pp. 20f.

46

slave and was found in the likeness and fashion of a man, those who are in Christ share in what he is by virtue of his exaltation. It is certainly clearer in Philippians than anywhere else that this is no simple exchange: the reversal of status belongs to Christ, and believers hope to share in this reversal.

Yet it is also clearer in Philippians than elsewhere that this idea of our participation is far from being automatic. Christ shares our humiliation, but if we are to share his glory, then we must share his humiliation. Once again this is not confined to the idea that we are baptized into Christ's death, but is worked out in terms of the Christian's attitude to life, and indeed the attitude of the whole Christian community. The introduction to the 'hymn' makes this clear. Paradoxical as it may seem, Christians are urged to become *like* Christ in his self-emptying – which meant, for him, becoming *like us*.[7] This is spelt out even more forcefully in chapter 3, where Paul describes how he has abandoned every source of confidence 'in the flesh', including even righteousness under the Law. Everything that he formerly prized he now considers as worthless and no better than rubbish for the sake of gaining Christ. He has identified himself with Christ's act of 'self-emptying', in order that he might be found in Christ (3.9); in doing so, he has forsaken the righteousness of the Law, which is based on claims about what one has, for the righteousness that comes from God through faith – a faith that has nothing else on which to rely except God himself. The meaning of the phrase πίστις Χριστοῦ in this verse has been the subject of much debate, and the context supports the arguments of those who wish to understand it as a reference to the faithfulness or faith of Christ himself;[8] this interpretation avoids the tautology that results from taking both occurrences of the word 'faith' in this verse as references to the faith of the believer. Moreover, it fits

---

[7] Some commentators argue that the passage is to be understood as an appeal to act in the manner appropriate to those who are in Christ, and not as an appeal to act in a manner similar to that of Christ himself. This distinction is an unnecessary one, however, resulting from a dogmatic dismissal of the notion of imitating Christ. See below ch. 7. Cf. also C. F. D. Moule, 'Further reflexions on Philippians 2: 5–11' in W. Ward Gasque and Ralph P. Martin (eds.), *Apostolic History and the Gospel, Biblical and Historical Essays presented to F. F. Bruce on his Sixtieth Birthday* (Exeter, 1970), pp. 264–76; and H. D. Betz, *Nachfolge und Nachahmung Jesu Christi im Neuen Testament* (Tübingen, 1967), pp. 163–9.

[8] See e.g. A. G. Hebert, '"Faithfulness" and "Faith"', *Theology*, 58 (1955), 373–9; T. F. Torrance, 'One aspect of the biblical conception of Faith', *Exp. Tim.* 68 (1957), 111–14, and comments by C. F. D. Moule, 177, 222; R. N. Longenecker in R. J. Banks (ed.), *Reconciliation and Hope* (Exeter, 1974), pp 146–8. The debate goes back to a suggestion made by Haussleiter in an article published in 1891. See also P. Vallotton, *Le Christ et la foi* (Geneva, 1960), and ch. 14, below.

well into the theme of participation with which Paul is here concerned. If it is correct, then Paul is saying that he abandoned the righteousness of the Law for the righteousness that came about through the faith of Christ himself, a righteousness that comes from God and is received by faith. 'Faith' sums up exactly Paul's description of Christ's self-emptying in Phil. 2, since in exchanging the form of God for the form of a slave, Christ was relying totally on God. This faith was vindicated at his exaltation, which proclaimed him righteous in God's sight. It is with this faith – this willingness to empty oneself of all pretensions and accept God's gift – that Paul now identifies himself, believing that by being found in Christ he will share Christ's righteousness. This interpretation is supported by the threefold use in this section of the verb ἡγέομαι, which was used in 2.6 in the first line of the passage about Christ. Paul counted, and continues to count, everything he once prized as loss and as rubbish, in order to gain Christ and be found in him. In him he is given the righteousness that comes through Christ's own faith – a righteousness from God, based on faith.

But this status of righteousness before God is not the end of the matter. Paul's purpose is to know Christ, to experience both the power of his resurrection and the fellowship of his sufferings; it is to be conformed to Christ's death, if only by doing so he may attain the resurrection from the dead. It is noticeable that the idea of knowing Christ and the power of his resurrection is here immediately qualified by the reference to sharing his sufferings. Possibly Paul is here opposing teaching that emphasized the experience of the risen Lord in such a way as to deny both future hope and present suffering: for Paul, life in Christ means experiencing the power of Christ's resurrection, but only as one experiences also his suffering. It was because Christ emptied himself that God exalted him (Phil. 2.9), and it is those who share his sufferings who share his resurrection. In order to attain the resurrection of the dead, one must become like him in death (3.10f). Those who do not recognize this are 'enemies of the Cross' (3.18). Although the image of being conformed to Christ's death reminds us of baptism, we notice that Paul uses a present participle, συμμορφιζόμενος, to denote a continuing process, with resurrection as a future goal. It is clear that Paul does not understand dying with Christ simply in symbolic terms. Those who hope to share in his resurrection must be conformed to his death – and that means sharing in his sufferings. It is through Christ's death and resurrection that the Christian is pronounced righteous: but this does not mean that Christ's sufferings are a substitute for ours. To say 'Christ died for us in order that we might live' is only half the story:

we need to die *with him* in order to live *with him*. Dying with Christ is a continuing process, and this means that resurrection can never be totally realized in this life. In Phil. 3.12–16, Paul stresses that it is still a future goal for which he must strive. He does not claim to have reached perfection: possibly he is alluding here to Christians who did make such claims. Paul himself is still aiming for the prize that awaits him at the end of the course. The image is similar to that which Paul uses in 1 Cor. 9.24–7, a passage that is of particular interest since Paul clearly envisages that there is a situation in which he might *not* win the prize.

It is clear from these passages that, however much Paul may stress the Cross as the decisive event in man's salvation, there is a sense in which, to use his own words, the Christian community must work out its own salvation (Phil. 2.12). Christ dies as man's representative, not his substitute – and this means not only that Christ's death embodies the death of others, but that they must share his dying.

It is of course in 2 Corinthians that we meet the most extended treatment of this theme of sharing in the sufferings of Christ. In the opening thanksgiving, Paul describes the way in which, though the sufferings of Christ overflow in his direction, the consolation that comes through Christ overflows in equal measure (1.5–7). In this case, however, the sufferings are not interpreted simply in terms of Paul's own experience, but in relation to that of the community in Corinth. Paul's affliction leads to the Corinthians' comfort and salvation, his comfort to theirs – when they patiently endure the same sufferings. Paul is confident that when they share his sufferings, they share also his comfort. It is interesting to notice that we have here a remarkable parallel to the pattern that we have found elsewhere. Just as Christ's death leads to life for Christians, so Paul's affliction leads to comfort and salvation for the Corinthians. Just as Christ's resurrection brings resurrection and glory (to those who are prepared to suffer with him), so Paul's experience of comfort brings comfort to the Corinthians (provided they share his sufferings).

Going on to describe the nature of the affliction that he has experienced, Paul says that although it was so severe that he despaired of his own life, this taught him to rely on God, who raises the dead to life. It was in sharing Christ's situation of helplessness that he learned to share his hope in God (2 Cor. 1.8–10). Under apparent sentence of death, Paul was delivered from danger, and so, in a sense, brought back to life. The difference between the two experiences of interchange referred to in 2 Corinthians, the one linked with Christ's death and the other with Paul's sufferings, is that the second experience derives from, and is dependent on, the first. It is because Paul shares in Christ's sufferings that his own are of benefit to others: it is those who are in Christ who experience the life that comes through death.

Paul takes this theme up again in chapter 4 of 2 Corinthians, a passage that follows on from the defence of his ministry in chapter 3 and may well reflect accusations from his opponents about his weakness and lack of dignity. Immediately after declaring that Christians are changed into Christ's likeness and glory, Paul describes how this 'treasure' is continued in 'earthen vessels' – once again, in order that we may learn to rely upon the power of God (v. 7). This passage provides us with Paul's fullest exploration of the theme of life-through-death. In a series of striking phrases, he describes various ways in which he is 'always carrying in the body the death of Jesus, in order that the life of Jesus may also be manifested' in his body (vv. 8–10). It is by sharing the dying of Jesus that he is able to experience the life of Jesus – a theme so important that Paul restates it in verse 11. Then once again he moves on to the idea that his own sufferings can benefit the Corinthians: 'So death is at work in us, but life in you' (v. 12).

He now introduces a quotation from the Psalms: 'Having the same spirit of faith, according to that which is written – "I believed, therefore I spoke" – we also believe, and therefore speak' (v. 13). In discussing the word 'same' here, commentators are divided between those who think that it refers to the psalmist[9] and those who suggest that it refers to the Corinthians.[10] The former suggestion seems awkward, since the psalmist's words are introduced into the argument as an ordinary proof-text,[11] while the latter suggestion does not really fit the context. It is important to note that Paul clearly understands faith here as faith in God, who raised Christ from the dead and brings life out of death. This is the faith that Paul claims to share. If he intends any answer to the commentators' question 'the same faith as whom?',

[9] E.g. C. K. Barrett, *The Second Epistle to the Corinthians* (London, 1973), *in loc.*
[10] E.g. R. H. Strachan, *The Second Epistle of Paul to the Corinthians* (London, 1935); W. Schmithals, *Gnosticism in Corinth*, trans. John E. Steely (Nashville and New York, 1971), p. 162.
[11] If the Old Testament quotation is intended to refer us to its original context, then it would certainly be appropriate here, for vv. 1–9 of the psalm describe the sufferings of the psalmist. However, the wording of the citation in 2 Corinthians reproduces exactly the LXX version, where what is Ps. 116.10 in the Hebrew text begins a new psalm – a psalm of deliverance. If Paul is quoting from the LXX, as the wording suggests, then it would seem that he is using the quotation atomistically. The Hebrew wording of the verse is difficult, and is variously interpreted, but its meaning seems to be significantly different from the LXX.

perhaps it is 'Jesus'. It is the death of Jesus that has just been mentioned in verses 10f. and is referred to again in verse 14, where Paul expresses confidence that the one who raised Jesus will raise 'us' with Jesus. If the interpretation of Phil. 3.9 given above is correct, then possibly we have here a parallel to the idea that in his death Christ demonstrated faith in the one who could raise him from the dead, and that those who are prepared to share his dying share his faith. It is significant that in 2 Cor. 4, as in 1.9, the theme of suffering with Christ is interwoven with that of faith in God who raises the dead.

In verse 15 Paul reiterates the thought expressed in verse 12 that his sufferings benefit the Corinthians. But not only the Corinthians. His temporary affliction is insignificant when compared with the eternal glory towards which it is working. As in Rom. 8.17 and Phil. 3.10f, we find Paul emphasizing that the sufferings of believers play a role in bringing about future glory. The process of glorification is not yet complete (cf. 3.18).

The opening verses of 2 Cor. 5 continue the theme of faith in God to bring life out of death (vv. 1–5), and lead on to the thought that the end of the process will mean not only glory but judgement (v. 10). This is a theme that is hinted at in Phil. 3.12–16 (cf. also 1 Cor. 9.24–7). Paul's doctrine of justification through faith does not exclude the idea of future judgement, and the reward and punishment of good and evil.

This chapter contains also a verse that sums up neatly some of the ideas that we have been examining. The statement that Christ has died for all in verse 14 might be understood – and has sometimes been understood – as substitutionary.[12] But Paul immediately adds the words 'therefore all have died', showing clearly that he understands Christ to have died as man's representative. Yet this death is something that men need to appropriate for themselves. Christ died for all, says Paul, so that 'those who live might live no longer for themselves but for him who for their sake died and was raised'. By living *for* him, they share his self-giving and are controlled by his love. This is why, if anyone is in Christ, there is a new creation (v. 17): just as death leads to life, so the old gives way to the new. The idea that dying with Christ means living under the control of Christ is spelt out also in Gal. 2.20f.

But Paul is concerned primarily in 2 Cor. 5 with his own apostolic calling. He has been entrusted with the ministry of reconciliation – reconciliation that resulted from Christ being 'made sin for our sake'

---

[12] E.g. Leon Morris, *The Cross in the New Testament* (Exeter, 1967), p. 220.

(v. 21). Inevitably, Paul's own ministry means sharing in the humiliation and suffering of Christ (6.4–10). Once again, however, we find Paul claiming to experience 'life' through 'death'; he comes to know joy through sorrow, and finds himself possessing everything through having nothing. Familiar, too, is the idea that this interchange of experience benefits others: although he is poor, Paul makes others rich. We have only to turn on to 8.9 to discover that this is not an experience that Paul claims for apostles alone. The Corinthians are exhorted there to give generously, and so to follow the example of Christ himself, who 'being rich, became poor for your sake, in order to make you rich by his poverty'.

The idea of imitating Christ is linked in 1 Thessalonians with the theme of suffering. In the opening thanksgiving, Paul describes the Thessalonians as having become 'imitators of us and of the Lord' in that they 'received the word in much affliction, with joy inspired by the Holy Spirit'. In the following chapter, he says that they 'became imitators of the churches of God in Christ Jesus which are in Judaea; for you suffered the same things from your own countrymen as they did from the Jews, who killed both the Lord Jesus and the prophets' (2.14f). Suffering is assumed, here, to be the lot of all who believe the gospel. If they are persecuted, the Thessalonians are following in the footsteps of the Lord himself, as well as of their apostle and of the churches in Judaea.

The suffering endured by the Thessalonians was caused by persecution, and was therefore the direct result of their Christian faith. Much of Paul's own suffering was clearly due to his apostolic call, and we are not surprised to find him describing it as a sharing in the sufferings of Christ. What *is* perhaps surprising is that he appears to make no distinction between this and what we might perhaps describe as 'ordinary' suffering – the pain that results from the simple fact of being human. It is as though *all* suffering, whether it is persecution or the thorn in the flesh of 2 Cor. 12.7–10, has been baptized into Christ, and can be transformed through the experience of interchange. In other words, the power of Christ's resurrection can be experienced in suffering that results from being 'in Adam', as well as in suffering that comes through being 'in Christ'.[13] Perhaps it is because he thinks of all suffering as due, ultimately, to Satanic powers opposed to God, that Paul makes no distinction between persecution and 'natural' events.

---

[13] See above, ch. 1, pp. 23f.

The most famous of all the passages in the Pauline epistles that refer to sharing the sufferings of Christ is Col. 1.24. Paul's own sufferings are described here as being ὑπὲρ ὑμῶν, and as 'filling up what is lacking of the afflictions of Christ'. Most commentators are concerned to stress what Paul does *not* mean here: in the words of J. B. Lightfoot: 'St. Paul would have been the last to say that [Christians] bear their part in the atoning sacrifice of Christ.'[14] Lightfoot went on to point out that 'the idea of expiation or satisfaction is wholly absent from this passage'. It is indeed only because commentators have approached Col. 1.24 with preconceived notions about the Pauline understanding of Christ's death that it has caused them difficulties. One can go further than Lightfoot and suggest that the ideas of expiation or substitution (which are not necessarily the same thing) are in fact far from central in Pauline thought, so that their absence here is by no means surprising. The interpretation of Christ's death as a once-for-all event is *one* model used by New Testament writers, but is not the only one. When Paul speaks of Christ's death in relation to sin, *then* he describes it in once-for-all terms. But the theme of dying-to-live is an ongoing process, in which Christians share. In describing his own sufferings as 'for you', Paul says no more than he says throughout 2 Corinthians. The belief that his sufferings can benefit others does not involve the idea that they also atone for the sins of others. Indeed, there are two occasions when Paul speaks about suffering ὑπὲρ Χριστοῦ. It might perhaps be possible to explain both away as meaning little more than 'as Christians'. But in 2 Cor. 12.10, Paul is acting as Christ's apostle and representative in accepting weakness, insults and hardships. And in Phil. 1.29, Paul uses the phrase twice, and writes that it has been granted to the Philippians τὸ ὑπὲρ Χριστοῦ πάσχειν. Paul speaks often of Christ suffering ὑπὲρ ἡμῶν: but here we find him using a parallel phrase in describing the sufferings of Christ's followers. It is not so surprising, then, in Col. 1.24, to find him writing of his own sufferings as 'filling up what is lacking in the sufferings of Christ', or describing this as of benefit to Christ's body, the Church.[15] A somewhat similar idea – albeit in this case a

---

[14] J. B. Lightfoot, *Saint Paul's Epistles to the Colossians and to Philemon*, 2nd edn (London 1876), *in loc.*

[15] It seems strange that τὰ ὑστερήματα τῶν θλίψεων is normally understood as a reference to the Church's quota of sufferings. Since Paul elsewhere regards it as part of his vocation to share Christ's sufferings on behalf of the Church, it seems more likely that it is Paul's own quota of sufferings, which he sees as still needing to be completed. See W. F. Flemington, 'On the interpretation of Colossians 1:24' in William Horbury and Brian McNeil (eds.), *Suffering and Martyrdom in the New Testament* (Cambridge, 1981), pp. 84–90.

hypothetical one – is found in Rom. 9.3, where Paul expresses his willingness to be ἀνάθεμα . . . ἀπὸ τοῦ Χριστοῦ ὑπὲρ τῶν ἀδελφῶν μου.[16]

Col. 1.24 provides an interesting example of the way in which commentators have allowed their theological convictions to influence their interpretation of the text. The belief that Christ's death is decisive and once-for-all has led some of them to shy away from the straightforward meaning of the words. Another example of this can be seen in the refusal to allow that Paul ever speaks of imitating Christ.[17] Col. 1.24 reflects the conviction that we have found elsewhere in Paul's writings, that it is necessary for the Christian to share in the sufferings of Christ, and that this participation in suffering can be of benefit to other members of the Christian community. This necessity is not based on the idea that there is a set quota of messianic sufferings that need to be completed. Rather it arises from the representative character of Christ's death. If Christ died for all, this means not only that all have died, but that they must continue to work out the meaning of dying with Christ. The acceptance of Jesus as Messiah means a willingness to share his experiences. In this sense, at least, the sufferings of Christ are no substitute for ours, but a pattern to which we need to be conformed.

The tendency to stress the belief that Christ's death was a substitute for ours to the exclusion of the Pauline conviction that Christians must participate in the suffering of Christ is perhaps a very early one. The Corinthians, for example, seem to have been unable to grasp the idea that there was any place for suffering and humiliation in their calling: for them, resurrection with Christ was a *past* event, and this meant that they shared already in his glory, fullness and riches (cf. 1 Cor. 4.8). Christ had suffered – and they experienced the resulting glory. He had become for them the substitute for humiliation and death. They failed to see the necessity to share his sufferings.

The failure of the antinomians to see the need to die with Christ to sin provides an interesting parallel. For them, too, the death of Christ was a once-for-fall act bringing them release. Neither group understood Paul's insistence that the Christian life was a continuous process of self-identification with Christ. The Corinthians wanted instant glory, the antinomians instant salvation. For Paul, these are the goal of Christian living, achieved through sharing Christ's sufferings.

In contrast to the Corinthian stance, Paul emphasized the gospel of

---

[16] The idea that Paul's sufferings can lead to salvation for others reappears in 2 Tim. 2:10. But the saying has lost the passion of Paul's own sayings and reads like an assessment of his apostolic achievements.

[17] Cf. above, n. 7, on the interpretation of Phil. 2.

Christ crucified (1 Cor. 1.23). This gospel is not a mere objective fact to be believed, however, but a way of life to be accepted. Christian discipleship means identification with the crucified Lord. Faith in God means faith in the one who raises the dead – a faith shown by Christ himself. In insisting that faith is the only way to find righteousness Paul was not being arbitrary, but spelling out the very nature of his gospel. For the way of the Cross, as it is set out in Phil. 2.6–8, is the supreme example of what Paul means by faith: those who accept this way make no claims upon God, and rely totally on his grace. Those who follow this path of faith must be prepared to share the humiliation and suffering that it brings, if they wish to experience also the glory that God gives.

4

Interchange in Christ and ethics

Every student of the teaching of St Paul is familiar with the fact that his ethics are grounded in his theology. It is not simply that, in writing to the congregations in his care, he tends to deal first with theological questions and then with ethical problems; rather, the one leads inevitably into the other. It is not that ethical questions are less important, and can therefore be dealt with in the tail-end of a letter; the truth is that ethical judgements can only be made on the basis of theological understanding. And that is why a closer analysis of Paul's letters shows that the neat division into theological and ethical sections is too simple, for he sometimes points the ethical moral while expounding theology, and he frequently drops theological nuggets into the argument when grappling with ethical problems: belief and behaviour belong together.

The best place for us to begin an attempt to understand Paul's approach to ethical questions is in his letter to the Romans, since this is the nearest thing we have in his writings to systematic theology. Here, the move from theological argument to ethical problems is plain: so, too, is the link between the two. Paul brings the former to a triumphant conclusion at the end of chapter 11, and immediately begins again with the words, 'I implore you, therefore . . .' Since we tend to read Paul in snippets, we often miss the significance of the links which hold his paragraphs together; his 'therefore' at the beginning of chapter 12 is often read as though it were simply a drawing of breath, a way of launching into the next section. But the word 'therefore' is a vital logical link in Paul's argument, for what he is going to say next depends on the case he has set out in the previous eleven chapters. Through the mercies of God (which Paul has been describing), Christians are now able to offer themselves to God as a living and holy sacrifice – one that is acceptable to God; indeed, this is the spiritual

The Second Annual JSOT Lecture delivered at the University of Sheffield on 20 February 1985.

service they owe him. Paul's logic holds divine grace and human response firmly together: without the mercies of God, men are not able to respond to God in true worship; when they experience them, then response to the demand to acknowledge God and to give him glory becomes both imperative and feasible.

Closer investigation of the text suggests that – whether consciously or not – Paul has chosen language which underlines the logic of his argument: 'I implore you, therefore, *offer* yourselves . . .' The verb 'to offer' is one that he used five times over back in chapter 6, where he spelt out the consequences of dying and rising with Christ:[1] those who are in Christ, and share his death and resurrection, must no longer put themselves at the disposal of sin, but must offer themselves to God, to be used as his instruments. In chapter 12, Paul begins to spell out what it means to offer oneself up to God. But what did it mean to offer oneself up to sin? For that, one must go back to the opening chapters of Romans, where Paul describes the plight of men and women without the gospel. The basic sin of mankind is the failure to worship God – the refusal to acknowledge him as God. In Rom. 1, Paul describes how men turned from the worship of the true God, and gave honour to false gods instead. The result was that God gave them up to all kinds of wickedness and vice: their *bodies* were dishonoured (v. 24); their *minds* were no longer able to discern what was right (v. 28). It is hardly accidental if now, in chapter 12, Paul implores Christians to present their *bodies* to God as a living sacrifice; as for their *minds*, they must be transformed and renewed.[2] And in order to understand what Paul means by transformation, we need to turn back once again to his earlier argument, this time to chapter 8, where he explains that their destiny is to be conformed to the image of God's son, and to be glorified with him.[3]

Paul thus introduces the ethical section of Romans in such a way as to remind his readers that the life they are now expected to live, and are able to live, is the very opposite of their former lives. The contrast between the two ways of life spells out what it means to live in Adam or in Christ, to be disobedient or obedient, to be a slave of sin or of

---

[1] Rom. 6.13 (twice), 16, 19 (twice).
[2] Rom. 12.2. When this happens, they will be able to discern (δοκιμάζειν) the will of God; see 1.28 for the reverse process.
[3] Rom. 8.29f. Cf. also 2 Cor. 3.18, which speaks of believers being transformed according to Christ's image, from one degree of glory to another, and Phil. 3.10 and 21, where Paul speaks of being conformed to Christ's death, and of the conformity to Christ's glorious body which awaits believers in the future.

righteousness, to live according to the flesh or according to the Spirit – the themes that have been set out in chapters 5, 6 and 8.

But he does not leave the matter there. In the pages that follow, Paul mentions various motives for adopting one mode of behaviour rather than another: the threat of judgement, with the implication of reward and punishment (13.4; 14.10, 12); the basic command to love (13.8–10); obedience to those whom God has appointed to rule (13.1–7); the demands set out in the Law (13.8–10); the promptings of conscience (13.5; 14.5). By far the commonest appeal, however, is to the gospel itself. This is Paul's use of the so-called 'indicative-imperative', which has been neatly summed up as the command to 'be what you are'. Those who are in Christ must behave accordingly. How should they behave towards fellow-Christians? They must remember that they are one body in Christ (12.3–8). What kind of behaviour is appropriate for Christians? They must 'put on the Lord Jesus Christ' (13.14). Should they observe holy days and abstain from certain kinds of food? They should do what they believe to be right, provided what they do brings honour to the Lord who died and rose again (14.5–9): for it is because he has been made Lord that Christians now do everything – living or dying – to him. How should they behave towards those with whom they disagree? They must welcome one another, since they have all been welcomed by God himself (14.1–3). They must be careful not to injure one another by their behaviour, since that would bring destruction on those for whom Christ died (14.13–21). On the contrary, the strong should bear the infirmities of those who are weak; they should not please themselves, for Christ did not please himself – indeed, he accepted reproach (15.1–3). They must therefore welcome one another, as Christ has welcomed them – Christ who, indeed, became a servant for their sakes (15.7–12).[4]

In these frequent appeals to the gospel, there is a logical link so persuasive as to suggest that the ethical conclusion is inevitable. Since Christ behaved in a certain way in order to bring salvation to Paul's readers, how can they *not* imitate him in that particular respect? To behave in any *other* way would be to deny the truth of the gospel. Being in Christ means sharing his righteousness: and that means, not simply his status before God – his vindication as the Righteous One – but his *moral* righteousness. The command to 'be what you are' is a command to be conformed to the image of Christ.

So far we have discovered a considerable amount of ethical teaching

---

[4] Paul states here that 'Christ became a servant to the circumcised', but goes on to show how this brought benefit to the Gentiles.

in Paul – but where, you may be wondering, is the notion of 'interchange'? Now 'interchange' is a term which some of us have used[5] for the idea which Paul sometimes uses, but which can perhaps best be summed up in some words of Irenaeus: 'Christ became what we are, in order that we might become what he is.'[6] It has to be admitted that the term 'interchange' is not entirely satisfactory, for it may suggest that Christ and the believer simply change places. According to my dictionary, the word 'interchange' means 'mutual give and take', but nowadays it is more likely to conjure up in our minds a picture of one of those complicated intersections of roads which occur when two motorways meet. If two cars converge at a motorway interchange, and if both change direction, they could be said to have changed places. Paul's statements could in some ways be more fairly described, if we continue with our motorway image, in terms of a breakdown van which joins the motorway, picks up a broken-down car, and tows it off at the next intersection in a new direction.[7] Two of the clearest examples of these interchange statements occur in 2 Cor., where, in 5.21, Paul says that Christ was 'made sin' by God, 'so that we might become, in him, the righteousness of God' and, in 8.9, reminds his readers of 'the grace of our Lord Jesus Christ, who was rich, yet became poor, so that you, through his poverty, might become rich'. We shall come back to those examples in a moment. First, we need to notice that there is an example of this idea in Rom. 8, even though the formula is incomplete. In verse 3, Paul, tells his readers that God has sent his own Son in the likeness of sinful flesh: the breakdown van has joined the traffic on the motorway. What is the result? If we read on through the rest of the chapter, we discover that those who had formerly been living according to the flesh, enslaved to sin, are now themselves acknowledged to be God's sons; their lives have changed direction, and they are conformed to the image of God's Son. We can find the same idea in Galatians, this time summed up very neatly in one of Paul's interchange formulae: 'God sent his Son, born of a woman, so that we might receive adoption as sons' (Gal. 4.4f).

If we probe a little further, we find another interesting link between the argument in Rom. 8.3ff and Gal. 4.4ff. In Galatians, Christ is said to have been born, not only 'of a woman', but 'under the Law';

---

[5] See above, chs. 1–3. | [6] See above ch. 1, n. 18.
[7] Paul's 'interchange' is not a simple exchange, since Christ does not cease to be Son of God in being 'born of a woman'; he himself remains righteous, even when he is 'made sin'. The image of a breakdown van is also inadequate, however, since the van does not share the 'brokenness' of what it rescues.

Christians, in turn, become sons of God, and are set free from the slavery of the Law. Now in Rom. 8 also, Paul links the sending of God's Son with the Law, but here he puts things rather differently. By sending his Son in the likeness of sinful flesh, God condemned sin in the flesh and did what the Law was unable to do: he found a way whereby the Law's requirement might be fulfilled in us[8] – and that requirement is presumably that we should be righteous.[9] Paul has indicated here the ethical implications of his notion of 'interchange': God sent his Son in the likeness of sinful flesh, and pronounced judgement on sin; those whose lives had been governed by sinful flesh have been made sons of God, and because they now live in the Spirit, they live in accordance with the Law's demands – not because they keep the Law's particular commandments, but because the Spirit is at work in their lives, making them like Christ: the requirement of the Law is thus fulfilled in them. Paul's quarrel with the Law is not that the Law is wrong, but that it is unable to achieve its aims; if now its requirements are fulfilled, that is not because the Law is still in force, but because its aims have been achieved – the goal has been reached, and the righteousness which the law demanded should, therefore, be demonstrated in believers' lives.

The basis of Paul's argument in Rom. 8, therefore, is that Christ became like us, in order that we might become like him; and this is why, when Paul turns to ethical teaching in the later chapters of Romans, he appeals back to the gospel: what Christians are depends on what Christ became: he shared human existence, and enabled men and women to share his. How does this mutual sharing take place? To answer that, we need to turn once again to Rom. 6, where Paul explains the significance of baptism. Through baptism, believers are united with Christ in death and resurrection. And though resurrection is still a future hope, death and resurrection are already being worked out in their lives. Since Christ died to sin, so must they; they are no longer slaves to sin, but instruments of righteousness (6.10–18). Thus while it is true that Christ's death brings us life, it is quite false to suppose that Paul's notion of interchange is a simple exchange. It is not a matter of substitution, whereby Christ dies and we live. Rather, he shares our life and our death; and we, in turn, share his death and his life, by dying to sin and living to God.

[8] The construction used by Paul here is similar to that found in the 'interchange formulae' in 2 Cor. 5.21; 8.9; Gal. 3.13f; 4.4f. God acted (by sending his son in the likeness of sinful flesh) in order that (ἵνα) . . . The result is spelt out later in the chapter: we, too, become sons of God. But more immediately, it is expressed in v. 4 in terms of the δικαίωμα τοῦ νόμου being fulfilled in us – an achievement which stands in contrast to the Law's failure in the previous verse.   [9] See. above, ch. 2, pp. 32f.

The link between Paul's notion of interchange and ethical behaviour is by no means confined to Romans. In Gal. 4, as we have seen, Paul talks about the Law rather differently: Christians are set free from the Law.[10] But why are they set free? Because there is no further need for the Law. Christians are sons – we need the sexist language to emphasize the link – and they have received the Spirit of God's Son, and through the Spirit they expect righteousness (5.5). Paul then goes on to explain just what he means by freedom (5.13–15),[11] and what he means by life in the Spirit (5.16, 22–6): 'to live in the Spirit' means 'to be in line with the Spirit' (5.25)[12] and *that* means 'love, joy, peace, patience, kindness, goodness, faithfulness, gentleness, self-control' (5.22f). Once again, interchange in Christ bears ethical fruit.

There is another example of 'interchange' in Galatians, and interestingly enough, that, too, is linked with both the Law and the Spirit. In Gal. 3.13, Paul declares that Christ became a curse for us, thereby redeeming us from the curse of the law; the 'us' here presumably refers to Jews, who were 'under the Law'.[13] But Christ's action affected not only Jews but Gentiles, who received the blessing promised to Abraham – namely, the gift of the Spirit.[14] There is, therefore, as Paul goes on to explain, no distinction between Jew and Gentile in Christ: by sharing the condition of men, Christ has set them free to share the blessing which belongs to those who are children of God, namely, life in the Spirit, and all that this means; and as we know from Gal. 5, part of what this means is appropriate behaviour.

Let us go back to our two examples of interchange in 2 Corinthians, and ask whether Paul links *them* with ethical teaching. The first, in 5.21, is a saying of major theological importance – and difficulty: 'Christ was made sin, in order that we might become the righteousness of God in him.' The verse is set in a passage where Paul describes his understanding of his own ministry among the Corinthians. This is then

[10] The notion of freedom from the Law is, of course, used in Romans also, in 7.1–6.
[11] Paradoxically, freedom from the Law is exercised in serving (δουλεύω) one another in love. Even more surprisingly, this love for one another proves to be the fulfilment of the Law from which they have been set free (cf. Rom. 8.4).
[12] The verb used here is στοιχέω.
[13] See, e.g. H. D. Betz, *Galatians* (Philadelphia, 1979), p. 148.
[14] Strictly, the logic of vv. 13f suggests that those under the Law were redeemed for the benefit of the Gentiles, who were thereby enabled to receive the 'blessing of Abraham'; cf. Rom. 15.8ff, where Christ is said to have become a servant to the circumcised, so that God's promises to the patriarchs might be confirmed, and the Gentiles glorify God for his mercy. In both passages, the salvation of Jews leads to mercy for the Gentiles, and since Paul is writing primarily to Gentiles, he is concerned to stress the benefit which came to them: the redemption of the Jews is thus not an end in itself, but is seen as a means to an even greater end.

followed, in 6.14–7.1, by an appeal for righteousness: 'Do not be mismatched with unbelievers. For what partnership have righteousness and iniquity? What fellowship has light with darkness? What agreement has Christ with Belial? . . .' Commentators have frequently argued that this paragraph does not belong here, and that it interrupts the flow of Paul's argument; they call it 'an erratic boulder'. But no one has ever explained who threw the boulder in at this point, or why.[15] It seems much more likely that Paul himself broke off his argument in 6.13 and picked it up again in the next chapter. But if Paul intended the paragraph to stand here, what was its relevance to his argument? Did he perhaps think that it was necessary to spell out what it meant – or what it *should* mean – to become 'the righteousness of God in Christ'? Is this paragraph perhaps the ethical outworking of the consequences of interchange in Christ? 'Therefore come out from them, and be separate from them, says the Lord, and touch nothing unclean . . . and I will be a father to you, and you shall be my sons and daughters' (2 Cor. 6.17f).

As for the second statement, in 8.9, that comes in a passage where Paul is trying to persuade his readers to give generously to the collection he is making for the poor: 'You know the grace of our Lord Jesus Christ: he was rich, but became poor, so that you, through his poverty, might become rich.' Here the ethical implications are clear and immediate. If that is what Christ has done for them, they must in turn contribute from their riches to help alleviate the poverty of their fellow-Christians.

My final example of the notion of interchange is to be found in Philippians. Once again, as in Rom. 8, the formula is incomplete. In chapter 2, in what may perhaps be a quotation from an early hymn, Paul describes how Christ, who was in the form of God and might have claimed equality with God, nevertheless emptied himself, taking the form of a slave, and was born in the likeness of man; and how he then humbled himself still further, dying on a cross – the form of execution used for slaves. It is only at the end of the next chapter that Paul describes how Christians in turn become like Christ; this time he speaks of a future event, when Christ will come from heaven and change our bodies of humiliation, conforming them to his own glory. Once again, however, the reason why Paul introduces the so-called 'hymn' in chapter 2 is in order to support an ethical appeal: 'Let your manner of

---

[15] For a useful summary of the arguments on each side, and an examination of possible links between the passage and its context, see M. E. Thrall, 'The problem of II Cor. vi.14–vii.1 in some recent discussion', *NTS*, 24 (1977–8), 132–48.

life be worthy of the gospel of Christ . . . Complete my joy by being of the same mind, having the same love, being in full accord and of one mind. Do nothing from selfishness or conceit, but in humility count others better than yourselves. Let each of you look not to his own interests, but to the interests of others. And this is the mind you are to have among you – the mind which you have in Christ Jesus . . .' So Paul launches into the hymn, and when he comes to the end, he continues: 'Therefore obey [my commands]. Do everything without grumbling or arguing, so that you may be blameless and innocent, children of God without blemish in the midst of a crooked and perverse generation.'

It is clear, then, that Paul's notion of interchange does not mean simply that Christians 'become what he is' in the sense that they share in Christ's status before God; if they are made 'the righteousness of God in him', that implies *moral* righteousness – and when we ask Paul what behaviour is appropriate for those who are 'in Christ', then he appeals to the example of Christ himself. So we discover that, paradoxically, the behaviour which is required of those who are in Christ and who wish to be like him conforms to the attitude which *he* showed in becoming like us.[16] he was obedient; he emptied himself; he humbled himself; he became poor; he identified himself with the sinful and with outcasts. And so, in describing his own ministry, Paul claims that he, too, has accepted all manner of humiliation and suffering for the sake of others; he, too, has accepted poverty and yet made others rich.

This emphasis on moral righteousness and 'Christian' character is an essential part of Paul's understanding of what it means to 'become like Christ', and we distort his teaching if we ignore it. And from time to time it *has* been ignored. When Paul writes about Christians being conformed to the image of Christ, he is often referring to a future hope – and that hope is that we will share the glory of Christ. Rom. 8 and Phil. 3 are good examples of that future hope. But the process of becoming like Christ has already begun – an idea which Paul stresses in 2 Cor. 3.18, where he speaks of Christians already sharing Christ's glory; or the process *should* have begun: Gal. 4.19 is a *cri de coeur* which suggests that Paul thinks the Galatians have a long way to go: 'My little children, with whom I am again in travail until Christ is formed in you.' But what does it mean to 'share Christ's glory' in *this* life? The great temptation was to think of it in terms of honour and status. But that was not how Paul saw it. 'Far be it from me to glory except in the

[16] See below, ch. 7.

Cross of our Lord Jesus Christ', he writes to the Galatians (6.14) – which means that his understanding of 'glory' is very different from theirs. Very different, too, from that of the Corinthians, who regarded everything they had received as a cause for boasting. Meanwhile, Paul appeals to the meekness and gentleness of Christ (2 Cor. 10.1) and he urges the Corinthians to imitate him, even as he imitates Christ (1 Cor. 4.16; 11.1). And that involves accepting weakness, enduring persecution, blessing those who revile him and attempting to conciliate when he is slandered (1 Cor. 4.10–13). It means trying to please others, and not seeking his own advantage (1 Cor. 10.33). It means putting up with all kinds of discomfort and danger for the sake of the Church (2 Cor. 4.15) – beatings, imprisonment and hunger are just a few of the trials he has to endure (2 Cor. 6.4f). It means showing in his life the activity of the Holy Spirit and the power of God – in purity, forbearance, kindness, genuine love and truthful speech (2 Cor. 6.6f). It means that the paradox of the Cross (1 Cor. 1.18–25) is seen in his own life: his affliction brings comfort to others (2 Cor. 1.4f), his dying brings life (2 Cor. 4.12), and his poverty brings riches (2 Cor. 6.10). 'Being like Christ' thus involves far more than moral 'goodness'. It has a great deal to do with 'life-style', and in particular with concern for other people. The Corinthians think that 'being like Christ' means living like kings, glorying in their new freedom, and boasting in the gifts God has given them (1 Cor. 4.8). With considerable sarcasm, Paul responds by describing his own experience as an apostle (vv. 9–13). He himself refuses to boast, except in his weakness (2 Cor. 11.30; 12.5–10); he accepts shame and humiliation as his lot (2 Cor. 4.7–12; 6.4–10): for it is in weakness that God shows his strength, and in humiliation that he displays his glory (1 Cor. 1.22–31). Paul's understanding of the Cross is remarkably like that of the Fourth Evangelist, for whom it is the revelation of God's glory. Paul 'boasts' in the Cross (Gal. 6.14); to him, it is both 'strength' and 'wisdom' (1 Cor. 1.24). As for the Corinthians, their problem is not simply that they have not grasped the link between the gospel and morality, but that they have not seen the implications for their own life-style. They are arrogant and boastful; they are treating Christ simply as a substitute: he died, we live; he became poor, we are rich; he suffered, we rejoice; he emptied himself, we live like kings. They see themselves only as recipients of grace – not as those who are commissioned to pass it on – for they have not grasped that the pattern of the gospel must now be stamped on their own lives. They think of the interchange between Christ and themselves in terms of simple exchange – he gives, we take – instead of in terms of mutual give and take. But how can one give to Christ? It is not so much a case of giving *to* Christ but giving *in* Christ – that is, sharing in *his* giving.

The Corinthians got things out of focus, and it is worth asking whether later Christian theologians have sometimes got Paul's teaching out of focus, too. They have certainly placed far more emphasis on his doctrine that men and women are saved by grace than on his exhortation that they are to 'work out their own salvation' in their lives (Phil. 2.12): the link between gospel and 'good works' has not always been clear. The Reformation slogan of 'justification by faith' can itself mislead, if Paul's insistence that no one is justified by works, but on the basis of faith, is taken out of context, and 'justification' is seen as the final goal of human existence. Being brought into a right relationship with God is the beginning of a new era, in which response to the gospel is demanded, and becomes possible, through the Spirit.

At times, too, emphasis on the unique character of Christ's death – especially when that death has been interpreted in substitutionary terms – has perhaps obscured Paul's belief that Christian living means sharing in the dying of Christ. The idea that Christians are called to imitate Christ has often been neglected – even denied – because it seemed to be a denial of the uniqueness of the Cross. But for Paul, the ultimate denial of the gospel of the Cross is the refusal to live according to the pattern of self-emptying love which it proclaims: the gospel demands conformity to Christ's death.

It is time to ask whether this particular aspect of Paul's teaching can help us in grappling with contemporary ethical problems. There are some, I suppose, who would assume that the answer to this question must be 'no', since Paul is so far removed from our own day. But Paul was the first Christian theologian, and his work was seminal for the later Church: he certainly cannot be ignored. Nevertheless, the particular ethical problems he had to tackle were the problems of his own time, and often seem remote from our own: we do not include the question of whether or not to eat meat that has been sacrificed to idols among the pressing moral questions which we have to answer. Equally, some of Paul's answers were governed by his own cultural presuppositions: for all his attempts to deal with the role of women in the Church in theological terms, his attitude was clearly influenced also by his first-century understanding of the place of women in society. How, then, can we hope to demonstrate – as I am charged to do – the relevance of his teaching to contemporary issues? What practical help can Paul offer us in dealing with problems such as embryo research, mass unemployment, heart transplants or nuclear arms control? I suggest that his teaching is in fact relevant in three ways.

First of all, we have seen that, in dealing with moral problems, Paul goes back to first principles – and that means, that he goes back to the gospel. Some rules are self-evident: the commandments – 'You shall not commit adultery, You shall not kill, You shall not steal, You shall not covet – hardly need justification, but are in fact all explained as examples of love for one's neighbour (Rom. 13.9). Similarly, immorality is out, because that is incompatible with Christian baptism, through which believers have been washed and sanctified (1 Cor. 6.9–11): 'The works of the flesh are plain', writes Paul to the Galatians (5.19). The fruits of the Spirit were perhaps less obvious, since meekness and gentleness were not universally esteemed; the guiding rule is again love for others, concern for the community as a whole. The vital question is thus whether an action builds up the community or destroys it, shows love towards the brother for whom Christ died or does him harm (Rom. 14.13–23; 1 Cor. 8.7–13; 9.19–23). This is why Paul regards love as the greatest of all spiritual gifts. For even spiritual gifts can be used in ways that benefit the individual rather than the community; this is why Paul is hesitant about the gifts of tongues (1 Cor. 14.1–33), and why he is cautious about those who claim to have faith and knowledge when it comes to questions about whether or not it is right to eat certain foods (Rom. 14.1–23; 1 Cor. 8.1–13; 10.23–33).

As a guiding principle, the notion of conformity to the gospel can take one a long way. The problem is that it does not offer very clear guidance when we come to those ethical questions which are matters of debate, since Christians often disagree on these questions, and can hold diametrically opposed views, while sincerely maintaining that they are working on the principle of conformity to the gospel and love for others: you can support or attack embryo research, for example, on the basis of love for your neighbour.

This brings us to our second point, for though Paul lived in a far less complicated world than our own, he, too, found himself dealing with ethical questions to which there were no clear-cut answers. Was it right or wrong to eat food that had been sacrificed to idols? In answering that one, Paul sides with first one group in the Corinthian Church, then the other, leading some commentators to conclude that such contradictory responses could only have been made in separate letters. Such a solution fails to explain why Paul should change his mind: I suggest that it also seriously misunderstands Paul's approach. When Paul regards the answer to an issue as clear-cut, he sets out the answer in no uncertain terms. On this occasion, he believes that neither side has the monopoly of truth: both sides are right. The strong or knowledgeable are right to say that idols do not exist; food cannot be 'unclean' or contaminated by being offered to non-existent deities. But the weak are right in saying that it is wrong to do something which is contrary to their consciences. Both sides are right – but are they both wrong? I think not. At *this* point, Paul sides with the weak, for though the strong are right in believing that all things are lawful, nevertheless all things are not helpful (1 Cor. 10.23). Their concern must not be their own good, but the good of their neighbour (10.24). Once again, we are back with first principles: which course of action matches up to the gospel? And notice that this guideline is not used in order to decide the original issue (since Paul himself seems to agree with the strong) but in deciding how to behave. The strong are to help the weak, for if they do not, then they *are* in the wrong, since they are not living in accordance with the gospel. So is Paul advocating that the whole Christian community must move at the pace of its most timid members? Must all be teetotallers or sabbatarians for the sake of a few? On the contrary, his advice is that each Christian should follow his or her own conscience. But there must be mutual respect between those with different views. And those who regard themselves as strong or knowledgeable have an obligation not to lead those who are weak or less knowledgeable into actions which are against their conscience. The obligation is on those who are wise or strong precisely because they *are* wise or strong. That is what the gospel is about. And that is why Paul spends a whole chapter in the middle of this discussion in 1 Corinthians establishing his rights and privileges as an apostle, in order that he may remind his readers that he has given them all up for the sake of the gospel. He is not wandering off the subject; nor is he being awkward; nor is he boasting. He is simply giving an example of what it means to be weak for the sake of the weak, to be poor, in hope of making others rich. When we turn to the parallel passage in Romans, we find Paul once again appealing to an example of the principle that the strong must bear with the failings of the weak; this time, the example is that of Christ himself (Rom. 15.1–3, 7–9).

My third and final point is this. I suggested earlier that Paul's notion of 'interchange' has sometimes been misunderstood. He is *not*, I suggested, speaking about a simple exchange between Christ and the believer. Christ died in order that we might live; he became poor in order that we might be rich. But in order to share that life, we must share his death. And what about his riches? Must we not share his poverty, in order to share his wealth? Remember Paul's sarcastic rebuke of the Corinthians, who boasted about the riches and spiritual gifts and wisdom they had received through the gospel. For Paul, being in Christ means sharing in the dying as well as the living, in the giving as well as the receiving, in the poverty as well as the riches, in the humiliation as well as the glory. That is why conformity to the gospel affects his whole life-style.

Contrast with this the promise of one of the evangelists who is well known to those who are familiar with the North American phenomenon known as 'electronic religion', who every week assures his audience on television and radio: 'Something good is going to happen to you today – spiritually, physically, financially.' It is fairly easy to see that something is wrong with this message, for what have promises of financial success to do with the Christian gospel? Why should Christians expect material benefit from the gospel? Such promises of physical and financial benefit are crude appeals to self-interest; religion is being sold to viewers as a way to success. Religious men and women will do well because God will reward them. What sort of a gospel is this? Christ died – and I am cured from my cancer. He became poor – and my bank balance gets steadily healthier. He was hung up on a gibbet – and I am a great success.

Now of course this is a travesty of religion – so much so, that we find ourselves amazed that anyone is taken in by it. But perhaps the travesty is only an extreme example of an attitude which is much more pervasive – and therefore much more dangerous. When Christianity is marketed in this way, then the Church has totally succumbed to the values of the outside world. Religion is being sold like any other commodity, and the vital question is 'What do I get out of it?' But what sort of values *should* Christians be maintaining – in a world which esteems self-reliance and applauds success? What sort of values should they be maintaining in a world where millions have no hope of being self-reliant or successful?

Christians are no more likely than anyone else to find the solution to problems of inflation and unemployment, injustice and famine. What they *can* do is to show the relevance of the Christian gospel to all these problems. When the world is divided between rich and poor, prosperous and starving, those with jobs and those without, strong and weak, where should Christians be found? Looking for something good to happen to them, spiritually, physically and financially – or concerned about the welfare of others? Maintaining the rights of the strong, or standing up for the weak? Enjoying the success that has come to them through their own efforts or through good fortune – or identifying with those who have no hope of ever experiencing anything good?

Such questions leave us all uneasy. No doubt we think that their implications are impractical. But they remind us that Paul's ethical teaching is as much concerned with 'lifestyle' as with answers to particular moral questions. And the 'life-style' is that of one who emptied himself, became poor, and identified himself with sinful mankind. *That* is the pattern of living to which Paul points Christians. Who will dare to say that his teaching is *not* relevant to our contemporary problems?

II
Adam

5

Adam in Romans 1

The phrase ἐν ὁμοιώματι εἰκόνος in Rom. 1. 23 is one which has long puzzled commentators and translators, who are compelled to paraphrase it in order to make sense of the verse. There is no obvious reason why Paul should have employed two words which in this context appear to convey an identical meaning, unless, as C. K. Barrett suggests, 'the reduplication emphasizes the inferior, shadowy character of that which is substituted for God'.[1] It is generally accepted that Paul has in mind here the words of Ps. 106 (LXX 105). 20, where the LXX reads:

καὶ ἠλλάξαντο τὴν δόξαν αὐτῶν
ἐν ὁμοιώματι μόσχου ἔσθοντος χόρτον.

Paul's version, however, is considerably longer:

καὶ ἤλλαξαν τὴν δόξαν τοῦ ἀφθάρτου θεοῦ
ἐν ὁμοιώματι εἰκόνος φθαρτοῦ ἀνθρώπου καὶ πετεινῶν καὶ τετραπόδων
καὶ ἑρπετῶν.

Paul has, in fact, expanded the second half of both lines from the psalm, using the words τοῦ ἀφθάρτου θεοῦ in place of αὐτῶν, which would be meaningless in his context,[2] and substituting for μόσχου ἔσθοντος χόρτον a more comprehensive list of the various forms of idolatry. It is clear from this comparison that the word in our phrase which needs explanation is not ὁμοίωμα, which is taken directly from the psalm, but εἰκών.

This fact leads us to compare Paul's use of εἰκών here with his use of the term elsewhere, and with the biblical usage in general. In the LXX, the commonest use of the word is in the sense of 'idol' (thirty-two

---

[1] C. K. Barrett, *A Commentary on the Epistle to the Romans* (London, 1957), p. 38.
[2] Paul's interpretation is in keeping with the current exegesis of his time, according to which 'their glory' is one of the eighteen 'corrections of the scribes', and the phrase really means 'his glory'. Some manuscripts of the LXX read αὐτοῦ, and the Targum has 'the glory of their Lord'.

73

times). It is found also six times with the specialized meaning 'image of God'.[3] It is used three times in a general sense approximating to that of 'shadow'[4] and once of Adam begetting a son 'in his own image'.[5] The general New Testament use is similar to that of the LXX. In the book of Revelation εἰκών is used ten times in the sense of 'idol'; akin to this is its use in Mark 12.16 (= Matt. 22.20 and Luke 20.24) of the image on a coin.[6] In Heb. 10.1 we find it used with the meaning 'shadow'.

Turning to Paul's use of the term, however, we find a totally different picture. Apart from Rom. 1.23 he uses εἰκών seven times, always in a sense corresponding to the use of the term in the early chapters of Genesis. Twice he refers the term to Christ, who is 'the image of God',[7] once to man, in an exposition of Gen. 1.27;[8] and four times to the future glorified state of the Christian, who is being changed into, or conformed to, the image of Christ or of the creator.[9] Thus εἰκών in Rom. 1.23 seems to stand in striking contrast with its use by Paul elsewhere. A closer examination of the context will perhaps suggest that this contrast is not so great as at first appears.

In a recent article in *New Testament Studies* H. P. Owen has examined Paul's argument in Rom. 1.[10] He maintains that Paul is not ascribing a knowledge of God *as creator* to the Gentiles, but a knowledge of him 'as an invisible, eternal Power of great majesty'.[11] Although 'Paul says in v. 25*b* that Gentiles have refused to *worship* the creator, he does not say that they have ever *known* him as such.'[12] Owen finds confirmation for this interpretation in Paul's speeches as they are recorded in Acts 17 and 14, where Paul proclaims God as creator – an idea which was apparently new to his listeners. Rom. 1 'is concerned with a knowledge that both can be and has been attained'[13] – but this knowledge is recognition of God θειότης, not proof of the existence of a creator. Owen writes:

> The more closely we look at Rom. i. 18–21 the more puzzling it appears. Are we to imagine that each Gentile generation, and each individual within each generation, first knows the truth and then suppresses it by a single, irrevocable act, so that it remains for

---

[3] Gen. 1.26, 27; 5.1; 9.6; Wisd. 2.23; Ecclus. 17.3. Cf. also Wisd. 7.26 – 'image of his goodness'. [4] Pss. 39 (38).6; 73 (72).20; Wisd. 17.21. [5] Gen. 5.3.

[6] This saying perhaps implies that man is made in the image of God, but this does not affect the meaning of εἰκών as it refers to the coin.

[7] 2 Cor. 4.4 and Col. 1.15. [8] 1 Cor. 11.7.

[9] Rom. 8.29; 1 Cor. 15.49; 2 Cor. 3.18; Col. 3.10.

[10] H. P. Owen, 'The scope of natural revelation in Rom. i and Acts xvii', *NTS*, 5 (1959), 133–43. [11] *Ibid.*, p. 141. [12] *Ibid.*, p. 134. [13] *Ibid.*, p. 138.

evermore suppressed? Hardly. Pagan behaviour gives no support for such a view. Gentiles did not turn to idolatry after rejecting a prior non-idolatrous revelation; they were born into idolatry which was the established norm of worship. Rather, I believe, we must suppose Paul to mean that every idolater, at *some* time, or times, has a measure of insight into God's θειότης, and that every idolater, instead of letting the insight grow, suppresses it.[14]

In conclusion, Owen states that he can think of no other exegesis of Rom. 1 which makes sense. Before suggesting an alternative exegesis which, we believe, not only makes sense, but also removes the cause of his puzzlement and is, moreover, biblical in its interpretation, we may perhaps point out two weak points in Owen's arguments. First, we may question the value of accepting Paul's speeches as they are recorded in the book of Acts as reliable evidence of his thought; it is particularly dangerous to interpret genuine Pauline writing on the basis of passages which are, at best, second-hand accounts of his thought. Second, we must query the way in which Owen minimizes all references to the idea of creation in Rom. 1. While it is true, as he says, 'that in Rom. 1.19–20 Paul does not describe God as the Maker of the world',[15] it is emphasized that the knowledge of God has been available ἀπὸ κτίσεως κόσμου – a phrase which suggests that Paul is thinking in particular of God's creative activity; a phrase, moreover, which links the revelation with an historical point of time, and which loses its significance if Paul is speaking of a rejection of God which is made 'by every idolater, at some time, or times'. It is also true that Paul does not say that God's δύναμις made the ποιήματα, but clearly the ποιήματα must have been made – and by God: moreover, it is through these ποιήματα that God's attributes are known. Owen maintains that Paul is being faithful to Gentile thought, which 'never reached a belief in God as κτιστής'.[16] But it must nevertheless be remembered that Paul was a 'Hebrew of the Hebrews', and it seems impossible that a Jew could speak in these terms without implying a knowledge of God as creator. Moreover, although Paul is undoubtedly thinking primarily of Gentiles, his remarks are not confined to them: he is speaking of men in general (ἀνθρώπων, v. 18), and his condemnation includes not only the Gentiles, but also the Jew who comes in for more particular castigation in the following chapter. In verse 25 Paul directly refers to God as creator. Owen makes a subtle distinction here between worship of the creator and knowledge of him as such. But this destroys the

---

[14] *Ibid.*, pp. 141f.   [15] *Ibid.*, p. 134.   [16] *Ibid.*, p. 138.

whole point of Paul's contrast between worship of the creator and worship of the creature: if men do not know God as creator, are they 'without excuse' when they confuse him with his creation?

Much of the confusion which surrounds this passage is probably due to the commonly-held assumption that Paul is here affirming a belief in natural revelation.[17] This would appear however to be too facile an interpretation. Paul does not say here that by a process of deduction men have come to a knowledge of God; what he *does* say is that from the very beginning God has clearly manifested the truth to them. In other words, he is speaking of a definite divine revelation which men have rejected, not of a knowledge of God to which men have by their reasoning attained.

The affinities between Wisd. 12 and Rom. 1 have been rightly emphasized, and it is probable that Paul had the former passage in mind when writing this epistle.[18] But the differences are no less important than the similarities, and Owen has rightly distinguished here between Wisd. 13, which speaks of a knowledge of God to which men should have attained through Nature but have not, and Rom. 1, which is concerned with a knowledge which was given to men but which they have suppressed.[19] We may correctly describe Wisd. 13 as an exposition of natural theology; it is dubious whether the term is applicable to Rom. 1. We must therefore inquire in what sense Paul can claim that men have been given a revelation of God which they have rejected.

The clue to the answer to this problem would seem to lie in those very references which Owen minimizes – namely in the references to creation. This does not mean, as we have seen, that Paul is arguing from Nature to Nature's God; rather he is describing man's sin in relation to its true biblical setting – the Genesis narrative of the creation and the fall.

We have already noted the connection between Rom. 1.23 and Ps. 106 (105). 20. It seems possible that other passages have influenced Paul's thought at this point – in particular the descriptions of idolatry in Jer. 2.11 and Deut. 4. 15–18. It has also been demonstrated recently by N.

---

[17] *Ibid.*, p. 133. Cf. the discussion in A. Nygren, *Commentary on Romans*, ET (London, 1952), pp. 102–9.

[18] See, in particular, W. Sanday and A. C. Headlam, *Romans* (*ICC*, Edinburgh, 1902), *in loc.*

[19] Owen, 'The scope of natural revelation', pp. 137f. See also G. Bornkamm, 'Faith and reason in Paul's Epistles', *NTS*. 4 (1958), 96.

Hyldahl[20] that the description of the creation of living creatures in Gen. 1.20–5 includes the three terms used by Paul: τὰ πετεινά, τὰ τετράποδα and τὰ ἑρπετά. Paul mentions these creatures in the same order as they occur in Genesis, though he omits the sea creatures (τὰ ἑρπετά again), fishes (τὰ κήτη), 'beasts of the earth' (τὰ θηρία) and cattle (τὰ κτήνη). Hyldahl argues further that Paul's use of ἄνθρωπος is a reference to Gen. 1.26f, and that in using the singular he has been faithful to his source, just as he has followed Genesis in using the plural for the three kinds of animals. Moreover, in Gen. 1.26 we find the terms εἰκών and ὁμοίωσις: Paul uses the first of these terms in Rom. 1.23, and for the second he substitutes ὁμοίωμα, with which, Hyldahl argues, it would probably be interchangeable in New Testament usage.

Our comparison of Rom. 1.23 with Ps. 106 (105). 20 has already shown that the phrase ἐν ὁμοιώματι echoes exactly the language of the psalm, and there would thus seem to be no necessity to follow Hyldahl in linking it directly with ὁμοίωσις in Gen. 1.26. When we turn back to that comparison, however, we notice a point of real significance – namely, that in the phrase which Paul has substituted for the μόσχου ἔσθοντος χόρτον of the psalm, every word except one (φθαρτός) is found in Gen. 1.20–6. It would appear that Paul, in describing the idolatry into which man has fallen, has deliberately chosen the terminology of the creation story.

The language of Rom. 1.23 is not the only connection, however, which this passage has with the early chapters of Genesis. In particular, the sequence of events outlined in Rom. 1 reminds us of the story of Adam as it is told in Gen. 1–3. Of Adam it is supremely true that God manifested to him that which can be known of him (v. 19); that from the creation onwards, God's attributes were clearly discernible to him in the things which had been made, and that he was thus without excuse (v. 20). Adam, above and before all men, knew God, but failed to honour him as God, and grew vain in his thinking and allowed his heart to be darkened (v. 20). Adam's fall was the result of his desire to be as God, to attain knowledge of good and evil (Gen. 3.5), so that, claiming to be wise, he in fact became a fool (v. 21). Thus he not only failed to give glory to God but, according to rabbinic tradition, himself lost the glory of God which was reflected in his face (v. 23).[21] In believing the serpent's lie that his action would not lead to death (Gen. 3.4) he turned his back on the truth of God, and he obeyed, and thus gave his allegiance to a creature, the serpent, rather

---

[20] 'A reminiscence of the Old Testament at Romans i. 23', *NTS*, 2 (1956), 285–8.
[21] Gen. Rab. 11.2; 12.6; Sanh. 38*b*; Apoc. Moses 20–21.

than to the creator (v. 25). Adam, certainly, knew God's δικαίωμα (cf. Rom. 5.12–14); by eating the forbidden fruit he not only broke that δικαίωμα, but also consented with the action of Eve, who had already taken the fruit (v. 32).

It would appear from this remarkable parallelism that Paul's account of man's wickedness has been deliberately stated in terms of the biblical narrative of Adam's fall. If so, however, we still have to explain why he pictures the results of that fall in terms of (a) idolatry (b) sexual licence and perversion, (c) wickedness in general.

The answer to the question, broadly speaking, is undoubtedly the simple one that these were the three forms in which Paul saw sin as particularly rampant in his time. There are reasons for believing, however, that they may also be linked with the Adam myth. According to Paul's account here the sin into which man originally falls is that of idolatry, and it is on account of this that God gives him up to other forms of sin. It may perhaps be objected that there is nothing in the narrative in Genesis to suggest that Adam ever offered worship to idols. He can, however, as we have seen, be justly accused of serving the creature rather than the creator, and it is from this confusion between God and the things which he has made that idolatry springs. Moreover, as we have already noted, the terms for these idols in Rom. 1.23 are taken from the Genesis narrative, and the animals mentioned are, in fact, among those over which man is expressly given dominion. In listening to the voice of the serpent, Adam has not only failed to exercise his rightful dominion over creation, but, by placing himself in subservience to a creature, has opened up the way to idolatry.

Therefore, says Paul, God gave them up to other sins. Although the verb which he uses is different, it may perhaps reflect something of the force of ἐξαπέστειλεν . . . ἐξέβαλεν in Gen. 3.23f. God gave men up to their own lusts, to the dishonouring of their bodies and to unnatural passions. Possibly there is in the phrase τοῦ ἀτιμάζεσθαι τὰ σώματα αὐτῶν an echo of the shame of Adam and Eve at their own nakedness (Gen. 3.7–11). More important, however, is the rabbinic tradition which associated the Fall with sexual desire: in several passages the serpent's temptation of Eve is explained as being a temptation to unchastity,[22] others speak of unnatural intercourse of Adam and Eve with demons.[23] Although late in date, these passages probably reflect

---

[22] See e.g. Sotah 9*b*; Sab. 146*a*; Yeb. 103*b*; Ab. Zar. 22*b*; Gen. Rab. 20.11; 22.2. In Gen. Rab. 18.6 and Aboth R. Nathan 1, 3*a*, the serpent is said to have acted out of a desire to kill Adam and marry Eve.   [23] Erub. 18*b*; Gen. Rab. 20.11; 14.6.

an exegesis current as early as the first century AD;[24] similar ideas are found in pseudepigraphical writings,[25] and Thackeray suggests that they lie behind 2 Cor. 11.2–13.[26] There is thus good evidence for suggesting that Paul would naturally have associated the Fall with sexual lust and perversion. Moreover, by obeying the serpent instead of exercising authority over it, man reduced himself to the level of the animals and therefore became prey to bestial passions; the woman, in particular, is condemned to a life which is wholly given up to this physical aspect, consisting as it does of the bearing of children, desire for her husband and subjection to him (Gen. 3.16).

The third result of man's suppression of the truth about God is summed up by Paul in a general catalogue of sins of every kind. The list he gives in verses 29–31 can be paralleled by similar passages in Hellenistic and Hellenistic-Jewish writings,[27] but he places it in the context of the biblical narrative. It is not necessary to discuss here exactly how Paul conceived of the relationship between Adam's fall and the sin of mankind in general; it is clear from Rom. 5.12–21 that he *did* regard them as related, that he believed that sin had entered the world through Adam, and that every manifestation of sin is thus in some sense ultimately connected with the initial sin of Adam.

Paul is not alone, of course, in condemning these three forms of sin and in linking them together. Thus the author of Wisdom regards idolatry as 'the beginning, the cause, and the end, of all evil',[28] the sin which leads to all others. To find a parallel to the order which Paul sets out in Rom. 1.24–32, however, we have to turn back to the early chapters of Genesis. There we find the same sequence as in Romans: first, we have worship of the creature (v. 25), parallel to Adam's sin in Gen. 3; following this, we have sexual perversion and unnatural intercourse (vv. 26f), which in Genesis is found in 6.1–4; this, in turn, leads to other forms of sin (vv. 28–31), which are, similarly, the immediate result of lust in the Genesis narrative (6.5), though the Hebrew states this, typically, in a much more pithy manner than does Paul in his Hellenistic catalogue. As we have already noted, there is nothing in the Genesis narrative itself to suggest that Adam was an idolater. It is perhaps not without significance, however, that when

---

[24] Cf. H. St J. Thackeray, *The Relation of St Paul to Contemporary Jewish Thought* (London, 1900), pp. 50–2; F. R. Tennant, *The Sources of the Doctrines of the Fall and Original Sin* (Cambridge, 1903), pp. 152–60.

[25] E.g. 4 Macc. 18.7f; Apoc. Moses 19. Cf. I En. 69.4–6; Slav. Bk. Enoch 31.6; Apoc. Abr. 23.

[26] Thackeray, *The Relation of St Paul to Contemporary Jewish Thought*, pp. 52–5.

[27] Cf. especially Wisd. 14.25f.   [28] Wisd. 14.27.

Paul repeats in verse 25 the charge originally made in verse 23, he does so in terms which are wholly applicable to Adam, and idols are not mentioned. Moreover, rabbinic tradition certainly associated Eve's downfall with idolatry, as well as with lust. The serpent, it is said, injected lust into Eve, with the result that idolaters remain lustful to this day, although the Jews, who turned from idolatry to the worship of the true God, lost this lust at Sinai.[29]

Further indications that Paul had the Genesis narrative in mind when writing this passage are found in the vocabulary which he uses. We have already noted that several words in Rom. 1.23 are used also in Gen. 1. 20–6. Other echoes of Gen. 1 are found in ἀόρατα in verse 20, and ἐσκοτίσθη in verse 22, with which we may compare ἀόρατος and σκότος in Gen. 1.2. Linked with ἐσκοτίσθη, which perhaps suggests a return to the primeval chaos, we find ἐματαιώησαν in verse 21; although this verb is used only here in the New Testament, we find ματαιότης later in this epistle, at 8.20. It is significant that the noun is used there of the futility to which the creation has been subjected as a result of man's sin; from this futility it will be set free as a direct consequence of the freedom arising from the glorified state of the children of God, who are conformed to the image of Christ.

The adjective ἀΐδιος, in Rom. 1.20, is not found in the LXX version of the Old Testament, but it does occur once in the book of Wisdom: in 7.26, where it is used in connection with Wisdom. In 2.23, moreover, some manuscripts read ἀιδιότητος.[30] This verse is of particular importance for our purpose, since it is concerned with the creation of man:

> ὅτι ὁ θεὸς ἔκτισεν τὸν ἄνθρωπον ἐπ' ἀφθαρσίᾳ
> καὶ εἰκόνα τῆς ἰδίας ἀιδιότητος ἐποίησεν αὐτόν.

In addition to ἀιδιότητος, we find two other words here which are echoed in Rom. 1.23 – ἀφθαρσίᾳ and εἰκόνα. The following verse, which speaks of death entering the world through the envy of the devil, is also of interest, since the contrast between ἀφθαρσία and θάνατος is repeated by Paul in the terms ἄφθαρτος . . . φθαρτός. The idea that man is φθαρτός goes back ultimately, of course, to God's decree in Gen. 3.16, even though it is expressed there in more graphic terms.

Returning to our initial problem of the meaning of the phrase ἐν ὁμοιώματι εἰκόνος, we find that our examination has lent additional

---

[29] Sab. 146a; Yeb. 103b; Ab. Zar. 22b.
[30] 248 and 253, followed by most patristic writers. ℵ, A and B have ἰδιότητος.

weight to C. K. Barrett's point that the words convey the impression of the shadowy nature of that which is substituted for God. For the contrast between the glory of God and the likeness of an image – which is further emphasized by the use of the definite article in the first clause, and its complete absence in the second – is the contrast between man's knowledge of God before the Fall and his imperfect knowledge of him afterwards. Adam spoke with God face to face in the Garden; when he had sinned, he hid from God's presence,[31] and it is not clear whether he emerged from hiding, even when God called to him.[32] Certainly, after Adam's expulsion from the Garden, it was no longer possible to speak face to face with God: mortal man may not look on God and live; he cannot stand the sight of God's glory.[33] Thus Paul, following the psalmist in his contrast between worship of the true God and that of man-made substitutes, emphasizes his point by stressing the difference between the real and the unreal, the incorruptible and the corruptible, the direct vision of God and the partial knowledge of him, imperfect because of man's sin.

Paul's desire to emphasize this contrast is no doubt one reason why he has used the term εἰκών in a sense which is for him unique, in preference to the word εἴδωλον, the term which he employs for 'idol' elsewhere. Another reason for his choice of this word, however, is

---

[31] Gen. 3.8: 'face' in both the Hebrew and Greek.

[32] Adam does not give a direct answer to the questions 'Where are you?'; instead, he explains *why* he hid himself – and this reason still exists. Gen. 3.9f.

[33] There are, of course, exceptions to this, but they are rare, and are noted as being exceptional. God appears to Abraham (Gen. 18), Jacob (Gen. 32.24–30), Gideon (Jud. 6.11–24), Manoah (Jud. 13.2–23), though always *incognito*. The elders of Israel are said to have seen God (Exod. 24.9–11), though it is from a distance (vv. 1, 2, 12–15). Moses alone is said to have spoken with God 'face to face' (Exod. 33.11; Deut. 34.10; Num. 12.8); according to Exod. 3.6, however, even Moses is afraid to 'look upon God' in the phenomenon of the burning bush (cf. Elijah in 1 Kings 19.13), and in Exod. 33.17–23, he is unable to see God's glory (here = his face). Some of the prophets claim to have seen God: Isaiah in 6.1, 5; Amos in 7.7 and 9.1; Ezekiel in 1 – though he describes only 'the appearance of the likeness of the glory of God'. There was a tendency in later times to minimize all suggestions that man was capable of seeing God. In the Old Testament, this appears in the alteration of the phrase 'see Yahweh' to 'appear before Yahweh', etc. (See, e.g., Exod. 23.15; Ps. 42.2 (3); Isa. 1.12. Cf. Gen. 16.13.) A similar influence is seen at work in the LXX, which has changed וַיִּרְאוּ אֵת אֱלֹהֵי יִשְׂרָאֵל to καὶ εἶδν τὸν τόπον, οὗ εἱστήκει ἐκεῖ ὁ θεὸς τοῦ Ἰσραήλ in Exod. 24.10. The Targum of this passage says that the elders saw the glory of God, while it changes 'face to face' to 'word for word' in Exod. 33.11 and Deut. 34.10; 'form' to 'likeness of the glory' in Num. 12.8, and 'God' to 'angels of the Lord' in Gen. 32.30. In apocalyptic and rabbinic theology, the vision of God is thrown into the future and becomes a feature of the messianic era. See, on the whole subject, K. E. Kirk, *The Vision of God*, Bampton Lectures, 1928 (London and New York, 1931), pp. 10–22; I. Abrahams, *The Glory of God* (Cambridge, 1925), pp. 39–52.

suggested by the fact which we have already noted, that εἰκών, together with the other terms which Paul has added to the quotation from the psalm, can be traced to the Genesis narrative; the only exception was φθαρτός, and we have now seen that there is reason to link that, too, with the story of Adam. It is significant, moreover, that the word is used in the singular, as is the phrase φθαρτοῦ ἀνθρώπου, whereas the terms later in the verse are plural. It is true that ὁμοίωμα is also used in the singular, but in this Paul is following his source. His dependence on Ps. 106 (105) suggests that the εἰκών is to be linked most closely with the two words which follow it, rather than with the ἐν ὁμοιώματι. Thus we should probably interpret the phrase: 'for a likeness of (a) an image of corruptible man, (b) various types of animals', rather than 'for a likeness of an image, both of corruptible man and of animals'.

This association of εἰκών with ἄνθρωπος points us once again to the Genesis narrative, and to the statement that man is made in the image of God. In 1 Cor. 11.7 Paul refers to Gen. 1.26f and says that man 'is the image and glory of God'; image and glory, although not synonymous, are here very closely connected. When we turn to other passages where Paul uses εἰκών, we find in almost every case a similar association with δόξα.[34] There is thus good ground for supposing that in Rom. 1.23 there is a particular contrast between the two phrases τὴν δόξαν τοῦ ἀφθάρτου θεοῦ and εἰκόνος φθαρτοῦ ἀνθρώπου.

What is the precise meaning of δόξα in this verse? From the context, both in the psalm, and in Romans, it is obviously used in a sense almost equivalent to 'worship'.[35] We have already noted that it suggests, also, the actual presence of God; this is in accordance, not only with Old Testament usage, but also with rabbinic tradition, which used the term 'glory' as a periphrasis for God. The contrast between δόξα and εἰκών suggests, however, that δόξα may here have yet another shade of meaning, and refer not only to the glory which God possesses in himself, but to that same glory in so far as it was originally possessed also by man. This suggestion receives support when we turn back once more to the verse as it stands in the psalm, and remember that there is a similar double interpretation there. As we have already noted,[36] although the glory is there said to be that of Israel, this was regarded as a scribal correction for 'his glory', made from motives of reverence, and Paul appears to have been aware of this double significance. Certainly

---

[34] See Rom. 8.29f; 1 Cor. 15.42–9; 2 Cor. 3.18; Col. 4.4.
[35] Cf. Isa. 42.8; 48.11.   [36] See above, n. 2.

he must have been familiar with the idea which is expressed both in the verse as it stands, and in the similar passage in Jer. 2.11, that the true glory of the people is to be found in God.[37] Jeremiah and the psalmist are concerned with the people of Israel, and trace this loss of glory to the nation's apostasy; Paul is speaking of mankind in general, and so takes the idea further back in history. The rabbinic tradition that at the Fall Adam lost the glory of God which had hitherto been reflected in his face, points us once again to Gen. 1–3. The same idea reappears in Paul two chapters later, at Rom. 3.23, where he speaks of all men lacking the glory of God.

Thus we find in this verse a triple contrast: man did not only exchange the worship of the true God for that of idols; he also exchanged intimate fellowship with God for an experience which was shadowy and remote, and he exchanged, too, his own reflection of the glory of God for the image of corruption. Paul – like the rabbis – does not say that man ever lost the image of God – though his references to the recreation of man after the image of God or of Christ show that he regarded it as being almost effaced. The things which man *did* lose were the glory of God and the dominion over Nature which were associated with that image; and he lost them when he forgot that he himself was εἰκὼν θεοῦ, and sought to find that εἰκών elsewhere. In so doing, he took on the image of corruption and became subject to death, thus obscuring the fact that he was originally created in the image of the incorruptible God.

The evidence which we have examined suggests that Paul's use of the term εἰκών in Rom. 1. 23 is of more significance than is generally recognized. The verse must, indeed, be considered in the whole context of Paul's theme in Romans, summed up in 1.16f – the gospel as the revelation of God's righteousness. This righteousness is revealed, says Paul, both in wrath (chs. 1–3) and in justification (chs. 4–5). In his argument he moves from all men (chs. 1.18–2.16) to the Jew (chs. 2.17–3.20), from the Jew (ch. 4) back to all men (ch. 5). The theme of chapter 5 is the same as that of 1.18–2.16, but considered from the point of view of justification instead of wrath, and it is framed in both passages in terms of man's solidarity with Adam. But just as, in the sections dealing with the Jew, the reference to Abraham is made explicit only when Paul turns from wrath to justification, so the reference to Adam is made explicit only when we come to chapter 5.

The results of this justification are outlined in the following chapters,

[37] Cf. Ps. 3.3.

and the climax of this part of the epistle is reached in chapter 8, where we find man glorified with Christ and conformed to his image, while Nature is set free from the futility to which she was subjected when man lost his dominion over her. So, in Christ, the tragedy of 1.23 is reversed: men who have sought for glory and incorruption (2.7), qualities which come from God alone (1.23), and which were lost at the Fall, will find them in Christ, as they are changed from the image of the earthly to the image of the heavenly.[38]

[38] 1 Cor. 15.49.

6

A further note on Romans 1

In the previous chapter, I suggested that in writing Rom. 1.18–32 Paul had the figure of Adam in mind, and that in these verses he deliberately described man's predicament in terms of the biblical narrative of Adam's fall. Not only does the language of this section echo that of Gen. 1.20–6, but the sequence of events is reminiscent of the story of Adam in Gen. 1–3. This idea has been accepted and developed by Professor C. K. Barrett,[1] who points out that for Paul the Fall itself is a religious or theological event, 'a lapse from God into idolatry', and that the moral wickedness described in Rom. 1 is the *result* of the Fall. The link between man's failure to glorify God and the moral wickedness which follows is underlined by Paul: three times, in verses 24, 26 and 28, the moral 'consequences' of man's fall are introduced by the verb παρέδωκεν, and 'in each of these verses the "consequence" introduced is essentially the same'.[2] The Fall itself, described in verse 23 in terms of idolatry, is referred to again in verses 25 and 28.

On this analysis, then, we find that Paul has three times referred to what Professor Barrett terms 'the prior, non-moral but religious or theological fall', and three times followed this with a description of the 'moral consequences' of the Fall. This pattern has been obscured by the paragraphing in Souter's text and the RV, but is seen more clearly in the arrangement of the Nestle text. At this point, however, we discover that there is not only a parallelism between the three references to the Fall (in vv. 23, 25 and 28), and a parallelism between the three accounts of the consequences (in vv. 24, 26f and 28), but also a verbal antithesis within each of the three paragraphs. This is best seen by setting out the verses in parallel columns:

---

[1] C. K. Barrett, *From First Adam to Last* (London, 1962), pp. 17–19.
[2] *Ibid*, p. 18.

A φάσκοντες εἶναι σοφοὶ ἐμωράνθησαν, καὶ ἤλλαξαν τὴν δόξαν τοῦ ἀφθάρτου Θεοῦ ἐν ὁμοιώματι εἰκόνος φθαρτοῦ ἀνθρώπου καὶ πετεινῶν καὶ τετραπόδων καὶ ἑρπετῶν.

διὸ παρέδωκεν αὐτοὺς ὁ Θεὸς ἐν ταῖς ἐπιθυμίαις τῶν καρδιῶν αὐτῶν εἰς ἀκαθαρσίαν τοῦ ἀτιμάζεσθαι τὰ σώματα αὐτῶν ἐν αὐτοῖς.

B οἵτινες μετήλλαξαν τὴν ἀλήθειαν τοῦ Θεοῦ ἐν τῷ ψεύδει, καὶ ἐσεβάσθησαν καὶ ἐλάτρευσαν τῇ κτίσει παρὰ τὸν Κτίσαντα, ὅς ἐστιν εὐλογητὸς εἰς τοὺς αἰῶνας. ἀμήν.

διὰ τοῦτο παρέδωκεν αὐτοὺς ὁ Θεὸς εἰς πάθη ἀτιμίας· αἵ τε γὰρ θήλειαι αὐτῶν μετήλλαξαν τὴν φυσικὴν χρῆσιν εἰς τὴν παρὰ φύσιν, ὁμοίως τε καὶ οἱ ἄρσενες ἀφέντες τὴν φυσικὴν χρῆσιν τῆς θηλείας ἐξεκαύθησαν . . .

C καὶ καθὼς οὐκ ἐδοκίμασαν τὸν Θεὸν ἔχειν ἐν ἐπιγνώσει,

παρέδωκεν αὐτοὺς ὁ Θεὸς εἰς ἀδόκιμον νοῦν, ποιεῖν τὰ μὴ καθήκοντα, πεπληρωμένους πάσῃ ἀδικίᾳ . . .

It can be seen that Paul says virtually the same thing three times over, in different ways, but that the language he uses seems to have been chosen every time in such a manner as to 'make the punishment fit the crime'. In A, man forsakes the true worship (δόξα) of God for the false glory of man and animals: the result is man's own dishonour (ἀτιμάζεσθαι); it should be noted that Paul regularly uses ἀτιμία as the opposite to δόξα.[3] There is possibly also another hint of the appropriateness of the punishment here: for those who worship animals (the great majority of which were considered unclean) are given up to uncleanness (ἀκαθαρσία); it is interesting to note that in Acts 10.12 the creatures which Peter refuses to eat because they are unclean are described in precisely the same terms as those used here – τετράποδα, ἑρπετά and πετεινά.[4] In B, the correspondence is brought out by the repetition of the verb μετήλλαξαν: one false exchange leads to another. The unnatural worship of the creature instead of the creator results in the unnatural use of sex, contrary to the natural created order; the exchange of the truth of God for a lie leads to a similar distortion in the relationships between men and women. In C, the link between cause and result is brought out by a play on words: man's failure to give

---

[3] 1 Cor. 11.14; 15.43; 2 Cor. 6.8.

[4] Paul's own use of the terms is probably to be traced to Gen. 1. 20–5. See N. Hyldahl, 'A reminiscence of the Old Testament at Romans i.23', *NTS*, 2 (1956), 285–8; see above, ch. 5, pp. 76f.

recognition to God (οὐκ ἐδοκίμασαν) results in a mind which is ἀδόκιμος: the absence of God ἐν ἐπιγνώσει leads to a mind which approves of all kinds of evil.

We have referred already to the connection in both thought and vocabulary between this passage as a whole and the early chapters of Genesis. Paul seems to have been influenced also by the theme and language of Ps. 106 (LXX 105). In addition to the quotation from verse 20 in Rom. 1.23 there are echoes of verse 14 (καὶ ἐπεθύμησαν ἐπιθυμίαν) in 1.24 and of verse 48 (εὐλογητὸς Κύριος ὁ Θεὸς ᾽Ισραὴλ ἀπὸ τοῦ αἰῶνος καὶ ἕως τοῦ αἰῶνος) in 1.26. Even more significant is the structure of the psalm, which lists alternatively the sins of Israel and the activity of God – in either deliverance or punishment. We find here the same link between man's sin and God's punishment which is found in Rom. 1:

> They made a calf in Horeb
> and worshipped a molten image.
> They exchanged the glory of God
> for the image of an ox that eats grass.
> They forgot God, their Saviour,
> who had done great things in Egypt,
> wondrous works in the land of Ham,
> and terrible things by the Red Sea.
> Therefore he said he would destroy them . . .

This link between sin and punishment (in vv. 23, 26 and 40f) is made in Hebrew by ו and in Greek by καί, though the RSV translators found it necessary to translate the sense by 'therefore'. Most interesting of all is verse 41, which is parallel to Paul's own repeated formula in Rom. 1.24, 26 and 28 – καὶ παρέδωκεν αὐτοὺς χεῖρας ἐθνῶν.

It seems probable, therefore, that this section of Rom. 1 is influenced not only by the account of Adam's fall in Genesis, but also by Ps. 106, and that it is the latter passage which lies behind Paul's threefold statement of man's sin and God's punishment. The nature of the sin (idolatry) and of the punishment (the moral consequences) has been worked out by Paul in terms of his understanding of Adam's disobedience and its meaning for mankind. In the close link which Paul makes here between sin and its results, we see his profound recognition of the fact that sin brings its own 'reward' in appropriate forms; behind individual acts of wickedness lies the basic sin of man's rebellion against God, and the 'sins' of which the moralist is aware are the consequence and symptom of that fundamental disobedience.

7

Philippians 2.6–11

One of my favourite quotations is a comment made by A. B. Bruce in 1876. Writing on Phil. 2.6–11 he remarked: 'The diversity of opinion prevailing among interpreters in regard to the meaning . . . is enough to fill the student with despair and to afflict him with intellectual paralysis.'[1] Nearly 100 years later, the cause of the despair has increased out of all proportion – but the paralysis has apparently still not overtaken us!

One of the most hotly debated questions among many is that of the meaning of the phrase οὐχ ἁρπαγμὸν ἡγήσατο. Is ἁρπαγμός to be understood as *res rapta* or *res rapienda*? Is it to be understood as equivalent to εὕρημα, meaning 'a piece of good fortune'?[2] Is it to be understood in an active sense, meaning 'snatching'?[3] A recent article by J. Carmignac[4] approaches the problem in a new way, by examining the position of the word οὐχ in the sentence; this, he maintains, belongs not to ἡγήσατο but to ἁρπαγμόν. Paul means that Christ considered equality with God as something which did not need to be usurped; it was his, by virtue of the fact that he was ἐν μορφῇ Θεοῦ. This interpretation not only does justice to the position of the negative in the sentence, as Carmignac demonstrates; it also allows the ἀλλά in the next verse to have its proper force. Every other interpretation of the phrase οὐχ ἁρπαγμὸν ἡγήσατο weakens the force of ἀλλά, since what Christ did *not* do in verse 6, and what he *did* do in verse 7, are

[1] A. B. Bruce, *The Humiliation of Christ* (Edinburgh, 1876), p. 8.
[2] For a summary of the various views which have been suggested, see R. P. Martin, *Carmen Christi. Philippians ii.5–11 in Recent Interpretation and in the Setting of Early Christian Worship*, SNTS Monograph, 4 (Cambridge, 1967), pp. 134–53.
[3] See the recent article by C. F. D. Moule, 'Further reflexions on Philippians 2.5–11' in W. Ward Gasque and R. P. Martin (eds.), *Apostolic History and the Gospel, Biblical and Historical Essays Presented to Frederick Fyvie Bruce on his Sixtieth Birthday* (Exeter, 1970), pp. 264–76.
[4] J. Carmignac, 'L'Importance de la place d'une négation OYX APΠAΓMON HΓHΣATO (Philippiens II.6)', *NTS*, 18 (1971–2), 131–66.

interpreted as different ways of saying the same thing. But if Carmignac is right, then the statement that Christ considered equality with God to be no act of robbery, is properly followed by the words: 'nevertheless, he emptied himself . . .'

But why did Paul put the sentence in this negative form at all? Why is it necessary to deny that equality with God might have been considered aggrandizement? Why is there this contrast in the ἀλλά between what Christ considered his right and what he actually did?

The difficulty of understanding this particular passage is increased by our uncertainty as to whether or not it had a prehistory. The introductory ὅς in verse 6 suggests immediately the beginning of a section which is separable from its context, and which is perhaps already known, not only to Paul, but also to his readers. The undoubtedly poetic character of the passage also suggests that it may have had a prior existence – though possibly we have here an example of poetic style rather than an actual 'poem' or 'hymn'. If the passage is *pre*-Pauline, then we have no guide-lines to help us in understanding its meaning. Commentators may speculate about the background, but we know very little about pre-Pauline Christianity, and nothing at all about the context in which the passage originated. It may therefore be more profitable to look first at the function of these verses in the present context and to inquire about possible parallels within Paul's own writings. For even if the material is non-Pauline, we may expect Paul himself to have interpreted it and used it in a Pauline manner. Certainly we may legitimately compare these verses with Pauline ideas, and hope to find some indication as to what he was doing with them, whether or not he is their author. I shall therefore consider the relation of these verses to Paul's argument in the surrounding chapters, before looking at the vocabulary and structure of the 'hymn' itself, so returning to the question of the contrast in verses 6–7.

Whatever the origin of Phil. 2.6–11, the passage belongs in its present context. Its vocabulary echoes that of the verses immediately preceding. It is introduced in verse 5 with the verb φρονεῖτε, which echoes φρονῆτε and φρονοῦτες in verse 2. The important word ἐταπείνωσεν in verse 8 picks up the term ταπεινοφροσύνη in verse 3; ἡγήσατο in verse 6 reminds us of ἡγούμενοι in verse 3. The verses are also firmly anchored in their context by what comes immediately after. In verse 12 Paul begins the next section with the word ὥστε – and when he writes ὥστε elsewhere it is because there is a logical progression in his thought, not because he considers it a suitable weak link word; in this case it is ὥστε ὑπηκούσατε – echoing the ὑπήκοος of verse 8. Thus four times over Paul links the behaviour of the Philippians (or rather the behaviour which he expects of them) with the behaviour of Christ himself, described in verses 6–8.

The traditional interpretation of these verses, which may be described as the 'ethical interpretation', and which is reflected in the AV's command to have the mind 'which was also in Christ Jesus', has come under attack in recent years. It is argued that Paul never appeals elsewhere to the earthly life of Jesus as an example to be imitated; he grounds his ethics in the saving events of the death and resurrection. Moreover, if Paul is referring to the self-humiliation of Christ as an example to be imitated, what, it is asked, is the relevance of the last three verses to this theme? Does Paul simply include them for the sake of completeness? Many modern exegetes therefore follow E. Käsemann[5] in interpreting the passage as setting out the events of salvation. The only appeal made to the Philippians is to act in the way which is proper to those who are 'in Christ'. R. P. Martin sums up this view in these words: 'the hymn is only loosely dependent upon the ethical admonition, yet . . . supplies the objective facts of redemption on which an ethical appeal may be made. The Apostolic summons is not: follow Jesus by doing as He did – an impossible feat . . . rather: become in your conduct and church relationships the type of persons who, by that *kenosis*, death and exaltation of the Lord of glory, have a place in His body, the Church.'[6] In this interpretation, the final verses describe the exaltation of Christ, which is part of the salvation event, and lead into an acclamation of the lordship of Christ.

If we are considering these verses in isolation, then it must be agreed that they are a recital of the events which are the ground of salvation. But I suspect that commentators have been so concerned to discover the original form and *Sitz im Leben* of the passage, that they have imposed their interpretation of this hypothetical pre-Pauline hymn onto Paul's own argument. I do not which to deny for a moment that Paul has a very profound understanding of the relationship between the saving events of the gospel and the conduct appropriate to those who are in Christ; of course he did not consider Christian ethics to be simply a matter of imitating the example of Christ; rather it is a conformity to the true existence which belongs to those who are in

---

[5] E. Käsemann, 'Kritische Analyse von Phil. 2,5–11, *ZThK*, 47 (1950), 313–60 (= *Exegetische Versuche und Besinnungen*, vol. 1, 5th edn, Göttingen, 1967, pp. 51–95): ET, in *JThCh*, 5 (1968), 45–88.   [6] Martin, *Carmen Christi*, pp. 290f.

Christ. In Käsemann's words, Christ 'ist Urbild, nicht Vorbild'.[7] But what is the character of this new humanity – this life in Christ? It seems to me nonsense to suggest that it is not the character of Jesus himself. It is only the dogma that the Jesus of History and the Christ of Faith belong in separate compartments that leads to the belief that the appeal to a Christian character appropriate to those who are in Christ is not linked to the pattern as seen in Jesus himself. It is perhaps worthy of note that Paul does *not* introduce this famous passage with the phrase ἐν Χριστῷ, but with the words ἐν Χριστῷ Ἰησοῦ. I believe that he is in fact using them in the same sense as his usual form ἐν Χριστῷ. But may it not be significant that in this particular instance he chose to add the name 'Jesus'? The life which should be demonstrated in the lives of those who are ἐν Χριστῷ, which is possible only because of the salvation events, is precisely the kind of life seen in Jesus Christ. If the Christians in Philippi fail to live in accordance with this pattern, then they are denying the validity of the events which made them Christian.

We have already noted the objection that Paul does not normally appeal to his readers to imitate Jesus Christ. This is true. But it is interesting to note that the closest parallel to the idea of Christ's self-emptying in Phil. 2 is found in 2 Cor. 8.9: 'You know the grace of our Lord Jesus Christ, that being rich he became poor for your sake, that you through his poverty might become rich.' Here we have another summary of the gospel events, much briefer than the passage in Philippians, tossed into the argument in a typically Pauline way; the context once again is concerned with Christian behaviour. The example of Christ is appealed to in urging the Corinthians to be generous in giving to the poor. Once again, it would be inadequate to describe this as simply *imitatio Christi*; their obligation to behave like Christ arises out of the fact that their lives are dependent upon him. But in this case there is no use of the phrase ἐν Χριστῷ. The appeal to act in a certain way is directly linked with the action of the Lord Jesus Christ. The example here is of course not that of the earthly Jesus; we are referred to the χάρις of the Lord Jesus Christ in becoming poor; but this is exactly parallel to the Philippian reference to Christ's self-humiliation – which in turn is parallel to the statement that the earthly Jesus became obedient to death by crucifixion.[8]

[7] Käsemann, 'Kritische Analyse von Phil. 2.5–11', 345; ET, 74.
[8] The theme of imitating Christ is found also in Rom. 15.1–7, 1 Cor. 10.31–11.1; 1 Thess. 1.6; cf. also Eph. 5.2. In all these passages, as well as in Paul's appeals to readers to imitate him (see 1 Cor 4.16; Phil. 3.17; 2 Thess 3.7, 9), the example to be followed is one of self-denial and suffering. On the theme of Christ as example, cf. E. Larsson, *Chrisutus als Vorbild*, *ASNU*, 23 (Uppsala, 1962).

The other objection we noted is the fact that the last three verses of our passage have no relevance to the theme of humility; it may be impossible for Christians to imitate Jesus Christ; it is certainly nonsense to speak of them imitating Christ in being exalted.

Once again, however, it is perhaps worth noting the relation of what Paul says here to his argument elsewhere in the epistle. The most interesting links are found in 3.20f. Here we have σύμμορφον echoing μορφή, ὑπάρχει echoing ὑπάρχων, and μετασχηματίσει picking up the word σχῆμα. The reference to humiliation in ταπεινώσεως reminds us of the verb ἐταπείνωσεν used of Christ in 2.8, and the words δόξα and πάντα both reappear, as does the phrase Κύριος Ἰησοῦς Χριστός. Even more significant is the thought of the passage; for here Paul spells out what is to happen to Christians at the appearance of the Lord Jesus Christ. The body of our humiliation (τῆς ταπεινώσεως ἡμῶν) is to be changed (μετασχηματίσει) and conformed (σύμμορφον) to his glorious body; he is to do this through the power which enables him to subject all things to himself. I have argued elsewhere[9] that we have a parallel here – and an extended one – to those passages where Paul uses the idea of 'interchange', e.g. 2 Cor. 8.9 and 5.21, Gal. 3.13 and 4.4; Christ becomes what we are, so enabling us to become what he is. The former idea is set out for us in Philippians in 2.6–8. Then in verses 9–11 we have a description of what Christ is. Now in 3.20f, we discover that the power given to him (by which all things were subjected to him) will enable him to transform us into conformity with him: we shall become like him.

Of course this is not imitation, it is conformity, and it is a central theme in Paul. It would be better, perhaps, to use this word 'conformity' also when speaking of the appeal Paul makes in 2.5–11; for what Paul urges the Philippians to do is to be conformed to what they ought to be in Christ, because of what has happened through his life, death and resurrection; but what they ought to be – and what they can become in Christ – results from what Christ is and did; one cannot separate the Christian character from the character of Christ himself.

The idea of imitation is not, however, entirely absent from chapter 3. In verse 17 Paul urges the Philippians to imitate *him*; 'you have us as a τύπος', he writes. In contrast they have things back to front – they glory in their shame. Paul's own manner of life is in conformity with the gospel of the Cross which he sets out in chapter 2. He has described it already in the earlier verses of chapter 3. Again, there is an interesting echo of 2.6–11 in verses 7–8 where we have ἥγημαι and ἡγοῦμαι (twice)

---

[9] See above, ch. 1.

– cf. ἡγήσατο in 2.6. Paul considered all the advantages of his Jewish birth as worth nothing by comparison with the riches found in Christ. The reward and goal are set before him – namely conformity with the glorious body of Christ.

Paul not only uses the so-called hymn, therefore, as the basis of his ethical appeal to the Philippians, but draws on its language in describing the goal of Christian life which he links with the Parousia. Whatever its origins, in its present context Paul links this description of Christ's self-emptying with the life of the Christian community. As so often happens, it seems that an unnecessary antithesis has been set up by interpreters, between a rather superficial interpretation of Pauline ethics on the one hand – an interpretation implying that Christian behaviour is simply a case of following Jesus – and on the other hand the conviction that the passage is to be understood only as a recital of saving acts, to which the Church responds in adoration. What in fact we have is a typically Pauline fusion of these two themes. The behaviour which is required of those who are in Christ is required of them – and possible for them – precisely because they are in Christ, and their being in Christ depends on the saving acts proclaimed in the gospel. The Christian response is not simply to join in the chorus of adoration and confess Jesus as Lord, but to obey the one named as Lord, and to give glory to God by being conformed to the image of his Son. The pattern for Christian obedience set out in chapter 3 and in many other passages of Paul's letters is conformity to the way of the Cross: Paul is content to be found in Christ – to know the power of his resurrection and the fellowship of his sufferings; to be conformed to his death, in confident hope of resurrection. We suffer with him, Paul writes, in order that we may be glorified with him – the theme elaborated at the end of chapter 3. It is of course paradoxical to suggest that Christians should be like Christ in his self-emptying and obedience – for these were his actions in becoming man – subject to human limitations. We shall go on to explore the even greater paradox which underlies this idea.

Another assumption of contemporary exegesis of Phil. 2 is that the verses with which we are concerned can properly be described as some kind of early hymn. Ever since Lohmeyer made his analysis of these lines,[10] attempts have been made to set out the structure of the passage. The fact that different scholars produce different poetic structures

---

[10] E. Lohmeyer, *Kyrios Jesus. Eine Untersuchung zu Phil.* 2,5–11, 2nd edn (Darmstadt, 1961).

makes one slightly hesitant about the value of this exercise; I myself have produced six or seven different analyses, and found each of them convincing at the time! One of our difficulties is in knowing what we are looking for. If this passage is poetry, it is certainly not Greek poetry; is it then a translation of an Aramaic 'hymn'? There have been attempts to translate it back into Aramaic,[11] and analyse it in terms of a triple stress in each line. One of the difficulties is that the passage as we have it never really fits the patterns into which the commentators try to push it; they therefore excise certain lines as Pauline glosses. But there is a dangerous circularity in this kind of method; I suspect that often those who analyse the lines have decided which words are Pauline glosses before they start their poetic analysis.

It is of course undeniable that there is something poetic about these lines. Whether this makes them a poem – or whether they would be better described as a piece of rhythmic prose – is a different matter. In many ways the latter seems more likely, and we may perhaps compare the Prologue of John's gospel, and the many attempts which have been made to analyse that.[12] At any rate it is perhaps dangerous to assume too readily that we can tell from the structure which words belong to an original 'hymn' and which are Paul's own comments. If we are dealing with rhythmic prose this kind of analysis does not allow us to make such a distinction. If it *is* a 'poem' or 'hymn', then I must analyse the material accordingly, and demonstrate that it is possible to set the passage out as it stands in a poetic form, without making any excisions. I therefore offer the following analysis for consideration. I am not committed to it – though I find it attractive. If these lines are indeed a hymn, then I find my reconstruction more convincing than others. But I offer it primarily in order to demonstrate that it is possible to set out the *whole* of Phil. 2.6–11 in poetic form. We cannot use the poetic tool as a way of deciding which pieces may be excised as Pauline glosses.

> ὃς ἐν μορφῇ Θεοῦ ὑπάρχων
> οὐχ ἁρπαγμὸν ἡγήσατο
> τὸ εἶναι ἴσα Θεῷ
> ἀλλὰ ἑαυτὸν ἐκένωσεν
> μορφὴν δούλου λαβών
> ἐν ὁμοιώματι ἀνθρώπων γενόμενος

---

[11] Most recently by P. Grelot, 'Deux notes critiques sur Philippiens 2,6–11', *Bibl*, 54 (1973), 169–86.

[12] Cf. the discussion of these attempts by C. K. Barrett, *The Prologue of St. John's Gospel* (London, 1971).

καὶ σχήματι εὑρεθεὶς ὡς ἄνθρωπος
ἐταπείνωσεν ἑαυτὸν
γενόμενος ὑπήκοος μέχρι θανάτου
θανάτου δὲ σταυροῦ.

διὸ καὶ ὁ Θεὸς
αὐτὸν ὑπερύψωσεν
καὶ ἐχαρίσατο αὐτῷ τὸ ὄνομα
τὸ ὑπὲρ πᾶν ὄνομα

ἵνα ἐν τῷ ὀνόματι ᾽Ιησοῦ
πᾶν γόνυ κάμψῃ
ἐπουρανίων καὶ ἐπιγείων καὶ καταχθονίων
καὶ πᾶσα γλῶσσα ἐξομολογήσηται
ὅτι *ΚΥΡΙΟΣ ΙΗΣΟΥΣ ΧΡΙΣΤΟΣ*
εἰς δόξαν Θεοῦ Πατρός

This particular analysis presents us with a chiastic structure. A six-line statement about Christ's *kenosis* in becoming man is followed by a four-line section continuing this theme in terms of his earthly life. The second part of the hymn reverses the form as well as the theme; a four-line statement of Christ's exaltation and receipt of the Name is followed by a six-line expansion of this theme. Each of my six line 'verses' can in fact be subdivided into two three-line sections, giving us six short sections; then it may be noted that the final line of each section fills out the meaning of the previous one. Thus: what was it that the one who was in the form of God did not consider a usurpation? It was equality with God. What did taking the form of a slave mean? It meant taking on the likeness of men. What was the death to which he became obedient? It was death on a cross. What was the name given to him? It was the name which is above all names. What is meant by every knee? Every knee in heaven and earth and under the earth. What does it mean to proclaim Jesus as Lord? It means the glory of God the Father. This pattern may perhaps not be quite so obvious in this final case, but is, I believe, significant here too; the proclamation of Jesus as Lord in no way deprived God of glory – it was in fact the centre of God's self-revelation; to proclaim Jesus as Lord and to give glory to God the Father are synonymous.

We may note also the linguistic links in this reconstruction. Μορφή in the first three lines is taken up by μορφὴν δούλου in the second three. The phrase in the sixth line, ἐν ὁμοιώματι ἀνθρώπων γενόμενος is taken up by the opening line of the next section, σχήματι εὑρεθεὶς ὡς ἄνθρωπος. A similar link occurs between the last line and the first line of the two main sections in the second half – τὸ ὄνομα τὸ ὑπὲρ πᾶν ὄνομα and ἐν τῷ ὀνόματι ᾽Ιησοῦ. The first half describes what Christ did – in the main verbs ἐκένωσεν and ἐταπείνωσεν: the second half describes the act of God – αὐτὸν ὑπερύψωσεν καί ἐχαρίσατο αὐτῷ. Notice also the small but important introductory words of each section: ὅς, ἀλλά, καί, διό, ἵνα, καί.

This kind of symmetry tempts me to join those who argue that we have here a carefully constructed passage which may properly be described as a hymn. More important, however, it conforms me in my opinion that we must look at the passage as a whole, and not think that we can pick out the Pauline garnishes to a pre-Pauline structure on the basis of literary form.

What, finally, of the meaning of our passage? The most widely held view at the moment seems to be that it reflects some form of Hellenistic Gnostic Redeemer myth, and recounts the descent of the divine hero and his ascent back into heaven. If our passage is indeed a translation of an Aramaic hymn, then this kind of speculation does seem a rather odd background for it! Other exegetes find the Old Testament a more likely background, and here the honours are divided between Adam and the Suffering Servant.[13] We cannot explore all these ideas in one chapter; I wish to concentrate my attention on Adam, who is certainly important for Paul elsewhere.

The starting-off point for the interpretation of this passage as a contrast between Christ and Adam has always been the *res rapienda* interpretation of the word ἁρπαγμός: Christ did not regard equality with God as something to be grasped. This has been seen as a deliberate contrast with the attempt of Adam in Gen. 3 to grasp at an equality which he did not possess. If we accept the *res rapta* interpretation, on the other hand, and regard equality as something which Christ did not cling to, then this particular contrast cannot be maintained; on Carmignac's interpretation, similarly, equality was something which did not need to be grasped.

I would like to explore this idea of a contrast with Adam in a somewhat different way. It has often been suggested that the phrase ἐν μορφῇ Θεοῦ is an echo of Gen. 1.26.[14] Ought we perhaps also to see the

---

[13] I discussed the difficulties of the latter view briefly in *Jesus and the Servant* (London, 1959), pp. 120f.

[14] Although the phrase itself is not found in the LXX version of that passage, the terms μορφή and εἰκών appear to be equivalent terms in the LXX. Cf. J. Jervell, *Imago Dei. Gen 1,26f. im Spätjudentum, in der Gnosis und in den paulinischen Briefen*, *FRLANT*, 76 (Göttingen, 1960), 204f, and the discussion by Martin, *Carmen Christi*, pp. 102–19.

words τὸ εἶναι ἴσα Θεῷ as an echo of the same verse? In Gen. 1.26 we read of God's intention to create man 'in our image, after our likeness'. The Hebrew words used are צלם and דמות|and the LXX reads κατ' εἰκόνα καὶ καθ' ὁμοίωσιν. If Carmignac is right (as I think he is) then in Phil. 2.6 we have a similar kind of parallelism: he who was in the form of God did not regard this equality with God (or this likeness to God) as something which needed to be usurped. Being in the form of God *meant* likeness or equality with God, as in the case of Adam in Gen. 1.26. The word ἴσα in Phil. 2.6 is normally translated 'equal', but it can be used in a much more general sense in the LXX to mean 'like',[15] and the phrase would therefore be appropriate as a reference to Gen. 1.26.

The phrase τὸ εἶναι ἴσα Θεῷ has often been compared with the very similar words in John 5.18 expressing the Jews' complaint that Jesus called God his own Father, ἴσον ἑαυτὸν ποιῶν τῷ Θεῷ. If our interpretation is correct, there is also a close parallel in meaning. For the Jews' objection in John 5 to Jesus' claim that God is his Father is that it is a usurpation, ἁρπαγμός, of a status which does not belong to him, whereas John, who sees Jesus as sharing the activity of God (5.17), recognizes the implications of this claim.[16] In John's presentation, Jesus does not regard his claims as the usurpation of status, but, paradoxically, as part of the obedience of the Son to the Father; Jesus is at once one with the Father, yet dependent upon him.

If Phil. 2 reflects the language of Gen. 1.26, then the question arises: why is the contrast between Adam and Christ expressed in this particular way? According to Gen. 3.5 and 22, the eating of the forbidden fruit meant that Adam became as God, knowing good and evil; according to Jewish tradition, however, his action meant that he *ceased* to be like God; in disobeying God's command, Adam ceased to be in the likeness of God. Gen. Rab. 21.2, 3, 4, for example, interprets Gen. 3.22 as meaning 'Behold, the man *was* as one of us'. By his sin, Adam lost his God-likeness; in particular, he lost his immortality. Similarly, we have the idea that this divine likeness, lost at the Fall, became a possibility once again at Sinai: Israel was like God ('Ye are Godlike beings', Ps. 82.6), just as Adam was like God ('Behold the man was as one of us', Gen. 3.22), but Israel followed Adam's footsteps, and therefore died as Adam died.[17] At the end, however, in the world to

---

[15] E.g. it translates the Hebrew כ ,in Isa. 51.23; Job 5.14; 10.10 (parallel to ὥσπερ); 13.28 (parallel to ὥσπερ); 15.16; 24.20; 27.16 (parallel to ὥσπερ); 29.14; 40.15., Cf. Wisd. 7.3. See also P. Grelot, 'Deux expressions difficiles de Philippiens 2,6–7, *Bibl*, 53 (1972), 495–507.

[16] Cf. C. K. Barrett, *The Gospel According to St. John* (London, 1962), *in loc.*

[17] Exod. Rab. 32.1; Num. Rab. 16.24.

come, the thing which Adam lost will be restored, and man will become like God: Gen. 3.22 will then be read: 'Behold the man *has become* as one of us'.[18] If Paul was aware of ideas like this, we can understand the logic which led him to write that one who was in the form of God, and who did *not* consider being-like-God as something which needed to be grasped (since it was already his), *nevertheless* deliberately put himself into a situation of being-like-Adam which led to Adam's death.

I suggest then, that the negative οὐχ is a deliberate contrast between Christ and Adam. Adam, created in the form and likeness of God, misunderstood his position, and thought that the divine likeness was something which he needed to grasp; his tragedy was that in seizing it he lost it. Christ, the true Adam, understood that this likeness was already his, by virtue of his relationship with God. Nevertheless, ἑαυτὸν ἐκένωσεν. This verb is usually translated 'he emptied himself' and so raises problems, as the translation leads us to ask: 'Of what did he empty himself?' It is worth noting that elsewhere in Paul the verb is used metaphorically, meaning to make null and void.[19] If we take it in the same sense here, we may translate: 'he made himself powerless.' This suits the context, since it offers a contrast with what went before: Christ, who was in the form of God, and knew that equality with God was his, nevertheless made himself nothing. This translation also leads us naturally into the next statement; making himself null and void, powerless, meant that he took the form of a slave; and as Professor Moule has recently reminded us, there can be no greater contrast than in this word δοῦλος – for the slave was the one who had no rights or privileges – who did not own even his own body.[20]

So Christ came in the likeness of men. The chief objection to the Adamic interpretation of this passage is perhaps the fact that at this point in the story the true Adam is said to *become* man; how can this be? One can understand a contrast between the two Adams, as in Rom. 5 or 1 Cor. 15; but what does it mean to say that the second Adam takes on the likeness of Adam? I suggest that it is precisely here that we see the paradox and irony of what the author of this passage is saying. At this point the one who is truly what man is meant to be – in the form and likeness of God – becomes what other men *are*, because they are in Adam. This explains the 'shadowy' language of the words σχῆμα and

---

[18] Gen. Rab. 21.7.

[19] The verb is used in the active in 1 Cor. 9.15 (with τὸ καύχημα), and in the passive in Rom. 4.14 (with ἡ πίστις), 1 Cor. 1.17 (with ὁ σταυρός) and 2 Cor. 9.3 (with τὸ καύχημα).   [20] Moule, 'Further reflexions', pp. 268f.

ὁμοίωμα. Men have ceased to be what they were meant to be; they have become slaves to sin and death and the Law, as Paul expresses it elsewhere; hence we have the paradox that when the true man becomes what they are, this human likeness is a travesty of what man is meant to be. In saying that Christ has become what men are, our passage is parallel to other christological summaries found in Paul, such as Gal. 3.13 and 4.4; 2 Cor. 5.21 and 8.9. Moreover, having put himself into this position of helpless enslavement, Christ is content to continue the path to the end. The inevitable end is death – the punishment which came upon Adam because of his grasping; again we see the irony of a situation in which one who refuses to take Adam's course nevertheless accepts the results of Adam's sin; and the death which he accepts is death on a cross – the particular form of punishment which in Roman law was considered proper for rebellious δοῦλοι. This final phrase should certainly not be excised as a gloss, as is now almost universally assumed. It is the climax of this section: the paradox has been pushed to the ultimate point, and the form of death is absurdly appropriate to the self-negation.

Therefore God exalted him. There are no echoes of Adam here – there cannot be! The second part is the reversal worked by God. Only when we come to the term κύριος are we reminded of what Adam was meant to be; he was commanded to rule the earth (κατακυριεύειν, Gen. 1.28). But Christ's rule is of every creature, not only on earth but in heaven and under the earth as well. This lordship in no way detracts from the authority of God – on the contrary, it brings glory to God, and Christ thus fulfils the original purpose for Adam.

It has sometimes been argued that the omission of a specific reference to the resurrection is un-Pauline; here all the emphasis is on the idea of exaltation. But Paul certainly speaks elsewhere of Christ's exaltation following the resurrection; Rom. 8.34 and 1 Cor. 15.27, for example, both speak of Christ's exaltation and reign, and it is perhaps significant that these two passages are both found in 'Second Adam' contexts. The emphasis on exaltation and lordship (an idea elsewhere linked with the resurrection[21]), is certainly appropriate in Phil. 2.

Christ is ἐν μορφῇ Θεοῦ and τὸ εἶναι ἴσα Θεῷ belongs to him. He does not cease to be ἐν μορῇῇ Θεοῦ by taking on the μορφὴ δούλου.[22] Here is

---

[21] See Rom. 10.9; 14.9.

[22] The concluding verses of Phil. 2.6–11 describe the open acknowledgement of the status of Christ, already indicated to us in the opening lines: the one who is ἐν μορφῇ Θεοῦ is exalted by God and acknowledged by the whole creation as Lord. We have here an interesting structural parallel with Rom. 1.3f, where we read of the gospel

the paradox: it is precisely because he is truly in the form of God (or God's image) that he is prepared to take on the form of a slave. This, then, is that deeper paradox which underlies the other paradox which we have already noted – namely that Christians are called upon to be like Christ in his self-humiliation which involved becoming like men. In becoming what we are, Christ becomes subject to human frustrations and enslavement to hostile powers; but his very action in becoming what we are is a demonstration of what he eternally is – ungrasping, unself-centred, giving glory by all his actions to God. It is because of this paradox, the absurdity of the form of God being demonstrated in the form of a slave, that Christians can become like Christ; it is because God's glory is demonstrated in shame and weakness (as Paul puts it elsewhere) that at one and the same time Paul can tell the Philippians to be like Christ in his action of ταπείνωσις and promise them that Christ will transform their bodies of ταπείνωσις to be like his own glorious body.

'about God's Son . . . who was declared Son of God in power according to the Spirit of holiness by the resurrection of the dead'. In each case the final designation makes known the true status of Christ, already referred to in the opening phrase; the intervening section describes Christ's life κατὰ σάρκα, though the contrast in Phillipians is more pointed than in Romans.

III
Wisdom

8

Hard sayings: 1 Corinthians 3.2

In this verse Paul appears to make a clear distinction between two types of teaching: the 'milk' on which he has fed the Corinthians in the past, and the 'meat' for which they are hankering. The contrast between milk and solid food offers an obvious metaphor for elementary and advanced teaching, and is used by other writers.[1] In the present context it is clear what Paul means by milk: it is 'the word of the Cross' (1.18), since that alone was what Paul preached to them (2.2). But what is the meat? It seems to be different from the milk, since Paul declares that the Corinthians are not yet ready for this solid food. Apparently it is to be identified with the wisdom of which he spoke in 2.6, where we find a similar contrast; there Paul declared that, although he did not use wisdom in preaching to the Corinthians, nevertheless he does speak wisdom to those who are mature. So the milk fed to babies is the simple message of the Cross; the meat for which the Corinthians are not yet ready is the wisdom which is fed to the mature.

The Corinthians appear to have accused Paul of giving them only milk to digest and not meat; this 'meat' they have found for themselves, in advanced philosophical speculations and esoteric wisdom. Paul is here denying their claim to be 'one up' on other Christians and to possess a wisdom which others lack. At first sight, it might seem that Paul, too, is distinguishing between a 'lower level' of Christian faith ('milk') and esoteric doctrine ('meat') which is reserved for selected Christians. The language he uses, with its references to 'wisdom' which is spoken in a 'mystery' to those who are *teleioi* (initiated/ perfect/mature?), reminds us of the mystery religions. It is much more probable, however, that Paul is using this language to *deny* that Christianity is a mystery religion: he does not speak of offering wisdom or secret knowledge by which men become *teleioi*, 'initiated'; on the

[1] See Heb. 5.12–14; Philo, *De Agric.* §2.

103

contrary, the wisdom which he offers is given to those who are already *teleioi*, 'mature'.

But if the 'meat' offered by Paul is not esoteric teaching, what is it? For a distinction is made here between this and the baby-food, just as in 2.1–6 there is a distinction between the wisdom which he speaks to those who are ready for it and the message which he preached in Corinth. The wisdom which Paul has in mind is further defined in 2.7 as the wisdom of God, spoken in a mystery. If Paul does not explain what this wisdom is, this is perhaps because his readers are still babes, and are not yet able to understand it (3.3). It is possible, however, that the Corinthians' failure to understand the wisdom spoken in a mystery is not due to the fact that Paul is withholding it from them, but is the result of their own inability to digest what he is offering them. If we, too, are unable to discern this wisdom, then it is perhaps because we, also, are 'babes'!

For if we look back at chapters 1–2, we find that Paul has already offered us an exposition of 'wisdom'. His idea of wisdom, however, is very different from that of the Corinthians. The wisdom he describes is the wisdom of God, which is folly in the eyes of the world – for it is the word of the Cross (1.23f), which turns all human values and judgements upside down, shames the wise and brings the things that are to nothingness (1.27f). The wisdom of God is Christ himself (1.30), who is for the Christian the source of all wisdom. It is precisely this wisdom to which Paul refers in 2.6, when he speaks of the wisdom which he expounds to the mature; for it is this topsy-turvy wisdom, so alien to this age, which had been decreed for our glorification and which was hidden from the rulers of this age who are passing away (2.8f); it is this topsy-turvy wisdom, so alien to the Corinthians' natural inclinations, that they have been unable to comprehend.

In his original proclamation of the gospel to the Corinthians, Paul offered them only Christ crucified; now, in this discussion of wisdom, he offers them an exposition of the same theme! His 'meat', then, differs very little, after all, from the 'milk' which he has already fed to them. But this is hardly surprising; he has already preached to them Christ crucified – what else *can* he offer them? For Christ is the wisdom of God, and nothing else is needed. Why, then, the contrast in 3.3? The answer must be that Paul is echoing a distinction which has been made by the Corinthians. Yet while he uses their language, the fundamental contrast in Paul's mind is not between two quite different diets which he has to offer, but between the true food of the gospel with which he has fed them (whether milk or meat) and the synthetic substitutes which the Corinthians have preferred. Similarly, in 2.1–6, the real contrast is not between Paul's elementary teaching for new converts and the wisdom intended for the mature, but between the folly of the gospel (which is wisdom) and the wisdom of men. Those who are mature can accept this true wisdom, for they realize the full meaning of the Christian gospel, and know that they have no need of other food, for Christ is all-sufficient; it is largely the attitude and understanding of the Corinthians themselves which made Paul's teaching seem like milk, and not meat. Those who despise the wisdom and strength of God, because they seem foolish and weak, will despise also the teaching which seems to them elementary, but which is in fact profound.

Paul's answer to the Corinthians' charge is therefore twofold. On the one hand, he shows them the true nature of the meat which is fed to the Christian: the strong food which Paul has to offer to those who are mature is found in the wisdom and strength of God – the wisdom and strength which seem to men like foolishness and weakness, the 'meat' which seems like 'milk'. On the other hand, he maintains that the diet he gave the Corinthians was the correct one, because of their immaturity in the faith; the divisions which have arisen in the Church as a result of their pursuit of wisdom are a proof of this immaturity (3.3f). It is because of their failure to develop that the Corinthians cannot see that true wisdom is to be found in Christ.

So Paul returns to the subject which led him to expound the meaning of wisdom in the first place – the divisions in the Church. For it is in seeking the wrong kind of wisdom that the Corinthians have split the Church into cliques and turned their backs on the true wisdom, which is a total reliance upon God. They have shown that they are still babes, for they have not yet grasped the implications of the basic truth of the gospel – 'Christ crucified'; until they realize that the scandal of the Cross has put an end to all human boasting, they will be unable to digest the diet which is offered to the mature, for this is unacceptable to those who think in terms of human achievement and glory. Paul has indeed wisdom to offer to the mature, but his wisdom can, by the very nature of the gospel, only be a deeper understanding of the message which he has already preached, a realization in the Corinthians' lives of the proclamation of Christ crucified, into whose death they have been baptized.

9

'Beyond the things which are written': an examination of 1 Corinthians 4.6

In 1 Cor. 3, Paul uses two of his favourite metaphors – the first agricultural, the second architectural – in the course of his attack on the divisions which had appeared in the Church at Corinth. After elaborating these metaphors – not always consistently – in connection with the position of Christian ministers, he explains, in 4.6, his purpose in applying them to Apollos and himself: it is 'that you may learn in us the "Not beyond the things which are written"', and 'that you may not be puffed up on behalf of the one against the other'. The second of these purposes is both reasonable and relevant to the context: it is precisely this tendency of the Corinthians to exalt one Church leader over another which Paul has been attacking. The first, however, appears to be nonsensical, and so difficult to reconcile with the context that many must have concluded, with Moffatt,[1] that the text is hopelessly corrupt. The various English versions illustrate the difficulty. The AV adds the words 'to think of men' after the negative – a translation which attempts to make the phrase relevant, but adds rather more than is permissible. The RSV paraphrases with 'that you may learn by us to live according to scripture', which fits neither the text nor the context. The translation of the NEB 'that you may . . . learn to "keep within the rules" as they say' – is even further removed from the Greek original. The most literal, though scarcely illuminating, translation is that of the RV, 'that in us ye may learn not to go beyond the things which are written': the revisers simply added a verb, which is a minimal requirement if we are to make any sense of the phrase.

None of the various attempts which have been made to explain these enigmatic words is particularly convincing.[2] It is possible that they are

[1] See his translation of the New Testament; also his commentary in 1 Corinthians in the Moffatt series.

[2] See, e.g., R. St J. Parry, *Cambridge Greek Testament: 1 Corinthians* (Cambridge 1916), *loc.*, who suggests that γέγραπται 'is used in a technical sense, but not the usual

a quotation from a letter written to Paul by the Corinthians; this might explain the elliptical structure, but without that letter we are no nearer to understanding the words' relevance to the context. Some have been convinced by the suggestion that the words τὸ μὴ ὑπὲρ ἃ γέγραπται are a marginal gloss[3]; W. F. Howard, advocating this theory, declared that it is the intrusion of this gloss which 'reduces the text to nonsense, from which no expository ingenuity has ever drawn a satisfactory meaning'. Without manuscript evidence, however, the suggestion must remain speculation, and many will consider that the theory regarding the incorporation of the gloss into the text shows ingenuity even greater than that of the expositors.

Let us, then, look at the context again and ask what Paul has been teaching in the preceding section. There appear to be two main points, the first of which is that Paul and Apollos are equal and undivided, fellow-workers of God; in illustration, they are described as gardeners, builders and stewards. The second point is the warning given in 3.10–20 about shoddy workers and people who are destroying the Church; this is a separate idea which causes Paul to alter and adapt his second illustration. The first point is taken up in 4.6 when Paul says that his purpose was to prevent the Corinthians exalting one leader at the expense of another; logically, therefore, we should expect the other ἵνα clause to take up his second point.

Turning then to 1 Cor. 4.6, we find that the second ἵνα clause appears to depend upon the first, rather than to be co-ordinate with it: we may expect, therefore, that the first will refer to the basic trouble which has given rise to the situation described in the second – that is, to the false teaching which has caused the rivalry and factions. The enigmatic phrase itself speaks of what is written, by which Paul clearly refers to scripture, so we must next ask whether there are any references to the Old Testament in 3.5–4.5. There are in fact two quotations, both of them in 3.10–20, the section which deals with Paul's second point, his warning against bad workmanship and the destruction of God's temple. They are used, in verses 19f, to show the foolishness of man's wisdom in the eyes of God – 'For it is written, He that taketh the

technical sense', and interprets it as the 'terms' of a teacher's commission. This interpretation is difficult in view of Paul's usage of γέγραπται in the 'usual technical sense' elsewhere. H. Lietzmann, *Handbuch z. N.T.: An die Korinther I–II*, 3rd edn (Tübingen, 1931), refers to Heinrici's suggestion that Paul is defending himself against an accusation of unscriptural teaching, and using his opponents' own motto. Such a charge seems unlikely, and its rebuttal would not fit the context here.
[3] See W. F. Howard, '1 Cor. 4.6', *Exp. Tim.*, 33 (1922), 479f, who summarizes the arguments of Weiss, Baljon and Bousset.

wise in their craftiness: And again, the Lord knoweth the reasonings of the wise, that they are vain' (Job. 5.13; Ps. 94.11).

In these quotations, Paul has returned to the theme of his first two chapters, which has never been far from his mind. For the false teachers whom Paul is condemning here are clearly those who have led the Corinthians astray with the philosophical speculations and empty wisdom disguised by rhetoric which Paul has derided in the opening chapters of 1 Corinthians. The men who build rubbish upon the true foundation laid by the apostle (3.11–13) are those who have taught the Corinthians to crave for 'meat' and to despise the pure 'milk' of the gospel (3.2), and who have replaced the preaching of the Cross with the 'wisdom of words' (1.17); it is they, too, who have caused the factions attaching themselves to individual Christians (1.12; 3.4–9; 4.6).

If we are right in suggesting that the first ἵνα clause in 1 Cor. 4.6 refers to 3.10–20, and to the false teaching which has resulted in rivalry, then 'the things which are written' may well refer primarily to the two quotations which Paul gives in that section. Since his argument here is so closely linked with that in chapters 1–2, however, it will be helpful to look also at the four Old Testament quotations which he uses there, for these, too, reflect the same theme of God's wisdom and man's foolishness. The first of these, in 1.19, is applied to the 'foolishness' of the Cross, which is, nevertheless, the power of God to those who are being saved – 'For it is written, I will destroy the wisdom of the wise, and the prudence of the prudent will I reject' (Isa. 29.14). While man's wisdom is brought to nothing, Christ is made 'wisdom from God, and righteousness and sanctification, and redemption. That, according as it is written, He that glorieth, let him glory in the Lord' (1 Cor. 1.30f; Jer. 9.23f). Paul declares this wisdom of God, which had been hidden from men but is now revealed through the Spirit: 'as it is written, Things which eye saw not, and ear heard not, and which entered not into the heart of man, whatsoever things God prepared for them that love him' (1 Cor. 2.9; Isa. 44.4). The man who does not have the Spirit regards these things as foolish, since he is incapable of grasping their meaning: 'For who hath known the mind of the Lord, that he should instruct him?' (1 Cor. 2.16; Isa. 40.13).

These are the scriptures to which Paul appeals in his argument against those who are perverting the faith of the Corinthian Christians. Can his warning in 1. Cor. 3.10–23 be described as 'Not beyond these scriptures'? Certainly it might be described as 'Not beyond (ὑπέρ) Paul's own teaching', since it speaks of those who add to that teaching, who build on ($\dot{\epsilon}\pi\acute{\iota}$) his foundation. But the foundation which Paul laid was none other than Christ himself (3.11): the gospel which he preached was 'the word of the Cross' which fulfilled the words of Isaiah that man's wisdom would be destroyed (1.18f); it was Christ Jesus, 'who was made unto us wisdom from God', so fulfilling what Jeremiah had written (1.30f); it was 'God's wisdom in a mystery', hitherto hidden and now revealed in fulfilment of Isaiah's prophecy (2.7, 9); it was something which was spoken, not in earthly wisdom, but in words comprehensible only to those taught by the Spirit, as Isaiah had understood (2.13, 16). This is the gospel which Paul declared to the Corinthians, but which the false teachers regarded as insufficient; they have added to it the 'persuasive words of wisdom' which were absent from his message (2.4) and which may well obscure the vital message and make the Cross void (1.17); they have treated his teaching as elementary – as milk for babies – and have added to it what they consider a solid diet for wise men (3.1f); they have thought themselves wise – and it is their wisdom which, in the words of Job and the psalmist, is foolish before God (3.19f).

The teaching which Paul gave to the Corinthians was the fulfilment of the scriptures. When he came to Corinth, he preached nothing there except 'Jesus Christ, and him crucified'; as he expresses it later, in 15.3 – 'I delivered unto you first of all that which also I received, how that Christ died for our sins according to the scriptures.' This was the wisdom of God, hidden in the Old Testament, revealed through Christ, foolish in the sight of man. It was to this 'simple gospel' that the Corinthian teachers attempted to add their philosophy and rhetoric – things which were not simply additions to the gospel which was 'according to the scriptures', but which were condemned in scripture itself as foolishness and vanity. This is the rubbish which they have added to Paul's teaching (3.12–15) – which, worse, may so obscure the gospel as to destroy men's faith (3.16f; 1.17). The 'wisdom' which was paraded by these teachers was something additional to Paul's own message of Christ crucified, the message which he saw as the fulfilment of God's purposes and of the 'things which are written'. It was a wisdom which was centred on ideas extraneous to the gospel, and which was therefore the wisdom of men, and not the wisdom of God. In following this worthless and harmful teaching the Corinthians were not simply adding to that of Paul, but were also going 'beyond the things which are written', and it was this search for additional 'wisdom' which had led to their divisions, and to the situation where one was 'puffed up for the one against the other'. In this tendency of the Corinthians to embrace fancy trappings of the gospel – the tendency which has been Paul's main object of attack throughout I Cor. 1–3 – we may surely find the explanation of his enigmatic words in 4.6: *Μὴ ὑπὲρ ἃ γέγραπται.*

If our interpretation is correct, then it may perhaps shed light on two difficult grammatical points in this verse. The first of these is the use of the verb *μετασχηματίζω* in a sense which Arndt–Gingrich describes as 'more or less unique'. Elsewhere in Paul[4] the verb is used in its basic meaning 'to change the form of'. Here, however, the words, *ταῦτα μετεσχημάτισα εἰς ἐμαυτὸν καὶ 'Απολλῶν*, are usually understood as meaning that Paul has substituted his own name and that of Apollos for those of the troublemakers. This explanation not only gives an unusual sense to the verb, but overlooks the fact that what is said of Paul and Apollos is not in fact appropriate to anyone else in Corinth: it was Paul alone who planted (3.6), and who laid the foundation (3.10); it is others who are adding 'wood, hay, stubble'. Moreover, although other leaders may perhaps have been exalted by particular groups, the predominant tendency must have been to exalt Paul and Apollos, who had planted and watered the seed in Corinth. How, then, can it be said that Paul has here 'transferred these warnings' from those who were to blame to himself and Apollos?[5] It is Paul and Apollos in particular who are in danger of being exalted, one above the other, and it is Paul alone who planted and who laid the foundation. He cannot have meant, then, that his readers should understand in 4.6: 'For Paul read X, and for Apollos substitute Y.'[6]

No other teachers or leaders are, in fact, mentioned in 4.6, and the object of the verb is the impersonal *ταῦτα*. If *μετασχηματίζω* is understood in its usual sense, then it is the *ταῦτα* whose form is changed, and they are changed *εἰς ἐμαυτὸν καὶ 'Απολλῶν*. Moreover, if we are right in understanding 4.6 as a summary of Paul's arguments in the previous section, then *ταῦτα* will refer to the things whose form has there been changed 'into Paul and Apollos' – namely the figures of gardeners, builders and stewards. One might, perhaps, suppose that the change is made in the reverse direction, and that it is Paul and Apollos who are changed into gardeners, etc.;[7] but of course Paul and

---

[4] Phil. 2.21; 2 Cor. 11.13–15.

[5] A. Robertson and A. Plummer, *I Corinthians*, 2nd edn (*ICC*, 1914), *in loc.*

[6] Cf. E.-B. Allo, *Saint Paul: Première Épître aux Corinthiens* (Paris, 1934), for a similar conclusion.

[7] For a change in form, cf. Philo, *Leg. ad Gaium* 80: *ἑνὸς σώματος οὐσίαν μετασχηματίζων καὶ μεταχαράττων εἰς πολυτρόπους μορφάς.*

Apollos did not in fact appear in these guises, and the changes are figurative ones. It is the metaphor, and not the outward appearance of Paul, which has been varied, and the εἰς indicates that the changing images have been applied to Paul and Apollos. The meaning seems to be: 'I have applied these figures of speech to myself and Apollos.' Although the verb is not used in this sense elsewhere,[8] σχῆμα and σχηματίζω can be used of figures of speech,[9] and Paul's usage is therefore a legitimate one. This translation is supported by our interpretation of the rest of the verse, for we have seen that it is precisely by using these figures of speech that Paul has done what he now declares to have been his intention: on the one hand, he has shown that he and Apollos are only workmen of God, on whose behalf the people must not be 'puffed up', and on the other he has warned those whose workmanship is not of the calibre of his own, and who are adding worthless material to his building, that what is 'beyond the things which are written' is fit only for the fire.

The second grammatical difficulty brings us back to the words τὸ μὴ ὑπὲρ ἃ γέγραπται. If, as we have maintained, they are relevant to the context, how are we to explain the elliptical structure, the negative construction, and the introductory τό? These features all suggest that Paul is here quoting some saying which is known to his readers: this is the only possible explanation of the article, and it is the most probable explanation of the omission of a verb, which would be unnecessary in such a saying; the use of the negative, instead of a positive command to confine themselves to what is written, is also explained if Paul is quoting – and denying – a saying which sums up the view which he is opposing. There is no need, and no evidence, to suggest that the words μὴ ὑπὲρ ἃ γέγραπται were ever a well-known saying or proverb.[10] The alternative solution is to suppose that they are a quotation of words known in the particular *milieu* of the Corinthian Church. There is, of course, no other evidence for their use in Corinth: yet it is clear from this passage alone that Paul expected the Corinthians to recognize them, and we have already shown their relevance to the Corinthian situation. We may conclude, then, either that the saying is one which Paul himself coined and had already used in opposition to those who

---

8 Cf., however, Plato, *Leg.* 906c, where ῥήματι μετεσχηματισμένον refers to the 'verbal change' whereby what is called 'disease' in the body is known as 'injustice' in the State.

9 E.g. Ps.-Demetrius, *De Eloc.* 298: περὶ μὲν δὴ πλάσματος λόγου καὶ σχηματισμῶν ἀρκείτω ταῦτα.

10 The suggestion is mentioned by J. B. Lightfoot, *Notes on the Epistles of St Paul* (London, 1895), *in loc.*

elaborated his teaching, or that the words are a misquotation, a deliberate denial of the maxim of others that one *should* go 'beyond the things which are written': in the former case, Paul is reminding the Corinthians of what he has already told them; in the latter, he is cleverly counter-attacking the troublemakers with one of their own slogans.

10

Authority on her head: an examination of 1 Corinthians 11.10

One of the many features in the Corinthian Church which caused disorder within the community and scandal outside was apparently the desire of some of the women to take part in Christian worship with uncovered heads. Paul's judgement on this matter, although based largely on contemporary custom, became the authoritative ground of a habit which has persisted to the present day: it is summed up in his statement in 1 Cor. 11. 10: διὰ τοῦτο ὀφείλει ἡ γυνὴ ἐξουσίαν ἔχειν ἐπὶ τῆς κεφαλῆς διὰ τοὺς ἀγγέλους. It will be noticed that Paul gives two reasons here for his statement that women must have 'authority' on their heads: the first – διὰ τοῦτο – refers back to his argument in the previous verses, while the second is an enigmatic reference to the angels. Before attempting to understand the central section of this verse we must try to see the relevance of these two phrases.

The reasoning which leads up to verse 10 depends in part on a play upon the word κεφαλή. The first stage in the argument, verse 3, is a statement of three parallel relationships:

> The head of every man is Christ.
> The head of the woman is the man.
> The head of Christ is God.

These relationships are not explained or elaborated, but simply stated as facts which Paul wishes the Corinthians to know. Man has a 'head'; so, too, has woman, and so, too, has even Christ: the relationship between man and woman is thus in some sense paralleled by that between God and Christ.

The second stage of the argument is found in verses 4–6, where we are given parallel statements regarding the man and woman who take an active part in Christian worship. Every man who prays and prophesies with his head covered dishonours his head, whereas every woman who prays or prophesies with her head *un*covered dishonours her head. The reason for this differentiation is given in verse 6, and is

113

based on social custom: in Paul's eyes an uncovered head is as great a disgrace for a woman as one that is shorn: 'For if a woman is not veiled, let her also be shorn: but if it is a shame to a woman to be shorn or shaven, let her be veiled.' In communities where it is no longer a disgrace for a woman to be 'shorn', the argument has lost its point. It is in these verses that Paul plays upon the meaning of κεφαλή: when he speaks of a head being covered or shorn, then it is obvious that he is referring to the man's or the woman's own head; but when he says that a head is dishonoured, we must ask whether the word 'head' is to be taken literally or metaphorically. Does the man dishonour his own head by praying with it covered, or does he dishonour Christ? The answer is probably that he does both, but the primary point is that he brings shame upon Christ. It is here that we see the relevance of verse 3 to Paul's argument: the man or woman who dishonours his or her own head in the literal sense brings dishonour also on his or her metaphorical head.

Verse 7 introduces a new point, made once again in the form of parallel statements regarding man and woman. The man ought not to cover his head, and the reason is that he is the image and glory of God: the woman, on the other hand, is the glory of man. Here Paul gives us the reason – to be taken up in the words διὰ τοῦτο – for the conclusion drawn in verse 10: it is because woman is the glory of man (a statement explained in the parenthesis of verses 8 and 9) that she ought to wear authority on her head. Paul's argument in this section is based upon the creation stories of Gen. 1 and 2, and must therefore differ from his previous argument, where the scheme of relationships included Christ. The Old Testament text to which Paul is referring here is Gen. 1.27, where we read: 'And God created man in his own image, in the image of God created he him; male and female created he them.' At first sight it may appear as if Paul has radically changed the meaning of this verse by narrowing its application from ἄνθρωπος to ἀνήρ: whereas Gen. 1.27 speaks of both male and female being created in the image of God, Paul uses this term only of the man. Yet Paul does not deny that woman, also, is the image of God, and it is possible that he omits the idea because it is irrelevant to his purpose, rather than because it is unacceptable to him. Paul's concern here is to point the contrast in glory:

> The man is the image and glory of God.
> The woman is the glory of man.

Since the idea of Adam's glory was closely linked in Jewish thought with that of the εἰκὼν θεοῦ – and was in fact dependent upon it – it is almost inevitable that the two should appear together. But at this point the parallelism breaks down, since though the woman may be the glory of man,[1] it would be nonsensical to say that woman is created in man's image: it is Adam's *son* who is 'after his image'.[2] In this contrast between man and woman Paul is making a distinction which is not found in Gen. 1.27, but which *is* found in Jewish interpretation of that passage.[3] Whatever Paul's understanding of εἰκὼν θεοῦ in Gen. 1.27, the essential point for his argument is the contrast which he sees in δόξα between man and woman: it is on this contrast that the different regulations regarding head-coverings are based.

The second basis for Paul's judgement is that it is διὰ τοὺς ἀγγέλους. Two explanations of this strange phrase have been given. The first is that the angels mentioned are evil, like the beings in Gen. 6.1ff who lusted after women; since the woman needs protection from this danger, she must have ἐξουσία – which can then be understood as meaning 'power' – on her head.[4] Her hat would therefore appear to be a kind of magic charm to frighten the evil angels away: alternatively, the covering is a veil which hides the woman's charms.[5] This interpretation of the angels as evil, however, is unsatisfactory for two reasons. First, nowhere else in the New Testament are angels thought of as evil,[6] second, and more serious, the idea is totally irrelevant to the context of the passage, which is concerned with Christian worship: what part have evil angels in the worship of God, and why should they constitute a danger to the woman who is engaged in prayer and prophecy? The alternative explanation of the phrase is that the angels who are present were 'good' ones, who were witnesses of the creation, and so expect to see the rule which Paul bases on the creation story maintained.[7] A comparison with other passages where Paul uses the term 'angels' suggests that he regarded them as associated with the

---

[1] Cf. Rashi on Isa. 44.13, who explains כתפארת אדם as a reference to woman, who is the glory of her husband.   [2] Gen. 5.3.

[3] Jewish exegesis interpreted Gen. 1.27 of Adam, and ignored Eve. For example, Life of Adam and Eve, 12–17.

[4] So H. Lietzmann, *Handbüch z. N.T.: An die Korinther I, II* (Tübingen, 1931), *in loc.*

[5] Cf. Test. Reuben 5.1, 5, 6: 'Evil are women, my children; and since they have no power or strength over man, they use wiles by outward attractions that they may draw him to themselves . . . Command your wives and your daughters, that they adorn not their heads and faces to deceive the mind . . . For thus they allured the Watchers who were before the flood' (trans. R. H. Charles, *The Testaments of the Twelve Patriarchs*, Oxford, 1908).

[6] Cf. Strack-Billerbeck, *Kommentar z. N.T.*, vol. 3, 2nd edn (Munich, 1954), pp. 437–40.

[7] W. Foerster, ἐξουσία, *TWNT*, 2, pp. 570f. R. St J. Parry, *Cambridge Greek Testament: 1 Corinthians* (1916), *in loc.*

'principalities and powers' who govern this world.[8] To some extent authority for the created order has devolved upon them, and we would therefore expect angels to be concerned with seeing that the ordering of things established at the creation is maintained.[9] In other words, the phrase διὰ τοὺς ἀγγέλους adds support to the reason which Paul has already given for his judgement in verse 7, and which was summed up in the words διὰ τοῦτο at the beginning of verse 10: the two explanatory phrases which we distinguished in fact belong together, and this explains why they have not been separated by καὶ but are linked together. On this interpretation the question which we asked above regarding the place of angels in Christian worship receives a meaningful answer: it is not surprising to find angels present as the guardians of the natural order, and indeed we might expect to find 'good' angels concerned in particular in seeing that the worship of God is conducted in a fitting manner.[10]

It is for this reason, then, that woman ought to have 'authority on her head'. In these strange words we see another change from the form which strict parallelism might have led us to expect: instead of saying that the woman should be covered – in contrast to the man who should not – Paul declares that she ought to have ἐξουσία on her head. What is this ἐξουσία and why does Paul use this word, instead of the verb κατακαλύπτεσθαι? The Latin versions ignored the difference and translated ἐξουσία as though it were κάλυμμα, veil; their example is followed by the RSV. G. Kittel traced both words to an Aramaic root, שלט, and saw the statement as another play on words.[11] This explanation is, one feels, too ingenious, for Paul would surely not have made his argument depend upon a pun which was incomprehensible to his Greek readers. Others refer to the protection which the veil

---

[8] Cf. Rom. 8.38. G. B. Caird, *Principalities and Powers* (Oxford, 1956), pp. 15–22, interprets the angels in 1 Cor. 6.3 and 11.10 as the powers behind the pagan world order. T. W. Manson (*On Paul and John*, London, 1963), pp. 19f., suggests that in Paul 'angels are not always nor even generally good'; he shows how in Gal. 3.18–4.9, they are the means by which the Law is given – and are therefore instrumental in bringing bondage (cf. Col. 2.18). Alongside Manson's interpretation of this passage, however, one must also remember that the Law was ultimately God-given, and that if Paul had been asked whether the angels concerned were evil, he would probably have replied (as he did in Rom. 7.7 in reply to the same question regarding the Law itself) μή γένοιτο. Ἄγγελος in itself is a morally neutral term, and can be used of a messenger from God (Gal. 1.8; 4.14) or from Satan (2 Cor. 12.7). But when the context, as here, is concerned with creation and worship, there is at least a suggestion of 'goodness'.

[9] Cf. E. Kähler, *Die Frau in den Paulinischen Briefen* (Zürich, 1960), pp. 59–65.

[10] The idea of angels witnessing men's actions is found in 1 Cor. 4.9.

[11] G. Kittel, *Arbeiten für Religionsgeschichte des Urchristentums* (Leipzig, 1920), vol. 1, part 3, pp. 17–30.

accords the eastern woman, and see in ἐξουσία a reference to the honour and dignity which it represents:[12] this is presumably the reasoning behind the NEB's marginal reading – 'therefore a woman should keep her dignity on her head, for fear of the angels.' This interpretation not only gives to ἐξουσία a forced meaning, but once again introduces an element which is irrelevant to the context. Another explanation gives to ἐξουσία the meaning 'control' as in 1 Cor. 7.37: the woman exercises control over her own head by veiling it.[13] This picture of woman having to control her rebellious head by covering it is, to say the least, a quaint one; it is especially difficult in a context where Paul has been playing on the meaning of the word 'head', for we may be sure that he does not mean to suggest that woman ought to exercise control over man!

The most widely held explanation of this passage is that the head-covering worn by the woman is a *symbol* of authority, and so can be described as ἐξουσία:[14] this authority is understood to be that of the woman's husband, to whom she is obedient. According to Jewish custom, a bride went bare-headed until her marriage, as a symbol of her freedom; when married, she wore a veil as a sign that she was under the authority of her husband. Once more, however, ἐξουσία is being given a very strange meaning, since the head-covering is not being understood as a symbol of authority but, quite the reverse, as a symbol of subjection.[15] Moreover, this interpretation leads one into difficulties: if the head-covering is seen as a sign that the woman is obedient to her husband, what of the unmarried, of whom there were apparently a number in the Corinthian Church? Were they to pray and prophesy with uncovered heads? Dr Else Kähler,[16] reminding us that it is this activity of prayer and prophecy which is all-important in the context, suggests that while praying or prophesying the woman is obedient to God alone – how, then, can she wear a symbol of obedience to her husband, even if she has one?

A further objection to this traditional explanation is that the

---

12 W. Ramsay, *The Cities of St Paul* (London, 1907), pp. 202–5. E.-B. Allo, *Saint Paul: Première Épître aux Corinthiens* (Paris, 1934), *in loc.*

13 A. Robertson and A. Plummer, *1 Corinthians*, 2nd edn (*ICC* 1914), *in loc.* Parry, *Cambridge Greek Testament*, *in loc.* Cf. Rev. 11.6; 14.18 and 20.6.

14 Foerster, ἐξουσία.

15 Ramsay, *The Cities of St Paul*, p. 203, protests that the equation of authority on the head with that to which the woman is subject is 'a preposterous idea which a Greek scholar would laugh at anywhere except in the New Testament'. Similarly, Allo, *Saint Paul*: 'Cependant il a été observé avec justesse (J. Weiss, Ramsay), que tous les emplois connus du mot ἐξουσία sont actifs, et se réfèrent à une *puissance exercée*, et non à une *puissance subie* par quelqu'un.' 16 Kähler, *Die Frau*, pp. 43ff.

reasoning which it presupposes is faulty. It is not impossible, of course, that Paul may have been illogical here, as elsewhere, but the *non sequitur* should at least cause us to question whether we have understood Paul correctly. His argument, then, runs as follows:

> Man is the glory of God.
>
> Therefore his head must be bare.
>
> Woman is the glory of man.
>
> Therefore her head must be covered.

If the head-covering is a sign that one is under authority, why should the rule regarding the woman differ from that for the man? For he, too, is under authority. Now it is true that a similar apparently illogical conclusion is given earlier, in verses 3–6, but Paul does not appeal there to the authority of the 'head', but to the idea of 'shame'. Why, then, should the covered head of the man bring shame to his 'head', whereas for the woman it is the uncovered head which brings dishonour? At this point we may ask whether there is not a closer link than is sometimes supposed between the various stages of Paul's argument, and whether the explanation of his views regarding what is shameful is not to be found in verse 7, where he speaks of the opposite quality, δόξα.

We must remind ourselves once again that the context of this passage is a discussion of Christian worship, and that the man and woman concerned are engaged in prayer and prophecy. The man, according to Paul, is the image and glory of God, and it is upon this that the 'ought' in verse 7 depends: he ought not to cover his head simply because he ought not to hide the glory of God. Since he is the reflection of God's glory, any attempt to disguise this fact in worship, where God is expressly glorified, would be shameful – especially when he is speaking to or from God in prayer or prophecy. Similar ideas are found in the Old Testament story of Moses (used by Paul in 2 Cor. 3), whose face shone with the reflected glory of God after speaking with him on the mountain, and who was then forced to wear a veil – which he removed every time he went in to speak to the Lord – because the Israelites were unable to bear the sight of this reflected glory.[17] For Paul then, the man's uncovered head is a reflection, both of God's glory (on the basis of creation), and (on the basis of the new creation) of the glory of Christ, his other 'head': its concealment would bring them not glory but dishonour.

In the same way, the obligation which lies upon the woman is based

---

[17] Exod. 34.29–35.

on the fact that she is the glory of the man. In her case, therefore, her uncovered head will reflect his glory, both because she is his 'glory', and because he is her 'head'. It is for this reason that the judgement in her case is different; her head must be covered, not because she is in the presence of man, but because she is in the presence of God and his angels – and in their presence the glory of man must be hidden.[18] If she were to pray or prophesy with uncovered head, she would not be glorifying God, but reflecting the glory of man, and in God's presence this must inevitably turn to shame. The glory of man must therefore be covered, lest dishonour is brought upon the woman's 'head'. Although Paul's argument is based upon theological premises, it may perhaps reflect practical expediency; it is likely that it was the men of Corinth, rather than the angels, who were attracted by the women's uncovered locks, and that it was in this way that attention was being diverted from the worship of God.

In the presence of the angels, whose concern is the worship of God, the glory of man must be hidden, and the woman must wear a covering on her head – but why should this be described as ἐξουσία? Once again, the answer may lie in Paul's use of the word δόξα. Since the words 'glory' and 'worship' are to some extent synonymous, to be the glory of God is in itself to worship him. According to Paul, however, it is man, and not woman, who is the glory of God, and who will therefore naturally play the active role in worship: if now woman also, in contrast to Jewish custom, takes part in prayer and prophecy, this is because a new power has been given to her. In Jewish thought the δόξα given to Adam was closely connected with his creation in the εἰκών Θεοῦ and with his authority over the rest of creation:[19] although Gen. 1.27f speaks of this authority being given to both male and female, Jewish exegesis did not in fact allow it to Eve,[20] and with this view Paul is clearly in agreement. Yet now woman, too, speaks to God in prayer and declares his word in prophecy: to do this she needs authority and power from God. The head-covering which symbolizes the effacement of man's glory in the presence of God also serves as the sign of the ἐξουσία which is given to the woman; with the glory of man hidden she,

---

18 According to one tradition, the angels worshipped Adam at the creation, either by mistake (Gen. Rab. 8.10, Eccles. Rab. 6.9.1) or by divine command (Life of Adam and Eve, 12–17). It is possible, then, that Paul thinks there is a danger that the angels might be misled into worshipping man if his 'glory' is displayed.

19 Cf. Ps. 8.4–8; Ecclus. 17.3f; Apoc. Moses 10–12; 21.6; 2 En. 21.3; Gen. Rab. 8.10; 12.6; Baba Bathra 58a; P.R.E. 11. Cf. J. Jervell, *Imago Dei* (Göttingen, 1960), pp. 37–40.

20 Eve is ignored in Life of Adam and Eve, 12–17, Apoc. Moses 24.4; 2 En. 58.3–6. Cf. Jervell, *Imago Dei*, pp. 40f.

too, may reflect the glory of God. Far from being a symbol of the woman's subjection to man, therefore, her head-covering is what Paul calls it – authority: in prayer and prophecy she, like the man, is under the authority of God. Although the differences of creation remain, and are reflected in the differences of dress, it is nevertheless true that in relation to God 'there is neither male nor female; for you are all one in Christ Jesus'.

11

Were there false teachers in Colossae?

It seems to be accepted by all commentators and writers on Colossians that the basic reason for the letter's composition was the existence of some kind of aberration in the Colossian community. Sometimes this is referred to as a 'heresy'; more cautiously it is described as 'false teaching' or 'error'. Its proponents are variously thought to be members of the Christian community spreading corruption from within, or outsiders attacking the Church's beliefs; the teaching has been interpreted as Jewish, as gnostic, or as a mixture of the two. But that the Church was under some kind of serious attack, and that the letter was written to meet this attack, does not seem to be questioned.

The content and character of this 'false teaching' have to be deduced from what appears to be Paul's rejoinder, and this, as always, is an extremely difficult task, as prone to misinterpretation as the incidental overhearing of one end of a telephone conversation. In this particular case we think we recognize the voice as Paul's,[1] but we know very little indeed about those to whom he is speaking; and from the snippets of conversation which we overhear it is very easy to make false deductions. However, when Paul says 'don't', it is logical to suppose that he thinks such a warning is necessary; and when he elaborates a particular aspect of Christian teaching, it seems likely that he considers that this is being neglected. So, from the christological 'hymn' in Col. 1, and from the warnings about regulations in Col. 2, there has emerged a picture of false teaching whose advocates do not recognize the uniqueness of Christ, but try to set him in some kind of hierarchy of powers, and who are attempting to subject the Colossian Christians to a strange mixture of Jewish and ascetic practices.

The attraction of this theory is that it offers an explanation of the epistle. It is an axiom of Pauline studies that every letter has a *Sitz im Leben*: the apostle always wrote to a particular situation, and for a

---

[1] If Colossians is non-Pauline (and its special relationship to Ephesians seems to us to make this very difficult to maintain), then the problem of understanding the letter becomes more complex, but our discussion here is not radically affected.

particular purpose, and the exegete's task is to recover that situation and purpose. If Paul did not write this letter because he felt that the Church was in danger from false teaching, then we are left wondering why he sent it at all. What was the situation in Colossae, and what was the relevance of what he says in this letter to that situation? Is Colossians an exception to the general rule, written by Paul when he was perhaps occupying his time in prison in writing pastoral letters without any particular or pressing purpose in mind?

A further advantage of the traditional explanation is that it offers some kind of link between the Christology of chapter 1 and the admonitions of chapter 2; in both sections, Paul is understood to be correcting beliefs integral to the Colossian error. It is because the false teachers believe that the world is governed by angelic powers that they think the way of salvation is through knowledge of these spiritual beings and observance of religious practices, such as fasting.

The strangest feature about this reconstruction of the situation behind the Colossian epistle is the extraordinary calm with which Paul confronts it. If there were within the Colossian Christian community any kind of false teaching which questioned the uniqueness of Christ, which suggested, for example, that he was a member of some kind of gnostic series of spiritual powers, then Paul would surely have attacked such teaching openly and explicitly. Even if such false teaching was as yet outside the Church, but constituted a real danger to the faith of the Colossians, we should expect a much clearer refutation of these false ideas. The teaching in Col. 1 is entirely positive, and it is only the assumption of some kind of situation such as has been outlined that leads commentators to assume that what Paul affirms, others have been denying. If false teaching exists, then it cannot be serious, either in character or magnitude; one glance at Galatians reminds us of the way in which Paul reacts when he feels that faith in Christ is being undermined. There is therefore no real basis for assuming that the Christology of chapter 1 is developed in opposition to false beliefs in the Colossian Church which could in any sense be described as 'heretical' or 'dangerous'.

It is, of course, fashionable to attempt to reconstruct some kind of pre-Christian 'hymn' behind the christological section in chapter 1.[2] There is, however, no real evidence, in spite of the ingenuity of exegetes, that such a hymn ever existed. And though the exclamations of recognition, surprise and illumination uttered by the Colossians

---

[2] See , e.g. E. Käsemann, *Essays on New Testament Themes* (London, 1964), pp. 149ff.

when they heard Paul's new version of something familiar to them may be that part of the conversation which is lost to us, such a reaction on their part is sheer speculation. Certainly Paul is here describing the supremacy of Christ, and the comprehensive character of his work in creation and redemption. This does not mean, however, that he is refuting teaching which has suggested that others have a role in this work. It is illuminating to compare Col. 1 with Heb. 1, a passage which it in many ways resembles. In Hebrews, the author leaves us in no doubt that he is arguing for the supremacy of Christ as compared with other, lesser, beings, such as angels; Heb. 1 offers us more evidence for the existence of a 'heresy' – in which angels could play a large role – than does Col. 1.[3]

One must also be cautious about constructing too much on the basis of Paul's warnings in chapter 2. In verse 2 he explains that he is reminding the Colossians of certain facts in order that no one should delude them. The warning is a general one, and we should not assume too readily that Paul believes that the Colossians are in imminent danger from particular 'false teachers'. In verse 16, he urges the Colossians to allow no one to condemn them on the basis of certain regulations. Here the situation is more specific, but there is no hint that Paul supposes that his readers have already succumbed to the possible danger, which is contrasted to what they have received through Christ. Exhortation to avoid a certain course of action certainly does not necessarily indicate that those addressed have already fallen prey to the temptation, as every preacher and congregation must be aware. Only in verse 20 is there a possible indication that his readers have allowed themselves to be misled by 'false teaching' consisting of various negative rules listed in verse 21. Δογματίζεσθε is often taken to mean that the Colossian Christians have already submitted to these regulations. It is probable, however, that Paul is asking 'Why subject yourselves?', or, 'Why submit?' – i.e. to any attempt which may be made to impose such regulations – rather than 'Why *do* you subject yourselves?'.[4] In view of the lack of any other indication that the Colossians have submitted to such regulations, it seems more likely that Paul is issuing a warning than an accusation.

In chapter 2, then, we do have indications of pressure upon the

---

[3] Cf. T. W. Manson, 'The problem of the epistle to the Hebrews', *BJRL*, 32 (1949), 160ff, who suggested that Hebrews was written by Apollos to Colossae.

[4] Cf. C. Masson, *L'Epître de Saint Paul aux Colossiens* (Neuchâtel and Paris, 1950), *in loc.* Note the present tense of the verb, which may be understood as middle or passive. For a possible parallel, see 1 Cor. 10.30.

Church. But it is by no means certain that this ought to be described as 'false teaching'. Since commands such as 'do not touch, do not taste', are clearly taught, and since Paul undoubtedly regarded such teaching as false, our objection may seem pedantic. Yet it is unfortunate if labels are used which imply too much; and the phrase, 'false teaching', does tend to imply a system of teaching, a particular school or religious sect. It is perhaps for this reason that commentators wish to link up the warnings of chapter 2 with the speculations supposedly attacked in chapter 1, although there is no necessary or obvious link. But were the pressures upon the Christian community in Colossae of this kind? In looking for particular 'heresies' and sects which we may categorize, it is easy to overlook the less obvious but possibly far greater pressures upon the young Christian community. Although we may not be able to reconstruct the situation of the Colossian Christian community, we may certainly conclude that one element in the contemporary scene was the general acceptance in pagan society of immorality; another was the – very different! – heritage of Judaism. To the newly baptized Christian, called to be 'holy and blameless and irreproachable' (1.22) and surrounded by the lax morality of the pagan life he had abandoned, the pressure to achieve purity by keeping the regulations of Judaism must have been enormous. The convert who accepted so much from Judaism would naturally tend to accept these also. There is no need to postulate the arrival in Colossae of 'false teachers' or 'Judaizers' to explain Paul's warnings.

We have noted the absence from Colossians of the distress which permeates Galatians. Nor is there any angry outburst, such as we find in Phil. 3.2, or hint of a problem of rebellion, as in the Corinthian correspondence. Indeed, a closer examination of Paul's language in Colossians suggests a situation very different from the troubled state of some of his churches. He thanks God specifically for the faith and love of the Colossians (1.4) who are described as πιστοί in the opening salutation (1.2), and he mentions the fruitfulness of the gospel among them (1.6) and their love in the Spirit (1.8). Since we often find hints of the theme of a Pauline letter in its opening paragraph, it may be that Paul is deliberately reminding the Colossians of the reality of their faith; but he in no way suggests that it is weak.

A similar impression is given in chapter 2, where we find Paul rejoicing because of the good order and the firmness of the Colossians' faith (v. 5), urging them to live as those who are 'rooted and built up in him and established in the faith' (v. 7). Again, Paul may be reminding his readers of the basis of their faith, but his language does not suggest that he regards them as in danger of apostasy.

The evidence which has led commentators to speak of false teachers attacking the Christian community consists, on the one hand, of the warnings in 2.4, 8 and 20, which we have suggested may be more general in their reference; and on the other hand, of the christological statements in chapter 1. Although, as we have seen, the idea of false teaching offers some kind of explanation of the existence of these two themes in one letter, it leads in turn to the difficulty of holding together in one system the different beliefs which Paul is said to be attacking. The regulations referred to in chapter 2 seem to be mainly Jewish in character; the Christology of chapter 1 is said to oppose beliefs which seem to be more 'gnostic'. We might expect to find syncretism in Colossae, and it is therefore possible that the two sets of ideas cohere; but they do not necessarily or inevitably belong together.

In attempting to reconstruct the situation behind Paul's writings, the danger of circularity is inevitable; it is all too easy to use what hints there are in a letter to build a false picture of events, and then read this back into what is said. Our own attempt to answer the problem of Colossians can, of course, like any other, only use the evidence of the letter itself, and is open to the same danger of circularity. We suggest, however, that there may perhaps be a sufficient explanation of the letter in the facts which are outlined in it by Paul. Clearly he regards the Colossian Christian community as part of his pastoral responsibility, although he has not been to the city himself; the gospel was brought to them by Epaphras, but he acted as Paul's representative (1.7).[5] Paul's ministry includes the Colossians: his sufferings are 'for your sake' (1.24); his commission was 'to you' (1.25); he is striving 'for you . . . and for all who have not seen my face' (2.1); although absent in body, he is present in spirit (2.5). It is natural that Paul should write to the Church in these circumstances if the opportunity arises. This opportunity is possibly afforded by the return of Onesimus to his master (4.9); the letter to the Colossians is actually sent by the hand of Tychicus (4.7), but he was perhaps travelling to the Lycus valley to accompany and support Onesimus.

Even if the letter is written out of a general pastoral concern for the Christians in Colossae, rather than because of some dangerous error

---

[5] Reading ὑπὲρ ἡμῶν with ⅌ 46, ℵ* A B D* G, against ὑμῶν read by C K L P. See C. F. D. Moule, *The Epistles to the Colossians and to Philemon* (Cambridge, 1958), p. 27, n. 1.

there, we may expect Paul's words to reflect knowledge of the state of the Church. Aspects of the gospel which he includes in his thanksgivings, as well as points which he emphasizes in his exhortations, may well indicate tendencies within the community, news of which has obviously reached Paul. We must therefore briefly look at the main theme of the epistle.

Paul begins, as usual, after the opening salutation (1.1–2), with the customary thanksgiving for his readers. He singles out their faith, which is ἐν Χριστῷ Ἰησοῦ, and their love to all the 'saints', both faith and love being dependent upon ἐλπίς (vv. 4–5): this, as Professor Moule has pointed out,[6] is remarkable – and significant; for at once the Colossians' faith (which they possess because they are in Christ) and their Christian love (which they are displaying) are linked with hope, the goal of Christian life, which is to be an important theme in the epistle. Paul reminds them that they have already heard[7] of this hope in the gospel, which is bearing fruit and increasing in them as in the rest of the world (vv. 4–6).

Thanksgiving merges into prayer, and Paul prays that the Colossians may be filled (πληρόω) with the knowledge of God's will, in all wisdom and spiritual understanding (v. 9); here we have language which has suggested that Paul may be contrasting true knowledge and wisdom with some false system. However, ἐπίγνωσις, σοφία and σύνεσις (the latter two especially) are all terms with an Old Testament background,[8] and ἐπίγνωσις is used by Paul in Romans of response to God's revelation (1.28 and 10.2); σοφία can certainly mean a human wisdom which is opposed to God's – see especially 1 Cor. 1–3, although it should be noted that no particular 'philosophy' or 'heresy' comes under attack there. These words do not necessarily refer to a particular rival philosophy, or represent the vocabulary of some gnostic system. Professor Moule cautions us: 'it is well to remember . . . that they can still be found in non-technical senses in the New Testament, and it is a mistake to assume that they must invariably carry some abstruse inner meaning.'[9]

---

[6] Moule, *Colossians, in loc.*

[7] Assuming, *contra* Lightfoot and Moule, that the hearing precedes the time of writing, and not the hypothetical false teaching. Since it is Epaphras, not Paul, who has preached the gospel to them, it is natural that Paul should refer to what they have already heard. Cf. E. Lohse, *Die Briefe an die Kolosser an Philemon* (Göttingen, 1968), *in loc.*

[8] Ἐπίγνωσις is not common in the LXX, though the verb ἐπιγινώσκειν is widely used; the verb γινώσκειν, similarly, is much more frequent than the noun γνῶσις. Both σοφία and σύνεσις occur frequently, especially in the wisdom books.

[9] Moule, *Colossians*, p. 159.

True knowledge of God's will leads to action, and this brings us to the second petition in Paul's prayer – that his readers may live worthily of the Lord, bearing fruit and increasing in the same knowledge (ἐπίγνωσις) of God, being strengthened according to the might of his glory – that is, of his revelation in Christ.[10] The relation between knowledge of God and of his will (v. 9) and behaviour (v. 10) is clear: the strength with which the Colossians are strengthened (ἐν πάσῃ δυνάμει δυναμούμενοι) is dependent upon him: κατὰ τὸ κράτος τῆς δόξης αὐτοῦ. The passage also seems to be intended to emphasize the completeness of the goal; as well as the verb πληρόω in verse 9, and the use of synonyms, Paul uses πᾶς five times in three verses (ἐν πάσῃ σοφίᾳ . . . εἰς πᾶσαν ἀρεσκείαν, ἐν παντὶ ἔργῳ ἀγαθῷ . . . ἐν πάσῃ δυνάμει . . . εἰς πᾶσαν ὑπομονήν).

In verse 12 we return to thanksgiving, as Paul summarizes the facts of their redemption, the basis on which his prayer is built: the Colossians have been qualified by God for a share in the inheritance of the saints in light, having been rescued out of the power of darkness, and transferred to the kingdom of God's Son. In him we have redemption – the forgiveness of sins.

It is at this point that Paul launches into what is often described as a christological 'hymn'. Whether or not the passage had an independent existence before its use here, we should expect it – like other, similar christological sections in the Pauline literature – to be relevant to the context. If we leave this passage aside for a moment, we see that the argument in verse 21 takes up again the theme of verses 13–14: those who were at one time alienated (v. 21) are those who have now been given a share in the inheritance of God's holy ones (v. 12); those who were hostile in mind and evil deeds (v. 21) are those who have been rescued from the power of darkness (v. 13) and whose calling is the knowledge of God and every good deed (vv. 9–10); those who are reconciled through the death of Christ (v. 22) are those who have been transferred into his kingdom (v. 13); those whom he now presents as holy, blameless and irreproachable (v. 22) are those who in him have redemption, the forgiveness of sins (v. 14). It is possible, of course, to argue that verses 15–20 are therefore an addition to the main theme; but if Paul placed this section here, it was because he thought it relevant to his argument. The theme of these verses is the position of Christ, first in relation to 'all things' in general, and secondly in relation to the church. Everything was created and continues to exist,

---

[10] Cf. *ibid., in loc.*

ἐν αὐτῷ . . . δι' αὐτοῦ καὶ εἰς αὐτόν. This is often interpreted as Paul's reaction to those who believe in a gnostic 'hierarchy' and see Christ as one of a series of spiritual beings. But the point which is made is as much their coherence in him as his supremacy over them;[11] and at least half the 'hymn' is concerned with Christ's relationship with the Church. We suggest that the themes which are found in these verses are intended to underline the points which Paul has made in verses 13–14, and which he will take up again in verses 21–3. The supremacy of Christ to all things in heaven and earth guarantees the reality of the Colossians' rescue from the power of darkness; they have been transferred to the kingdom of one who is stronger than any spiritual powers which may have enslaved them in the past. The statement that all things were created in, through and for Christ tells us something about the final scope of his kingdom: in Christ, God's purpose for the world is being fulfilled, and everything finds its existence and meaning in him. The fact that Christ is head of the body, and that he is first-born from the dead, means that he is in everything pre-eminent. Interestingly enough, it is only at this point in these verses that statements about Christ lead to the conclusion that he is therefore pre-eminent, and it is in relation to the Church, not the spiritual powers, that this deduction is now made. The final statement that through him all things are reconciled (ἀποκαταλλάξαι) to him, defined in terms of 'making peace by the blood of his cross', confirms the earlier statement in verse 14 that in him 'we have redemption, the forgiveness of sins', and is echoed in verse 22, 'you . . . he has now reconciled (ἀποκατήλλαξεν) in his body of flesh by his death'.

These verses, then, give us christological statements which back up the reality of what Paul has said about the Colossians' redemption in verses 12–14, a theme which he takes up again in verses 21–3. Their redemption is guaranteed by Christ's relationship to God, to the world, and to the Church. It is worth noting that the introductory clause, ὅς ἐστιν εἰκὼν τοῦ Θεοῦ τοῦ ἀοράτου, is probably a deliberate echo of Gen. 1.26;[12] Christ, not Adam, is the one who is the image of God, at once the revealer of God's will to the world, and himself obedient to that will. Since Christ replaces Adam as God's vicegerent on earth, we should expect him to be supreme over the whole of creation.[13] Similarly, as the first-born from the dead, and head of the new humanity, it is not surprising to find that other men are dependent upon him.

---

[11] Note how language used of Christ in 1.15; 3.2; 1.13, 18 echoes terms in 1.16.
[12] Moule, *Colossians, in loc.*
[13] Cf. M. D. Hooker, *The Son of Man in Mark* (London, 1967), pp. 11–74.

Why did Paul think it necessary to write these things to the Colossians? Was it because false teachers were insisting on the authority and role of other powers besides Christ? Or was it because, living in a world which took the existence of such spiritual powers for granted, and wrested from their pagan beliefs and superstitions by Christian preachers, the Colossians would naturally have qualms about these beings, and wonder whether they still had power to influence their destiny? To suppose that belief in such forces can only be the result of explicit 'false teaching' in the Colossian Christian community is to underestimate the pressures of the pagan environment, and to forget the background of these converts. Paul himself does not deny the existence of the supernatural forces; for the Colossians, living in a world seemingly inhabited by hostile men and hostile spiritual beings, the reminder that Christ was greater than all others, and the one who had all things in his control, must have been very necessary. The reassurance which Paul gives seems more suited to calm such fears than to correct veneration of angelic powers. A Christian pastor in twentieth-century Britain might well feel it necessary to remind those in his care that Christ was greater than any astrological forces; if Christians succumb to the temptation to read their horoscopes in the newspaper, then they are yielding to the pressures of contemporary society and falling prey to superstition, not to false teachers who are deliberately invading the Church. Astrological powers and predictions which today are treated only semi-seriously were, in first-century Colossae, undoubtedly forces to be reckoned with – but forces which, according to Paul, had come under the control of Christ. Col. 1 is not the only place where Paul states this conviction; in Rom. 8.31–9 Paul declares that since God is on our side (in Christ) no one can be against us; no disaster or spiritual power can separate us from the love of God in Christ Jesus our Lord. It is worth noting that these verses form the climax to a section in Romans in which Paul has worked out the significance of what he said about Christ and Adam in 5.12–21, in relation to both mankind and creation. We are sons of God, and therefore heirs with Christ (8.14–17); we have received the Spirit, and wait for the completion of our adoption, the redemption of our body, for which we still hope (8.23–5); we are destined to be conformed to the likeness of God's Son, who is therefore πρωτότοκος (8.29–30). Here we have the idea of Christ as true Man, the prototype of the new humanity which becomes – in and through Christ – what Adam was intended to be from the beginning. Creation, too, is to be released from bondage and to be set free (8.18–22). In view of this certain hope – in which you have been saved (v. 23) – it is not surprising that Paul declares that no force in heaven or earth, physical or supernatural, can separate Christians from God's love. It is this cosmic understanding of the role of Christ that lies behind the assurances of Col. 1 also.

The 'hymn' of Col. 1 does, of course, move beyond Rom. 8 in that Christ is now seen as the agent of creation. Already, however, we have met the idea that Christ is the one in whom and through whom mankind and creation are restored (cf. also 1 Cor. 8.6). Moreover, since this restoration fulfils the original intention of creation, it is perhaps a natural development to say that Christ is the one in whom and through whom all things were *created*. This step seems to have been made within the context of a developing 'Wisdom Christology'.[14]

Paul, then, stresses the position and the power of Christ, in order to remind his readers of the importance of what has already happened and of what will happen; in verse 23 we have again a reference to the hope of the gospel. He urges them to remain faithful and firm – a general warning which is perhaps more relevant to the kind of situation which we have suggested, than in the more urgent situation assumed by most commentators, which would require a more pointed warning. The gospel in which they hope has been preached ἐν πάσῃ κτίσει – a further echo of the theme of its universal scope, already elaborated in verses 15–20.

At this point Paul somewhat abruptly introduces the theme of his own ministry. He is a servant of the gospel, and his ministry is 'to you' (v. 25). He refers first to his sufferings, which are 'for your sake', and which are in some mysterious way linked to the sufferings of Christ. One is puzzled not only by the meaning of verse 24, a notoriously difficult passage, but also by its sudden introduction. Is Paul, in prison, trying to understand the meaning of his ministry in this situation, and seeing his sufferings as his share in the 'messianic woes', the necessary preliminary to the fulfilment of the hope of the gospel, and the final working out of the picture in verses 15–20?[15] He speaks also of another aspect of his ministry, however, namely the task of making fully known the word of God – the mystery of God, which is Christ in you, the hope

---

[14] The suggestion of C. F. Burney in 'Christ as the ΑΡΧΗ of creation', *JTS*, 27 (1926), 160ff., that the background of the hymn is to be found in a combination of Gen. 1.1 and Prov. 8.22, and that Paul gives us here a rabbinic exposition of *běrêshîth*, is a very attractive one. If he is right, the very Jewish character of such an exposition would make any reference to 'gnostic' terminology even more unlikely.

[15] In Rom. 8, too, Paul reminds us that we must share the sufferings of Christ if we are to share his glory. See Rom. 3.17, and cf. 2 Cor. 1.5 and 4.7–18, where the comfort and glory which come though suffering are already a present experience.

of glory. Again we have the theme of the hope of the gospel, a hope which is dependent upon Christians' union with Christ. Paul's mission is to all men – the phrase πάντα ἄνθρωπον comes three times in verse 28 – and we note again how this aspect of his ministry, like suffering, is a sharing in the work of Christ; his aim is to present (παραστήσωμεν – cf. v. 22) all men mature (τέλειον) in Christ.

In 2.1–5, Paul turns from his wider ministry to his concern for those in the Lycus valley in particular. He desires their encouragement, and their possession of the understanding which consists in knowledge of Christ. Once again, we meet this emphasis on Christian knowledge, which suggests that Paul is well aware of the temptation to which the Colossians might succumb, of pursuing other varieties of knowledge. This danger is specifically mentioned in verse 4, although with no indication that Paul has any particular false teacher in mind. Paul, who has never visited the Colossians, nevertheless regards himself as their apostle, and naturally feels anxiety for these converts; although physically absent, he is with them in spirit (2.5), 'warning every man and teaching every man in wisdom, that we may present every man mature in Christ' (1.28).

From their relationship to himself, Paul turns to the more fundamental relationship of the Colossians with Christ. As they received Christ Jesus the Lord (through the preaching of Epaphras) so they must live, 'rooted and built up by him and established in the faith, just as you were taught' (2.6–7): Paul confirms the teaching which the Colossians have already been given. They are to beware lest anyone now kidnap them through philosophy and empty deceit. Paul's vivid metaphor of 'kidnapping' perhaps looks back to the imagery of 1:13, where the Colossians' conversion was spoken of in terms of a rescue from the powers of darkness, and a transference to the kingdom of Christ. They must beware lest they are snatched out of this kingdom. But who is it that might 'kidnap' the Colossians? Paul uses the indefinite τις, and although Lightfoot points out that he sometimes uses this word to refer to exponents whose name he knows, this does not exclude the possibility that here it simply means 'anyone'. Lightfoot also notes that the form of the sentence – βλέπειν μή with the indicative – 'shows that the danger is real'.[16] We would not for a moment deny that Paul believes that the dangers surrounding the Colossian Christian community are real, or that he thinks it necessary to warn

---

[16] J. B. Lightfoot, *St Paul's Epistles to the Colossians and to Philemon*, 2nd edn (London, 1876), *in loc*. The indicative is, however, a future one.

them against the temptation to turn to various theosophies. What we are questioning is the theory that they are under attack by a specific group of teachers who are advocating a particular doctrine which can properly be termed 'the Colossian error'. Paul's warnings here seem to us to be just as applicable to the situation which we have suggested existed in Colossae, in which all kinds of alternative philosophies and doctrines might assail the young convert. Here, Paul defines the 'philosophy and empty deceit' as being 'according to human tradition, according to the στοιχεῖα of the universe, and not according to Christ'. There has been much debate regarding the meaning of στοιχεῖα, and also concerning the precise nature of the opposing teaching, which from this description might be either 'gnostic' or Jewish. Perhaps the answer to this second question is that it is unnecessary to choose between 'gnostic' and Jewish, or to solve the problem by speaking of an amalgam; Paul has in mind *any* 'philosophy' which looks for salvation anywhere outside Christ: 'For in him the whole fullness of deity dwells bodily, and you have come to fullness of life in him' (vv. 9–10). There is no need for the Colossians to look anywhere else for completion. He is the head of all ἀρχαί and ἐξουσίαι (v. 10) – for he has disarmed them, triumphing over them in the Cross (vv. 14–15). Once again, what Paul has to say about ἀρχαί and ἐξουσίαι seems to suggest that the Colossians are still worried about the power of these spiritual beings, and need encouragement to be confident in Christ's power over them. Paul also refers, however, to the fact that the Colossians have been circumcised in Christ. Once dead in trespasses and the uncircumcision of their flesh, God has made them alive with Christ; their trespasses have been forgiven, and the bond with its legal demands has been cancelled. Here Paul's argument seems more appropriate to meet fears that salvation in Christ is not complete, that something more is needed to qualify the Colossians to be full members of the community of the saints (1.12), and that some method of dealing with trespasses is still needed. This suggests that Paul has in mind pressures on pagan converts to 'complete' their conversion by accepting Judaism and all its demands. This seems confirmed by the following verses, 16–19, which urge the Colossians not to allow anyone to condemn them in matters of 'food and drink, or with regard to a festival or a new moon or a sabbath' – scruples which, on the whole, seem to be Jewish in character. Paul's reference to these as the 'shadow of what is to come' reminds us of the argument of the epistle to the Hebrews (cf. 10.1); the shadow which is contrasted with the reality in Christ probably refers to Jewish regulations, recognized now by Paul to be futile and unnecessary.

The Colossians must therefore beware those who advocate these religious practices, for by pursuing them one can be disqualified (v.18; cf. 1.12). To rely on such things is to be puffed up by a mind of flesh, the very opposite of the attitude which should be seen in Christians, which is the holding fast (κρατῶν, v.19; cf. κατὰ τὸ κράτος τῆς δόξης αὐτοῦ, 1.11) to the head, from whom the whole body takes its strength and in whom it grows. Failure to hold fast to him means a failure to grow to maturity.

The fact that Paul refers in this chapter both to the defeat of the ἀρχαί and ἐξουσίαι, and to the futility of religious practices, has been interpreted by some commentators as an indication that the error comprised these two elements of belief in spiritual powers and the search for salvation through ritual observances. It is perhaps Paul himself, however, who has deliberately fused these two themes. If in Galatians he can describe the circumcision of Christians as a return to bondage to the στοιχεῖα, similar to their previous enslavement to beings which are not gods (Gal. 4.8–9), it is not surprising if his warning to the Colossians is couched in similar language. They, too, had formerly been in bondage to these spiritual powers; the submission of all spiritual powers to Christ means not only that the Colossians can be free from fear of the forces which oppressed them in the past, but also that they need not submit to any others.[17]

If, then, they have died with Christ from under the power of these στοιχεῖα τοῦ κόσμου, why should they submit to δόγματα about what may be touched and what may be eaten? These same δόγματα have been abolished through Christ's death (2.14). Such precepts are human in origin, and have only the appearance of wisdom, being unable to achieve what they claim to do. We have already suggested that the verb δογματίζεσθε does not necessarily indicate that the Colossians have already submitted to these regulations, though certainly the urgency of Paul's appeal suggests that he fears they may do so. The danger, however, seems to be one familiar in the Pauline literature – the temptation to succumb to pressure from Jews or Jewish Christians, and to seek Christian perfection by means of religious observance. There is no indication here of an 'error' which is unique to the Colossians.

In chapter 3, Paul states his case positively: if the Colossians have been *raised with Christ*, who is at the right hand of God, they must seek

---

[17] Cf. E. Percy, *Die Probleme der Kolosser- und Epheserbriefe* (Lund, 1946), pp. 160–9. Percy interprets the θρησκεία τῶν ἀγγέλων of Col. 2.18 in this light. Cf. Gal. 3.19.

and set their mind on the things which are above, not things which belong to the earth. At this point Paul reminds his readers once again of the Christian hope – a hope which is not limited to life on the earth, but which looks for a final conformity to the glory of God (vv.1–3).

The logical outcome of this dying and rising with Christ is that they must put to death desires belonging to the earth, and put away the evil practices of their old lives. They have put off the old man, with all its practices, and put on the new man, which is being renewed according to the image of its creator (vv. 9f). Paul here takes up the familiar theme of Christ as the Second Adam,[18] and also takes us back to the imagery of 1.15–20. The renewal of Christians is conformity to Christ, who is *the* image of the creator, the invisible God: in him, Christians have become what he is.[19] Paul also picks up again the theme of knowledge in the enigmatic phrase εἰς ἐπίγνωσιν, indicating perhaps that it is in this conformity to God's purpose that men come to true knowledge of him. In this new humanity, created in Christ, there is neither Greek nor Jew, circumcision nor uncircumcision; a reminder not only of the unity found in Christ, but of the fact that circumcision is not necessary, and that Gentiles are no longer excluded from God's people. Those who (v. 12) are the chosen of God, holy and beloved (as Christ is, 1.13), must put on attitudes belonging to the Lord, into whom they have been called in one body (vv.13–15). It is perhaps worthy of note that the final ethical section in 3.18–4.6, often seen as entirely separate from the main argument of the epistle, continues this theme of unity in Christ, and order in creation.

Paul's teaching in Colossians, then, seems to us to be quite as appropriate to a situation in which young Christians are under pressure to conform to the beliefs and practices of their pagan and Jewish neighbours, as to a situation in which their faith is endangered by the deliberate attacks of false teachers; in view of the absence from Colossians of any clear reference to the supposed error, or hint of distress on Paul's part, this explanation seems to us far more probable. Paul's emphasis on Christian hope and on maturity in Christ is understandable if the Colossians were subject to the obvious temptation to look for perfection in the regulations of Judaism. Even after reading his pastoral letter, these converts from paganism may well have found themselves wondering *how* they were to obey his exhortations to put off the things belonging to the old man and put on those belonging to the new; a code of rules is much simpler to obey, and

---

[18] Moule, *Colossians, in loc.*   [19] Cf. above, ch. 1.

enables one to measure one's progress! The christological section in chapter 1 is equally relevant to this situation, since it confirms both the reality of the redemption which already belongs to the Colossians in Christ, and the scope of their Christian hope: if Christ is supreme over all powers, then the Colossians need neither fear them nor obey them, for they have been set free from those powers which dominated them in the past, and must not submit to others now.

If our interpretation is correct, then this has certain consequences for our understanding of the christological passage in Col. 1. If no Colossian 'error' existed, then Paul's christological statement here was not, as has been suggested, developed or formulated in any attempt to combat false teaching. It may, however, have been developed and formulated (whether composed specifically for its present position or not) in order to demonstrate that both creation and redemption are completed in Christ because he has replaced the Jewish Law. Paul's argument that Christians need neither fear nor obey other 'powers' depends upon the supreme authority of Christ, of whose kingdom the Colossians are members; legal requirements have been done away with because they are only a shadow of the reality which exists in Christ. The logic of Paul's argument is clear, and the link between the Christology of Col. 1 and the exhortation of Col. 2 is explained, if this section in 1.15–20 is, as has been suggested, an exposition of Christ as the replacement of the Jewish Torah, in terms which have been taken from the Wisdom literature.[20] It is Christ, in whom all treasures of knowledge and wisdom are hid (2.3), who is the true Wisdom of God (1 Cor. 1.24, 30), who was with God from the beginning and through whom and by whom the universe was created (1.15–18; cf. Prov. 8.22 and Gen. 1.1). But for the Jew, the Wisdom of God is identical with the Torah.[21] In claiming for Christ what has been said of Wisdom, Paul is claiming that he has replaced the Jewish Torah; it is Christ, not the Torah, who is older than creation, the instrument of creation, the principle upon which creation itself depends and to which it coheres.[22]

---

[20] See W. D. Davies, *Paul and Rabbinic Judaism*, 2nd edn (London, 1955), pp. 147–52, 172–5.

[21] Cf. *ibid.* p. 170: 'It is important to emphasize that in the Judaism of Palestine in Paul's day and elsewhere the identification of the Torah with Wisdom was a commonplace.' For examples, see Ecclus. 24.23 and Baruch 4.1.

[22] For the role of Wisdom in creation, see Job 28.23–7; Prov. 8.22–31; Ecclus. 24.1–12. Davies, *Paul*, pp. 170–1, points out that various characteristics of Wisdom in relation to the creation are ascribed to the Torah in rabbinic writings. In particular, Prov. 8. 22f is applied to the Law in Sifre Deut. 11. 10; the Law is described as the instrument by which the world was created in Pirqei Aboth 3.15; and it is said that the world was created for the sake of the Torah in Gen. Rab. 12. 2.

This kind of reinterpretation, although startling in the audacity of its claims regarding Jesus of Nazareth,[23] is nevertheless precisely the kind of development which we should expect to take place in a period in which Christian thinkers were grappling with the problem of the relationship between Judaism and the person of Jesus Christ. Although Jesus is for them the Messiah, the fulfilment of the promises made in the Torah itself, he is nevertheless also greater than the Torah: what the Law could not do, God has achieved in his Son (Rom. 8.3); the ministry of the new covenant is more glorious than that of Moses (2 Cor. 3.4–18); it is Christ who is 'our wisdom, our righteousness and sanctification and redemption' (1 Cor. 1.30) – these things belong to those who are in him, not to those who are obedient to the Law. The Colossians have been brought into the inheritance of God's people, not through obedience to the Law, but because they have been transferred into the kingdom of God's beloved Son, and have redemption in him (1.12–13). In working out what these claims meant – a traumatic experience for those nurtured in the Jewish faith – it was perhaps inevitable that the role of Christ in relation to creation and redemption should in time be expressed in the kind of language which we find in Col. 1.15–20: Jesus Christ had indeed replaced the Torah as the revelation both of God's glory and of his purpose for the universe and for mankind. It is this fundamental truth which is expressed in Colossians, in terms which demonstrate its relevance for those who have been rescued from the grasp of alien powers, and who are subject to the constant temptation to look for perfection through religious rites and regulations, instead of simply relying upon the one in whom all the fullness of God dwells, and in whom they find fulfilment and the confident assurance of final glory.

---

[23] As Professor Moule aptly points out *Colossians*, pp. 3–4. Paul has already taken a vital step towards this interpretation, however, in speaking of Christ as the counterpart to Adam, whose behaviour and destiny affect the universe as well as mankind. Cf. Rom. 5 and 8; 1 Cor. 15. In 2 Cor. 3–4 we find the idea of Christ as εἰκὼν θεοῦ in whom God's glory is revealed, in a context which contrasts the lasting glory of Christ with the fading glory of Moses; it was natural that the theme of δόξα should form a bridge between Christ as Second Adam and as greater than the Law. See also the discussion of the theme of Christ in relation to creation in C. F. D. Moule, *Man and Nature in the New Testament* (London, 1964).

IV
Old and new

12

Beyond the things that are written?
St Paul's use of scripture

It seemed appropriate that a lecture given to honour a scholar whose concerns have been centred on the Old Testament, by someone whose field is the New Testament, should link together these two topics. I have therefore chosen to consider one aspect of the problem of the way in which the Old Testament is interpreted by New Testament authors: more specifically, the authority ascribed by one of them – St Paul – to the Old Testament in relation to the revelation of God in Christ.

Any New Testament scholar who is any way interested in the problem of hermeneutics is well aware of the dichotomy between the approach of New Testament authors to 'scripture' and our own. A study of their methods of exegesis must surely make any twentieth-century preacher uncomfortable, for they tear passages out of context, use allegory or typology to give old stories new meanings, contradict the plain meaning of the text, find references to Christ in passages where the original authors certainly never intended any, and adapt or even alter the wording in order to make it yield the meaning they require. Often one is left exclaiming: whatever the passage from the Old Testament originally meant, it certainly was not this! Yet we cannot simply dismiss their interpretation as false, for they were certainly being true to the exegetical methods of their day. Moreover, although the biblical scholar's primary concern will always be with the original meaning of his material, the present tendency in hermeneutics is to emphasize that 'meaning' can never be limited to the intentions of an author. We may consider that the meaning which Paul gave to the prohibition to muzzle an ox in Deut. 25.4[1] would have seemed as foreign to the original author as it seems far-fetched to us; but it is at least worth asking *why* Paul interprets scripture in this kind of way. What was his underlying hermeneutical principle if, indeed, he had one?

The Henton Davies Lecture delivered at Regent's Park College, Oxford, on Wednesday, 14 March 1979.
[1] 1 Cor. 9.9.

The phrase which I have borrowed as the title for this lecture is a well-known *crux interpretum* in Paul.[2] He tells the Corinthians that he wishes them to learn what this means: 'not beyond what is written.' Alas! If only we *knew* what it meant! The most ingenious theory is, of course, that the phrase is a gloss, so that to ask what Paul meant by it is to chase a red herring. My own hunch is that Paul means, 'You Corinthians must learn to keep to scripture', i.e. you must not start trying to add philosophical notions to the basic Christian gospel.[3] If the phrase, 'nothing beyond what is written', seems an odd way of putting this, it is worth remembering that for Paul the death and resurrection of Christ were 'in accordance with the scriptures', and that throughout these early chapters of 1 Corinthians, he is concerned to demonstrate – from scripture – the folly of human wisdom, with which the Corinthians want to clothe the gospel. For Paul, to stick to *this* understanding of scripture *is* to stick to the gospel.

But does Paul himself really stick to scripture? Or can he in turn be accused of going beyond what is written? Does he not often use scripture simply as a convenient peg on which to hang his arguments? Although he may frequently quote from scripture, the interpretation he gives it often lies beyond the obvious meaning of the text. His somewhat artificial exegesis leaves one wondering whether there is anything which it would not be possible for him to argue on the basis of scripture. Is there some unifying factor which explains his approach and sets limits to his imagination?

Perhaps the clearest example of Paul's apparent ability to do what he will with scripture is seen in his arguments about the Law. For in thumbing through the pages of a Greek text, one is soon aware of the fact that the greatest concentration of quotations from the Law is to be found in those passages where Paul is arguing *against* the Law. If Paul uses the Law to refute the Law, is he not quite blatantly wishing to have his cake and eat it? Is he really following his own advice to 'keep to what is written', or is he twisting its meaning to make it mean whatever he wants?

One of the key passages for understanding Paul's position on this matter is 2 Cor. 3, and I would like to take some time in exploring this passage. Needless to say, it is full of problems, ambiguities and pitfalls. Nevertheless, it certainly repays closer examination.

The chapter begins with a brilliant metaphor: brilliant because Paul, in trying to defend his apostleship, describes the Corinthians

---

[2] 1 Cor. 4.6.   [3] See above, ch. 9.

themselves as his own credentials; since they owe their Christian faith to Paul, they cannot deny his apostleship without denying their own Christian standing. It is not long, however, before Paul's metaphor – typically – becomes a mixed one. '*You* are our letter of recommendation,' he says, 'a letter written not with ink but with the Spirit of the living God; not on tablets of stone but on hearts of flesh.' Paul has jumped from one image to another; put them together, and he is clearly in a mess, for while it is possible to speak metaphorically of the Spirit of God writing on men's hearts, it really is not much use trying to write on stone with ink! Nevertheless, we can see how he got there, via a clear echo of Jer. 31.

The chapter which follows is concerned with this same theme of Paul's ministry. Like other crucial passages in the Pauline epistles, the argument here is based on a comparison and contrast: not between Law and gospel, nor between Moses and Christ, but between the ministry of Moses and that of Paul. With amazing audacity, Paul defends his own ministry, and his ability to fulfil that ministry – albeit an ability which is given to him by God – by comparing himself favourably with Moses. Paul is minister of a new covenant, ratified not by letters engraved on stones, but by the Spirit at work in men's hearts. The argument is of course based on Exod. 34, the story of Moses' descent from Mount Sinai with the two tablets of the Law, and quickly becomes an exposition of that passage. New Testament scholars at the moment delight in applying the term *midrash pesher* in a multitude of inappropriate places; if anything may properly be described as *midrash pesher*, however, 2 Cor. 3 certainly qualifies. Paul gives a running commentary on the passage from Exodus, explaining it, not in terms of Moses, but in terms of its fulfilment in Christ.[4] He begins, however, by contrasting the glory of Moses' ministry, which was concerned with letters engraved on stone – a ministry which, he says, brought only death – with that of the ministry of the life-giving Spirit: if the ministry of Law, which was able only to condemn, was accompanied by glory, how much *more* glorious is the ministry of righteousness – so much so, that the glory of the former pales into insignificance by comparison. It will be noted that Paul does not *deny* glory to Moses; indeed, he reminds

---

[4] It has been argued that Paul is here adapting an earlier Jewish–Christian *midrash* on Exod. 34, which extolled the figure of Moses and the Mosaic Law. See S. Schulz, 'Die Decke des Moses', *ZNTW*, 49 (1958), 1–30, D. Georgi, *Die Gegner des Paulus im 2 Korintherbrief* (Neukirchen, 1964), pp. 274–82. But Paul's own Jewish background, together with his opposition to those who still gave a central role to the Law, is sufficient to explain his argument here.

us that, according to the Exodus story, the glory which shone from his face when he came down Sinai was such that the children of Israel could not gaze at it.[5] Nevertheless, says Paul, this glory was καταργουμένη (v. 7), in the process of abolition, transient, temporary. Moreover, if one could measure the strength of glory with the appropriate instrument – a doxameter perhaps? – the glory seen on Moses' face is nothing by comparison with the glory which belongs to the ministry of the Spirit, a ministry which endures. After all, when one is plugged into the mains, candles seem a pretty inefficient form of lighting.

Well then, if the new glory is so much greater than the old, surely this, too, will be too dazzling for human eyes to bear? If Moses was forced to cover his face with a veil, will not the Christian minister also need to cover *his* face, since now the irradiation hazard must be infinitely greater? This would be the logical conclusion of Paul's argument, but in fact Paul makes precisely the opposite point. Unlike Moses, Paul does *not* cover his face; he is in no way ashamed, and makes no concealment, but acts boldly – a sign of the liberty that comes through the Spirit.[6] Earlier Paul's argument seemed to imply that he accepted the explanation for Moses' veil which is found in Exodus, that is, that it was worn to protect the children of Israel, because they were unable to gaze on the glory reflected from his face. Now, however, he gives a totally different explanation: Moses wore a veil in order to conceal the end of what was being done away with – by which he seems to mean the glory. It is true that some commentators try to reconcile these two explanations by understanding the second as meaning that Moses deliberately concealed from Israel 'the fulfilment of the Law', i.e. Christ, whose glory is greater than that of the Law.[7] If the end of the Law is its fulfilment, this too will be too dangerous for human eyes. But there are great difficulties with this interpretation. Moreover, even if we were to accept it, we still would not have solved the basic inconsistency in Paul's picture. For he has told us that Israel could not

---

[5] A similar interpretation is given in Philo, *De Vita Mosis* II, 70. Both Paul and Philo in fact go beyond what is said in Exodus, which is that the people were afraid to come near Moses.

[6] For the link between boldness and the absence of a veil, see W. C. van Unnik, ' "With Unveiled Face", an exegesis of 2 Corinthians III 12–18', *Novum Testamentum*, 6 (1963), 153–69. Brevard S. Childs, *Exodus* (London, 1974), p. 623, suggests that meekness might have been associated with Moses via Num. 12.3, which is also an account of a theophany.

[7] E.g. J. Héring, *The Second Epistle of Saint Paul to the Corinthians* (ET, London, 1967), *in loc.*; R. P. C. Hanson, *II Corinthians* (London, 1954), *in loc.*; A. T. Hanson, *Jesus in the Old Testament* (London, 1965), pp. 28f.

gaze on Moses' glory: how, then, does it come about that Christians can now gaze on the overwhelming glory which belongs to Christ?

We need to recognize that Paul has – typically – moved in the course of his argument from one interpretation of the Old Testament image to another. In verses 7–11 he compares the glory of Moses and of Christian preachers, and maintains that the latter far exceeds the former; if he were to pursue the 'how much more' theme he would be in trouble, for clearly Christian preachers ought to need much thicker veils than Moses ever wore! But in fact if we read Paul carefully we see that, like the narrative in Exodus itself, he does not mention Moses' veil at all at this stage of the argument: he simply refers to the dazzling glory which presumably necessitated the veil which is referred to later in the Exodus story. In this paragraph Paul concentrates on the superiority of the 'new' covenant to the old, and he does not explain how it is that Christians can gaze without danger on the overwhelming glory which is now revealed. In verses 12ff, however, he concentrates on the theme of concealment, symbolized by the veil, and explains why it is that he, unlike Moses, does not wear a veil. He seems to have overlooked the fact that his opponents, following on from the logic of verses 7–11, might well give a very different explanation and retort: the reason why you, Paul, do not wear a veil is quite simply that you do not have any glory to conceal!

It is remarkable that none of the commentaries I have consulted acknowledges that there is a *non sequitur* in Paul's thought at this point, though several of them struggle to reconcile the conflicting motives which he attributes to Moses. But they cannot be reconciled – and they ought not to be. Paul is using the idea of glory in two different ways in the two paragraphs, and we shall misunderstand him completely if we try to combine the two arguments. And why *should* anyone expect Paul to apply the image consistently, after beginning the whole section with a glorious mixed metaphor? It is typical of Paul to explore an idea in this confusing but very rich way.[8]

In verses 6–11, then, Paul makes four basic contrasts between the ministry of the new covenant and the ministry of the old. The old one functions through letter, γράμμα, the new through Spirit, πνεῦμα; the former kills, the latter gives life; the former brings condemnation, the

---

[8] These inconsistencies do not in themselves provide evidence for the view that Paul has taken over an earlier *midrash* and failed to adapt it sufficiently for his purpose. Indeed, if he were doing this, one might perhaps expect him to produce a more consistent interpretation than he would if he were composing the *midrash* himself and incorporating traditional Jewish interpretations of the Sinai story.

latter justification or righteousness; the former is temporary and the latter permanent. If even the former is accompanied by glory, then of course the latter will possess much greater glory.

In verses 12ff, on the other hand, Paul explores the significance of the veil. Whereas Paul is bold (as indeed his opponents complain), Moses hid his face in order to conceal the end of what was being abrogated. But what was being abrogated? Is it the glory, as in verse 7? Now the logical answer to this question must be 'yes', since what Moses hid was his shining face; it is therefore the end of the glory which Moses concealed. But the word meaning 'glory', δόξα, is feminine, and the participle used here for 'abrogated' is either masculine or neuter; so it seems that Paul must be thinking also of what that glory represented, namely, the ministry of Moses and the old covenant. But the words for both covenant, διαθήκη, and ministry, διακονία, are also feminine! The answer to this grammatical puzzle may be that Paul has used the phrases τὸ καταργούμενον and τὸ μένον in verse 11 of 'what is temporary' and 'what is permanent', and he repeats one of those phrases here to sum up everything which belongs to the old covenant. Moses concealed everything that was on the way out. Or perhaps Paul is referring back to τὸ γράμμα, for that is certainly being abrogated.

So Moses hid his face. 'But,' says Paul, 'the minds of Israel were hardened.' Once again, we seem to have a strange *non sequitur* in Paul's exposition. Why the 'but' at this point? And what is the logical connection between Moses' veil and the hardening of Israel's minds? The solution, I suggest, is found if we look back at the story of Moses' shining face in Exodus, and see how it is expounded by Paul in 2 Cor. 3.14 and 15. According to the account in Exod. 34.29ff, Moses came down from Mount Sinai carrying the two tablets of the Law, unaware of the fact that his face still shone as a result of his encounter with God. The people were naturally afraid to approach him, but Moses summoned them to him, and gave them all the commandments which the Lord had given to him. It is only at this stage, when the Law has been delivered to Israel, that Moses is said to have covered his face. After that, we are told, Moses always wore a veil, except when he went in to speak with the Lord. Then he would take off the veil, and keep it off until he had come out – with shining face – to tell Israel whatever the Lord commanded him; only when that was done would he cover his face again. Now it is immediately obvious that there is something rather odd about this narrative in Exodus: the reason which it offers for Moses' veil – namely the splendour of his face – does not fit what actually happens, since he fails to wear it when he addresses Israel.[9] The picture given by the Exodus narrative seems to be of Moses wearing a veil *except* when he is receiving or passing on the commands of Yahweh, that is, when he is acting as the mediator of the Law; at such times, the veil must be removed, presumably in order that nothing may impede the revelation of God to his people. It is perhaps not surprising to find Paul giving two contradictory interpretations of this story. The first, which seems to be assumed by Paul in his first paragraph, starts from the statement in Exod. 34.30 that Israel was afraid to come close to the glorified Moses; the veil conceals from them this terrifying symbol of the presence of God. This is probably the way in which the passage was understood by Paul's contemporaries, since there is a Jewish tradition which speaks of the glory of Moses as remaining until his death.[10] The other explanation is that which Paul offers in his second paragraph: when Moses is the 'conductor' of divine revelation, then he cannot wear a veil; but the glory which shines from his face is the reflection of God's glory, a glory which is presumably renewed when he speaks with God, and which could therefore well be understood – though Exodus does not say so – to fade at other times. Since, according to the Exodus story, Moses veiled his face at those times when he was not being 'charged' or passing the 'charge' on, Paul's interpretation is at least logical, even if the notion of Moses concealing what did not exist is a little quaint. Paul's whole argument in both sections is in fact based on the assumption that the glory on Moses' face did not last, an assumption which he does not bother to prove, perhaps because he is not arguing with Jews in 2 Corinthians; it seems unlikely that Jews would have accepted his bald statement that the glory of Moses was in any way temporary.[11]

It is, then, this account of Moses removing and replacing his veil which Paul expounds in verses 14–15. The clue to Paul's statement, 'But their minds were hardened', is found in the words which follow: 'for until this very day the same veil remains unlifted at the reading of the old covenant – for it is in Christ that it is done away with.' What Paul is doing, I suggest, is to explain how it comes about that – contrary to the pattern set out in Exodus – the veil now obscures the old covenant when it is read. The reason, he says, is that the minds of

---

[9] Cf. Childs, *Exodus*, pp. 618f.   [10] Targum of Onkelos, Deut. 34.7.
[11] Childs, *Exodus*, pp. 621f, suggests that Paul does not argue the point because his exegesis reflects a well-known Jewish tradition. However, there is no evidence for this.

Israel were hardened. *That* is why the veil could not be removed when the old covenant was read. Once again, we see how Paul makes a statement about Judaism which certainly would not have been accepted by his Jewish contemporaries, namely, that the true meaning of the old covenant is hidden from them. In talking about a veil which is not lifted at the reading of the old covenant, Paul would no doubt have in mind not only the veil on Moses' face in the Exodus story, but the curtain which hid the Torah in the synagogue and which was of course removed whenever it was read.

What Paul describes is a two-way process – or rather non-process: the veil – the barrier which prevents something being seen – goes hand-in-hand with a refusal to see the truth. This same argument is used elsewhere in the New Testament of men's refusal to respond to the gospel, most notably in Mark 4 and Rom. 11. So here: if Moses wore a veil, and if the veil remains unlifted from scripture to this day, it is because Israel's minds were hardened. Paul repeats his argument in verse 15, but now the veil seems to have moved to Israel's heart; it is still the barrier which conceals the truth, however: 'Until this day, whenever Moses is read, a veil lies on their heart. But whenever he turns to the Lord, the veil is taken away.' At this point Paul returns to the Exodus story, and actually quotes from it, but he does not explain whether it is Moses who turns to the Lord – as in the original story – or Israel or Christian believers or perhaps all three; nor does he explain whether 'the Lord' means Yahweh (as in Exodus) or refers to Christ (as is normal in Paul). However, the close parallelism between verses 14 and 16 gives us a clue to this problem. The veil, says Paul, is done away with in Christ (v. 14); it is removed when someone turns to the Lord (v. 16). His statement is an exposition of Exod. 34. 34: Moses removed the veil when he went in to the Lord. In so far as the words refer to Moses, 'the Lord' must refer to Yahweh. But Paul is also applying the passage to the present situation. And since the veil is now on the heart of Israel, he must be thinking also of Israel turning to the Lord, that is to Christ, with whom the veil is abolished. The text from Exodus is given a new meaning, as it is applied to the time of fulfilment: Israel turns away from the letter to the Spirit.

But just as it seems as if the veil is being lifted from our minds, too, and we think that we begin to grasp Paul's meaning, he confounds us all by declaring: 'Now the Lord is the Spirit.' Paul is not, of course, concerned here with the niceties of trinitarian theology. Rather, he is returning to the contrast with which he began, the contrast between letter and Spirit. The Lord is the Spirit who writes directly on men's hearts. In turning to the Lord, Israel not only experiences the removal of the veil, but moves from a relationship with God which is based on letter to one which is based on Spirit.

So the chapter concludes with a clear contrast between Moses and Israel on the one hand and Christian apostles and believers on the other; the latter gaze with unveiled face at the glory of the Lord, and are changed from glory to glory. At this point, we perhaps see at last what Paul is doing; returning to the theme of the contrast between the two kinds of glory, he now demonstrates that the first was derivative, the second direct. Moses caught a glimpse of God's glory, and it was this which was reflected from his face, and which was seen by Israel, until even that was hidden from them; but Christians gaze directly at the glory of the Lord, a glory which, as Paul goes on to explain in chapter 4, is seen in Christ, who is the image of God. Moses plays a mediating role; this is why he is compared with Christian apostles and not with Christ, who is the source of glory. Whereas Moses concealed the glory which was reflected from his face with a veil, Christians wear no veil, but reflect the glory of the Lord constantly, as though in a mirror,[12] as they become like him in character; nor does their glory fade, for they are made progressively more glorious, as they are transformed into Christ's image.

Those who are entrusted with this ministry, then, have renounced underhand ways and cunning; they do not tamper with God's word, but declare God's truth openly. One is somewhat surprised by Paul's vigorous language here; it seems more likely that he is defending himself against attack than bringing an accusation against Moses. Certainly he is defending himself when he goes on to say, 'even if our gospel *is* veiled, it is veiled only to those who are perishing'. But if *his* gospel is veiled, is he not in the same situation as Moses? The answer seems to be that, as Paul puts it, 'in their case the god of this world has blinded the minds of the unbelievers, to keep them from seeing the light of the gospel of the glory of Christ'. In the case of the Jews it was Moses – presumably acting under divine instructions – who veiled his face; but now it is Satan who tries to hide the light of the gospel from men and women. Once again, Paul states his case, rather than arguing it. The gospel is nothing less than Christ himself, and the glory which we

---

[12] Many commentators understand κατοπτρίζεσθαι here to mean 'behold', but the parallel with Moses suggests that it is used with its alternative meaning 'reflect'. The difference in meaning is not great. It is only as they *gaze* at Christ that Christians are able to *reflect* his glory. If they are said to be changed from glory to glory through *looking* at the glory of Christ, then they are clearly understood to be *reflecting* that glory.

see in him is the glory of God himself, who at the creation said, 'Let light shine out of darkness.' Paul here links the light of Gen. 1.3 with the glory revealed in Christ, which eclipses that of Moses. Interestingly enough, he is not the only New Testament author to do so. It is well known that the Fourth Gospel begins with a clear echo of Gen. 1; the opening verses explore the themes of creation, of life and light. But the author then goes on to link this with the figure of Moses, and to explore the account of the theophany in Exod. 33 and 34;[13] he contrasts the giving of the Law through Moses with God's self-disclosure in Christ. No one – not even Moses – has ever seen God, but the only Son has declared him to men, and we have seen his glory, a glory which makes known the character of God himself. The theme set out here is one which underlies the whole of John's gospel: Moses was the mediator of the Law, the one through whom God made his glory known, but the Son has not only seen God's glory, he is himself the *source* of divine glory. Christ is a much greater figure than Moses – the real contrast is therefore between Christians and Moses, since both are the recipients of revelation. The glory of Christ is greater than that of Moses, but it is nevertheless continuous with it, and Moses therefore bears witness to Christ, the lesser to the greater.[14]

In John 1, then, we find ideas very similar to those which Paul is handling in 2 Cor. 3–4. But whereas John begins with the light of creation in Gen. 1 and moves from that to the story of Moses on Sinai in Exodus, Paul begins with Moses and uses Gen. 1.3 as the climax of his argument. It seems likely that both authors are making use of a common tradition here, and it may well be that both of them are using the idea of wisdom, which has come to be associated in Jewish thought with the Law. The divine plan was with God from the beginning, and was revealed to Israel on Sinai, just as the divine glory was reflected by Adam in the Garden, and then glimpsed again when the Law was given. Later rabbinic writings describe the Torah as having been hidden with God since before the creation.[15] It is clear that for Paul the secret wisdom of God, hidden from creation and now revealed, is not the Law but Christ; he is the divine plan for mankind, the image to which we are being conformed, and the glory of God – and John expresses the same belief in his own terms. Over against the Jewish claim that God's eternal purpose was finally revealed at Sinai, we have the Christian claim that the Torah only pointed forward to the

---

[13] See M. D. Hooker, 'The Johannine Prologue and the messianic secret', *NTS* 21 (1974), 40–58.   [14] John 5.39.   [15] E.g. T. Bab. Sab. 88b.

revelation made in Christ. As the result of a gigantic take-over bid, we find all the functions of the Law attributed to Christ.[16]

2 Cor. 3–4 is an important passage, not simply because it is an interesting example of Pauline exegesis, but because in its central section it raises the question of the role of scripture. Now we must be careful at this point not to make too much out of what Paul says. His primary concern is not, after all, with scripture, but with the ministry of Moses. When he refers to the old covenant in verse 14 he of course means the account of the covenant made between God and Israel, not our Old Testament – though commentators sometimes fall into the trap of interpreting the phrase in this anachronistic way; nevertheless, Paul refers to the reading of the old covenant, and to Moses being read, so he is certainly thinking of the recital of scripture. The covenant is, after all, based on obedience to the demands of Torah, which are written in 'the book of the covenant'; in Paul's writings, 'Moses' and 'Law' are almost synonymous. Yet it is clear that Paul – however inconsistent he may sometimes be – could hardly have referred to scripture itself as 'abolished', when scripture provides him with his primary witness to Christ.

But if Paul's primary concern here is not the role of scripture, neither is it the role of that part of scripture which is more specifically known as the Law, though part of the confusion in this passage arises, I believe, from Paul's ambivalent attitude to the Law. Attempts have been made to find in rabbinic writings indications of an expectation that the Law would be abolished by the Messiah, or replaced by a new Law,[17] but the whole idea runs counter to Jewish belief in the Torah as the revelation of God. If the Torah expresses God's eternal plan, set out in heaven before creation, it is scarcely likely that it will be subject to second thoughts! Paul himself, asked if he is abrogating the law, replies with a characteristic $\mu\grave{\eta}$ $\gamma\acute{\epsilon}\nu οιτο$![18] Closer to Paul's attitude is the idea that the age of the Law will be succeeded by the age of the Messiah, an idea which suggests fulfilment rather than cancellation. What is it, then, that is done away with in 2 Cor. 3? What is it that possesses this characteristic of built-in obsolescence? It is not the Law itself, but what Paul terms the ministry of Moses. Now it is undoubtedly true that if we were to unpack what Paul meant by this, we should find ourselves talking about a relationship with God which is based on works of the

---

[16] Cf. Rom. 8.3f; 10.5ff.
[17] A full discussion can be found in W. D. Davies, *Torah in the Messianic Age* (Philadelphia, 1952). [18] Rom. 3.31.

Law, and of obedience to the letter of that Law. But Paul is not concerned with that issue here, and there is no indication that his opponents in Corinth were demanding obedience to the Jewish Law. His principal concern here is the nature of his ministry which, like the gospel itself, is a matter of πνεῦμα, not γράμμα.

However, it is precisely because the question at issue is the nature of Christian ministry that the role of scripture is fundamental: for Moses and Paul are both ministers of God's word. But whereas in the Mosaic dispensation the word is enshrined in the written page, in the Christian dispensation it is embodied in Christ. What the veil hides from Jewish eyes is the temporary character, not of scripture, but of the Mosaic covenant; when the veil is removed, then at one and the same time the temporary aspect of the Law and its abiding character are revealed – temporary, in so far as it is understood in terms of commands which claim to offer life to those who obey them, abiding in so far as it is seen as a witness to Christ. Christ has replaced the Law in Paul's thinking as the expression of God's purpose, character and glory; but Paul cannot simply ditch the Law. He transfers to Christ his former beliefs about the Law without denying the Law itself a role. If he seems to denigrate the Law, it is because he is concerned to emphasize the superiority of Christ: 'What once had splendour has come to have no splendour at all, because of the splendour that surpasses it' (v. 10). Moses was a minister of the Law. Paul is a minister of Christ; Moses' ministry was temporary, not because the *Law* was temporary, but because the Law's *true* role is to be a witness to Christ – this is why, when Christ comes, the Mosaic ministry is superseded. At that stage it is abrogated, because the Law takes on its true role.

In looking at this passage in 2 Corinthians, we have noted several times that there are blatant contradictions and *non sequiturs* in Paul's argument. From our point of view, his exposition is inconsistent. His arguments do not stand up logically, and he juxtaposes conflicting images and interpretations of the biblical text. Yet I have no doubt whatever that from his point of view, Paul's argument seemed proper and acceptable. He is, after all, using a well-known method of biblical exegesis; and in this particular case the apparent contradictions in what he says are in part due to the peculiarities of the text which he is expounding, peculiarities which do not worry him in the way that they would worry us, and no doubt, were *we* expounding the passage, we would feel bound to deal with them. In our terms, Paul's own arguments about glory do not hold together; in his terms, both are valid interpretations of the text of Exod. 34. New Testament scholars perhaps need to take warning from this example of one of the dangers into which we easily fall when interpreting Paul, the danger of presupposing that all his exegesis will be consistent, and furthermore, that *his* form of consistency will be similar to our own. In spite of warnings against the *Wörterbuch* approach, writers of monographs often tend to assume that Paul will always use words in the same way, always take a consistent line in handling a topic, always fight the same battles on the same basis. In fact, of course, there are plenty of examples of cases where Paul does nothing of the kind. The fact that in a single passage he can develop a clear line of argument and at the same time apparently tie himself in knots, can combine several images into a mixed metaphor, and apply one image in several different ways, is a salutary reminder that one should not try to force Paul into the strait-jacket of a systematic theologian.

There is something else which we can observe in this passage, and that is Paul's way of approaching scripture. Paul starts from Christian experience and expounds scripture in the light of that experience, quarrying the Old Testament where he will. It is perhaps not accidental that, though Paul writes a *midrash* on this particular Exodus text, he does *not* write a commentary on the book of Exodus. In this respect, his approach is somewhat different from that of the sectarians of Qumran, even though both employ the so-called *midrash pesher* method, and both understand the text as fulfilled in their community. Once again, Paul's method is radically different from that of a modern biblical scholar, who will think it proper to try to discard all his presuppositions when he approaches the text. The difference in our approach is, of course, the result of our own conditioning, for we are trained in the historical method; we are quite confident that the Deuteronomic command to leave an ox unmuzzled was *not* intended as a hidden command about Christian ministers, that the story of Moses' veil has nothing to do with the refusal of Jews to recognize the truth of the gospel, that it is improper to read back Chalcedonian definitions into New Testament terminology. Paul's exposition of Exod. 34 illustrates clearly the difference between his approach and ours. For him it is axiomatic that the true meaning of scripture has been hidden, and is only now made plain in Christ; for the modern biblical scholar it is axiomatic that the biblical writings must be interpreted in relation to their contemporary setting, not treated as secret texts which make sense only to later generations. What seemed to Paul to be the true interpretation often seems to us to be a bizarre reinterpretation.

In treating scripture as holding a hidden meaning Paul was not, of course, alone. Indeed, to some extent, much of Christendom took the same view for centuries to come. Rabbinic exegesis presupposed meanings which had to be uncovered. Among Paul's contemporaries, Philo expounded the allegorical meaning of scripture, and the sect at Qumran adopted the technique of *midrash pesher* on the assumption that scripture contained a hidden eschatological meaning. The principle on which they worked is summed up in this passage from the Habbakuk commentary:[19]

> God commanded Habakkuk to write the things that were coming upon the last generation, but the fulfilment of the epoch He did not make known to him. And as for the words, *so he may run who reads it,* their interpretation (*pesher*) concerns the Teacher of Righteousness, to whom God made known all the mysteries (*razim*) of the words of His servants the prophets.

A similar idea is reflected in apocalyptic writing, for the basis of apocalyptic is that what is written contains a hidden meaning; the fact that apocalyptic writers wrote in the name of Old Testament characters, using Old Testament material and deliberately concealing their message in symbolic language, suggests that they understood the prophets also to have been writing material which contained secret meanings which needed to be unlocked. We find the book of Daniel, the one example of apocalyptic writing in the Old Testament, using the same terms as those found in the Qumran writings. When Daniel interprets the dream of King Nebuchadnezzar he says:[20] 'This mystery (*raz*) has been revealed to me in order that the interpretation (*pᵉshar*) may be made known to the king.' Again, the king says to Daniel:[21] 'I know that the spirit of the holy gods is in you and that no mystery (*raz*/μυστήριον LXX and Theodotion) is too difficult for you; here is the dream which I saw; tell me its interpretation (*pᵉshar*).' Daniel is full of riddles; my guess is that the famous Son of man passages in 1 Enoch are attempts to unlock the meaning of one of them – namely the vision in Dan. 7.[22]

The significant difference between Paul and his contemporaries is not, then, a question of method, since he uses techniques which would have been familiar to them, even though they are strange to us. Rather it is seen in his underlying assumption that Christ himself is the key to the meaning of scripture. It is not that Christ expounds the scriptures –

---

[19] I Q p Hab. 7.1–5.   [20] Dan. 2.30.   [21] Dan. 4.9.
[22] Cf. M. D. Hooker, *The Son of Man in Mark* (London, 1967), pp. 43–7.

as did the Teacher of Righteousness at Qumran, and as was perhaps expected of the Messiah – but that he is himself the one about whom all scripture spoke. He is himself the μυστήριον, hidden by God through all ages and now revealed to men,[23] he is the 'Amen' to all God's promises.[24] In 2 Cor. 3, Paul has moved beyond the idea of Christ as the passive *content* of scripture, to seeing him as the active *agent*; he is the Lord, whose glory is reflected in scripture; he is τὸ πνεῦμα, the life-giving spirit, the one who writes in men's hearts the truth to which scripture bears witness. The writers of the New Testament were convinced that God had acted in Christ; but they were convinced, too, that God had revealed himself in the Hebrew scriptures. It was necessary for them to hold together the divine origin, both of what they had received from the past, and of what they were experiencing in the present. One way was to speak of Christ as the fulfilment of scripture. Another was to see Christ as the blueprint, and regard the Law as the witness to him; the roles of the Law and the Messiah are then in effect reversed, for though Christ followed the Law in time he is understood to have preceded it and ordered it. When this second approach is adopted, it means that Christ is seen as the key to the whole Old Testament; all scripture can be used, because it is all christological. This is why one does not need to go beyond the things that are written. And it is why Paul himself, however fanciful his interpretation may appear to us, would not consider his exegesis to be eisegesis, for his interpretation of the text accords with his experience of Christ, and therefore does not stray beyond what is written.

I promised to look at Paul's use of scripture, and I have looked at only one passage: time has been too short for more than one exploratory dig. But, one may ask, does this particular academic exercise have any relevance to our own situation, and our own problems in interpreting the Bible? The two tasks must not, of course, be confused. I cannot use Paul's first-century methods of exegesis, and I therefore inevitably read and use the Old Testament in a different way. Yet the way in which New Testament authors tackled the problem of hermeneutics will necessarily be of concern to Christians.

In Brevard Childs' commentary on Exodus, I came across this comment on Paul's use of Exodus 34:[25] 'Paul's interpretation of 2 Corinthians 3 is a classic example of genuine theological dialectic. He brings to the text the perspective of faith which had learned to hope in Christ . . . but he brings from the text a witness which conversely

---

[23] 1 Cor. 2.7; Col. 1.26.   [24] 2 Cor. 1.20.   [25] *Exodus*, p. 624.

forms his understanding of God and shapes the Christian life through his Spirit.'

When I read these words I found myself saying 'Snap!', for in a lecture given last year I had written these words:[26] 'We judge the Bible – but we ourselves are shaped *by* it; our Christian experience and attitudes are themselves shaped by the Bible, so that though we interpret the Bible from our own standpoint, that standpoint is itself a response to the Bible. The Bible and the believer are engaged in a continuing dialogue.'

It is no accident that for Paul, as for us, scripture exercises this function of standing over against us, representing the givenness of the past, the otherness of God. What has often happened in the course of history, however, is that there has been no genuine dialectic between the text and experience. Sometimes enthusiastic eisegesis has run riot without any check – and as I typed these words, my front-door bell was rung, with a splendid sense of timing, by a member of the Jehovah's Witnesses! But let us not imagine that it is only the fringe sects that misuse scripture in this way: it is all too easy for Christians to misrepresent scripture by reading back into it the beliefs of a later age. Sometimes, again, the text has been interpreted in a rigid way which has left no room for ongoing Christian experience: it has been understood, not as a witness to the truth, but as the embodiment of truth. One of the ironies of history is that Paul's own writings have often been fossilized, turned to stone and treated as $\tau\grave{o}$ $\gamma\rho\acute{a}\mu\mu\alpha$. Paul's own exposition of scripture demonstrates the absurdity of using him in this way. For him, God's word is living, not static, and scripture is the witness to that word, not its embodiment. As for his own words, they were addressed to particular Christian communities; he certainly did not imagine that he was writing universal principles which would be treated as valid in all ages and in every circumstance.

Like Paul, we need to learn *from* the text all that it can teach us, but we need to bring *to* the text our own experience of the ongoing activity of God. Only in this way can the dialogue continue.

[26] M. D. Hooker, 'The Bible and the Believer', Peake Memorial Lecture 1978, *Epworth Review*, 6 (1979), 88.

13

Paul and 'covenantal nomism'

In the introduction to his monumental work on *Paul and Palestinian Judaism*, E. P. Sanders discusses the problems of comparing two religions, and warns against the dangers of picking out similarities in particular elements within them. It is safer, he argues, to compare entire religions, by analysing two 'patterns of religion' and comparing the ways in which these two religions are believed by their adherents to function.[1]

Beginning with Palestinian Judaism, Sanders argues persuasively against the very negative view of Judaism which has dominated much Christian biblical scholarship. His conclusion is that Judaism is not a 'legalistic' religion, since salvation is seen as a matter of God's grace, not of works: the 'pattern of religion' which emerges from the great majority of Jewish writing of the period 200 BC–AD 200 is that of 'covenantal nomism'. Whether Sanders is correct in his definition as to what constitutes a 'legalistic religion', and whether his assessment is therefore true, are questions which we must leave on one side. Possibly his attempt to redress the balance in assessing Judaism goes too far. However, the balance certainly needed to be redressed, and we may be grateful to Sanders for his careful analysis of the material.

We must leave it to experts in Judaism to judge the accuracy or otherwise of Sanders' picture of Judaism. What is of interest to Pauline scholars is the close similarity between the 'pattern of religion' which emerges from his study of Palestinian Judaism and what is commonly believed to be the religion of Paul. No doubt many will have thought that they recognized Paul in the pages of the first part of Sanders' book, and will have concluded, as they turned to part 2: 'So Paul is thoroughly Jewish after all.' Yet it is at this point that Sanders springs his surprise, and argues that the pattern of Paul's religion, also, is quite different from what we had imagined: we end with Paul and Palestinian Judaism as far apart as they have ever been.

[1] E. P. Sanders, *Paul and Palestinian Judaism* (London, 1977), pp. 1–24.

155

In a short article it is obviously impossible to consider the many questions raised by Sanders' book. With much that he says we would wish to agree. Here we can discuss only this central question as to whether or not Paul's 'pattern of religion' is, as Sanders claims, essentially different from the covenantal nomism of Palestinian Judaism. In contrast to this pattern, Sanders sets out the pattern of 'participation theology': it is by dying with Christ that one obtains new life, and by being a member of the body of Christ that one belongs to the redeemed community.

Sanders' insistence on the central role of 'participation theology' is more than welcome: many will endorse his conviction that this is the heart of Paul's understanding of salvation. But is he right when he sets this in opposition to what he terms 'covenantal nomism'? Are the two approaches necessarily mutually exclusive? May they not perhaps to some extent overlap? By comparing what he terms 'patterns of religion' Sanders hopes to avoid the danger of distortion which comes through drawing parallels between ideas which in fact play very different roles in the two religious systems. But has he himself avoided this danger? In contrasting Jewish covenantal nomism and Pauline participation theology, is he in fact comparing like with like?

Before we attempt to answer this question, however, we need to consider whether the idea of covenantal nomism is, after all, in any sense appropriate for an understanding of Paul's view of religion. Now in so far as Paul is protesting against a religious system based on fulfilment of the Law, and arguing that man is justified in Christ *apart* from the Law, and that those who are so justified are not required to keep the Law – and indeed, that Gentiles must not attempt to keep it – he clearly *cannot* be maintaining covenantal *nomism*. In Gal. 3 he describes the Law as something which came 430 years after the agreement with Abraham, and which therefore cannot annul it. Certainly, for Paul, the Law cannot be the proper response of man to God's gracious act in Christ.

On the other hand, just as Palestinian Judaism understood obedience to the Law to be the proper response of Israel to the covenant on Sinai, so Paul assumes that there is an appropriate response for Christians who have experienced God's saving activity in Christ. Those who now partake in the blessings brought by Christ are expected to respond in certain ways. The demands are spelt out in a series of imperatives. They are not *the Law*, but they are *the law of Christ* (Gal. 6.2), and they can even be described as a fulfilling of the Law (Rom. 13.8–10). When Paul speaks about 'the obedience of faith' in

Rom. 1.5, he is clearly thinking about man's *response* to God's grace. The demands upon God's people are no less because they are now understood in terms of living in the Spirit instead of living under the Law. In many ways, the pattern which Sanders insists is the basis of Palestinian Judaism fits exactly the Pauline pattern of Christian experience: God's saving grace evokes man's answering obedience. If one were to ask Paul, 'How is one saved?', his answer would no doubt be framed in terms of what Sanders terms 'participation theology'. It is in Christ that one is justified, and it is by baptism into Christ that one responds to God's call; it is those who are in Christ who belong to the community of God's people, and who therefore behave in accordance with his Spirit; it is those who belong to Christ who will be saved by him from wrath on the day of judgement. Yet clearly this participation language is in no way incompatible with an understanding of Christian experience which can be set out in terms of divine initiative→human response→obedience or adherence to the divine will→final judgement.[2] Sanders argues in the first part of his book that the Jewish emphasis on judgement according to works does not exclude the belief in salvation by grace; it is equally true – as Sanders himself recognizes – that Paul's insistence on salvation by grace does not exclude belief in a final judgement according to works.

In Judaism, the pattern is that of covenantal nomism. The response demanded to God's electing grace was obedience to the Law, and the Law was therefore the means of staying within God's covenant people. If salvation depends on God's election and covenant, reward and punishment are dependent on obedience to the Law. There is an interesting parallel here with the apparent anomaly in Paul's thought whereby, alongside his insistence on justification by grace, he continues to hold a belief in judgement according to works. There are plenty of references in his epistles to future reward and punishment as dependent on one's deeds, and this recompense will be no light affair. Indeed, in Phil. 3, the critical nature of this judgement is such that Paul envisages the possibility of missing out on future salvation altogether. References to future judgement are found in Rom. 2.1–16; 14.10–12; 1 Cor. 3.10–15; 4.1–5; 2 Cor. 5.10. The day of judgement is a day of wrath, from which Christ will save those who belong to him (1 Thess. 1.10; Rom. 5.9f). But in order to escape this wrath it is necessary for Christians to be what they are – God's holy people. The fact that Paul

---

[2] Cf. G. M. Styler's analysis of Paul, 'The basis of obligation in Paul's Christology and ethics' in B. Lindars and S. S. Smalley (eds.), *Christ and Spirit in the New Testament*, essays in honour of C. F. D. Moule (Cambridge, 1973).

understands response to God's grace in terms of Spirit rather than Law, therefore, does not do away with the idea of final judgement. If the pattern of Israel's religious experience, as it is expressed in Judaism, can be seen in terms of God's election and salvation of Israel→Israel's response to the covenant at Sinai→life within the covenant, in obedience to the Law→final judgement→reward and punishment, this is remarkably close to the pattern which emerges from Paul's writings: God's gracious act in Christ→response to this act through baptism→life in Christ, in accordance with the Spirit→final judgement→reward and punishment. Although 'nomism' may not be the appropriate term for Paul's 'pattern of religion', therefore, it is clear that his understanding of how salvation 'works' is not so far from that of Judaism as his rejection of the Law might suggest. Indeed, one might well sum up his approach in the words of Leviticus: 'Be holy, for I am holy.'[3]

But what of Sanders' other term – the adjective 'covenantal'? Is he right in arguing that the idea of the covenant is not a central one for Paul? Now it is true that the word διαθήκη occurs rarely in Paul's writings, and that on the one occasion when he deals at length with the theme of the contrast between the old and new covenants he is concerned with ministers of the covenant, and it is not Christ who is compared with Moses, but Paul himself. Christ is so much superior to Moses that he is seen as the source of the covenant, not its minister. In Rom. 9.4 there is a reference to the fact that God made covenants with his people Israel,[4] and in Rom. 11.27 we find a quotation from Jer. 31.33 referring to the future establishment of God's covenant with his people. In 1 Cor. 11.25 the death of Christ is described as 'a new covenant in his blood' in a clear contrast with the covenant on Sinai, but this is the only use of this particular idea in Paul, and even that may be a quotation of traditional material. The contrast between the two covenants is made with the help of an allegory in Gal. 4, but the terms 'old' and 'new' are not used, perhaps because both covenants are here traced back to Abraham. It is his descendants through Ishmael, not Isaac, however, with whom the covenant on Sinai was made, and the true sons of Abraham – the children of Isaac – are those who have inherited the promises made to Abraham through the other covenant. Paul does not spell out his allegory here, but presumably he is referring to the covenant ratified in Christ's blood. However, by tracing the line of descent through Isaac, he reminds us that what happens in Christ is the fulfilment of the covenant made with Abraham.

---

[3] Lev. 11.44f.   [4] Cf. also Eph. 2.12.

The term διαθήκη is used also in the argument in Gal. 3, once again in connection with Abraham, but here it seems to have the meaning 'will' rather than covenant,[5] though presumably Paul is playing on the word's double meaning. Once again, the emphasis is on the superiority of the promises made to Abraham over the Law given to Moses. The provisions of the Mosaic Law could not annul the provisions of the earlier agreement with Abraham.

This meagre evidence might perhaps suggest that Sanders is right in concluding that the idea of the covenant is not central for Paul. Yet it is clear that Paul is far from suggesting that God has withdrawn from the covenant. The provisions of a διαθήκη – whether it is a 'will' or a 'covenant' – cannot be annulled once ratified, and any suggestion that God's promises have failed is met by Paul with an indignant μὴ γένοιτο! If the idea of the covenant is in any sense played down by Paul, it is only by contrast with the 'new covenant' which fulfils the promises made to Abraham before the Law was given. When Sanders writes that, '*Paul in fact explicitly denies that the Jewish covenant can be effective for salvation*',[6] he is right only if by 'Jewish covenant' he means the covenant on Mt Sinai, which Paul regards as being of temporary validity, an interim measure until God's original promises are fulfilled. What is perhaps surprising is that Paul does not speak of these original promises in terms of a covenant, even though, as we have seen, he twice uses the word διαθήκη in discussing them. In Gal. 3 he does indeed describe the agreement with Abraham as a διαθήκη, but almost certainly in the sense of 'will', not 'covenant', and in Gal. 4. the διαθήκη is made with the descendants of Isaac, though of course it has its origins in the promise made to Abraham. Now it may well be pure chance that Paul never describes God's promise to Abraham as a 'covenant'. But possibly it is because he in fact prefers to speak of it in terms of promise, and to use the term 'covenant' for what happens in Christ. The emphasis in both Gal. 3 and 4 is on the future fulfilment in Christ.[7] God's promises to Abraham are promises for the future, and it is in Christ that the promised blessing comes.[8]

Although Paul refers to the agreement with Abraham in terms of

---

[5] Cf. E. Bammel, 'Gottes διαθήκη (Gal. 3.15–17) und das Jüdische Rechtsdenken', *NTS*, 6 (1960), 313–19; cf. J. Behm, *TDNT* ii, διαθήκη, pp. 129f (*TWNT* ii, p. 132).

[6] Sanders, *Paul and Palestinian Judaism*, p. 551.

[7] Perhaps this explains Paul's use of the verb προκυρόω in Gal. 3.17, a term which seems to fit the legal vocabulary of this passage, but which J. Behm (*TWNT* iii, p. 1099; *TDNT* iii, p. 1099) describes as 'legally meaningless'. It is usually interpreted as meaning that the διαθήκη with Abraham was ratified before the giving of the Law; perhaps, however, it signifies its ratification before it came into force – in Christ.

[8] Cf. the phrase 'covenants of promise' used in Eph. 2.12.

promise rather than covenant, the term used in this connection by Sanders himself – 'covenantal promises' – is certainly an appropriate one. Moreover, these 'covenantal promises' refer forward to a covenant which proves 'effective for salvation'. Paul certainly does not deny that God's covenant with his people is effective for salvation – quite the reverse, for much of his argument is aimed at demonstrating that God's covenantal promises remain sure. Rather he is concerned to show that it is *not the covenant on Mt Sinai* which brings salvation. Possibly this is why he does not make a great deal of use of Exodus typology. For the conversion of Gentiles has, in Paul's view, demonstrated the temporary nature of the Mosaic Law. It is the promises to Abraham which are primary in the divine scheme.

Once again, then, Sanders' assertion that Paul's understanding of religion is far removed from the covenantal nomism of Judaism seems misleading. The term itself may not be an appropriate one for Paul's view, but the basic approach is very similar. The covenantal nomism which Sanders traces in Judaism is only one form of a more fundamental pattern, in which divine election and promise lead to human acceptance and response. Certainly Paul's pattern is more complicated, since what is begun in Abraham is completed only in Christ. The covenant on Sinai and the Mosaic Law, which form the heart of Judaism, are now seen as an interlude, sandwiched between the promises and their fulfilment. But the election of Abraham, and the promises made to him – which cannot fail – are part of God's covenant with Israel, and come to their conclusion with the 'new' covenant in Christ's death. The pattern begins with Abraham, who believed the promises of God, absurd though they appeared; it reaches fulfilment in Christ, the true son of Abraham, and in those who live 'in Christ'. In contrast to Judaism, however, what marks out this community as God's people is faith, not acceptance of the Law, and what governs their behaviour is life in the Spirit, not obedience to the Law's commands. This pattern of covenant/promise→fulfilment/faith embraces both Abraham and those who are now, in Christ, his children and heirs.

It is not the 'pattern of religion', then, that separates Paul from Judaism, but the pieces which make up the pattern. Clearly we cannot speak of covenantal nomism in Paul's case, since that would run counter to Paul's basic quarrel with the Law. But the point is that for Paul, the Law has been replaced by Christ – or rather, since the Law was an interim measure, it has been shown in its true character as a stand-in, now that the reality has arrived. The questions 'Who belongs to the covenant? and 'How does one respond to the covenant?', are answered by Paul in terms of Christ, by Judaism in terms of the Law.

Almost without noticing it, we have arrived at the notion of 'participation theology', which Sanders not only sees as the heart of Paul's religion, but sets in opposition to 'covenantal nomism'. The two ideas are, he argues, quite different, since[9] in one case 'one ratifies and agrees to a covenant offered by God', in the other 'one dies with Christ, obtaining new life'; the former involves 'becoming a member of a group with a covenantal relation with God and remaining in it on the condition of proper behaviour', the latter means 'that one is a member of the body of Christ and one Spirit with him, and that one remains so unless one breaks the participatory union by forming another'. The problem with this analysis, however, is that we are not really comparing like with like. The differences are partly due to the fact that the covenant ratified on Sinai was an agreement with a group, the call of Israel to be the people of God, whereas what Paul describes in his 'participation' language is the way in which men and women are included in a group which already exists in the person of Christ. What Paul has to say about participation is, as Sanders himself argues, primarily 'transfer terminology':[10] it describes how one is transferred from the power of sin to the dominion of Christ, from bondage to liberty. The question with which Paul is wrestling is: 'How does it come about that Gentiles are responding to the gospel, and are receiving the blessings promised to Abraham, while Jews remain outside the Christian community?' Clearly the normal Jewish understanding as to who belonged to God's chosen people must be wrong. It was not, after all, those who had accepted the Sinaitic covenant and who obeyed the Mosaic Law.

But if Gentiles were now found enjoying the covenantal promises, how had this come about? The answer was that they were there because they had been transferred into God's covenant people through union with Christ, and were now sons of Abraham and inheritors of the promises made to him. Sanders is right to stress the fundamental importance of 'participation theology' in Paul. But it is important precisely because it is an integral part of his understanding of the activity of God. The notion of participation explains how the promises made to Abraham can be relevant to Gentiles, and how the salvation which is effected through the 'new' covenant in Christ's death is worked out in the lives of particular individuals.

[9] Sanders, *Paul and Palestian Judaism*, p. 514.   [10] *Ibid.*, pp. 463–72.

It would seem that Sanders has fallen into the very trap which he attempted to avoid, in that he has taken something which is only a part of Paul's theology – central though that may be – and compared and contrasted it with a pattern of religion which he has traced in Judaism. But if this notion of participation is emphasized by Paul, it is because it is his solution to the question that preoccupied him: *How* can one receive the promises of God? Participation in Christ explains how it is that one particular group of people – namely those who believe in Christ – are members of God's covenant people. Jesus has been raised from the dead and declared righteous, acknowledged as God's Son. But this has taken place *apart from the Law*. This means that it is not, after all, on the basis of obedience to the Law that one is declared righteous. The inclusion of the Gentiles goes hand in hand with the demotion of the Law. The promises of the covenant are not confined to those to whom the Law was given. These promises were made to Abraham's seed, and Abraham's seed turns out to include all those who are in Christ. Gentiles are therefore included in the covenant from which the Law had excluded them. The idea of participation in Christ explains how it is that God's saving grace is not confined to Israel. But we must understand this participation in Christ within the context of the covenant with Abraham and the promises made to him.

There is another way in which Sanders, by contrasting Judaism's 'covenantal nomism' with Paul's 'participation theology', is not comparing like with like. For one very important difference between Judaism and Paul's theological understanding is that, for Paul, history has moved on a stage with the life, death and resurrection of Christ. The Messiah has come: what belongs in Jewish thinking to the End of days has in a sense already taken place. This is why, in contrast to Judaism, Paul thinks of Christians as those who have *already* been declared righteous. This explains what Sanders regards as an important difference between Paul and Judaism, namely that 'righteousness in Judaism is a term which implies the *maintenance of status* among the group of the elect; in Paul it is a *transfer term*. In Judaism, that is, commitment to the covenant puts one "in", while obedience (righteousness) subsequently keeps one in. In Paul's usage, "be made righteous" ("be justified") is a term indicating getting in, not staying in the body of the saved.'[11] But it is precisely this concern with 'getting in, not staying in the body of the saved', which we have already seen to be central in Paul's thinking. And the reason why

[11] *Ibid.*, p. 544.

righteousness is associated with this initiatory act, rather than with what follows, is that by incorporation into Christ, men and women share the status of Christ, who has already been raised from death. If the verdict of acquittal has already been pronounced, then it is not surprising if 'being made righteous' is a 'transfer' term describing the process of removal into the sphere of salvation, namely Christ. Logically, we might perhaps expect there to be *less* similarity between Paul's understanding and the pattern of covenantal nomism than there is! For if eschatology were fully realized, then the resurrection of Christ, which declares him to be righteous, and enables those who are in him to be sharers in his righteousness, would be the final act in the drama. But the End is *not* yet; the day of judgement still lies in the future – which means that there is an interim period between what has happened in Christ and what will happen in the future, an interim period which is in many ways parallel to the present age in Jewish thought. The redemption which takes place in Christ must inevitably be interpreted more in terms of the initial act establishing man's status before God, rather than as the final declaration of his condition. If there is still room in Paul's thinking for a future judgement on the basis of men's deeds, this is the result of the uncomfortable fact that what happens in Christ is not, after all, the end of salvation history but a new beginning, so that we go on living in this present age, as well as in the age to come. This means that something more must be said about man's response to God's grace than the fact that it is made ἐκ πίστεως. Inevitably, Paul must say something about the manner of life which is appropriate for God's people, and the obedience which springs from faith. As long as Christians continue to live in this present aeon, their religion will inevitably bear many similarities to covenantal nomism.

Finally, we may note that in spite of his contrast between Paul's understanding of 'participation theology' and Judaism's 'covenantal nomism', Sanders fails to explain how Paul relates the two views of salvation. For Paul, he says, 'righteousness *cannot* be by law, *since it is by faith* . . . If the death and resurrection of Christ provide salvation . . . *all other means are excluded by definition.*'[12] But *why* is it 'by definition'? What is it about the death and resurrection of Christ which *excludes* salvation by the Law? What Sanders fails to bring out is the inner logic which leads Paul to argue that the death and resurrection of Christ mean the end of the reign of the Law. Granted that Sanders is right in maintaining that there is nothing in Jewish thought to explain why the

---

[12] *Ibid.*, p. 484.

coming of the Messiah should dethrone the Law, why have the *death and resurrection* of Christ done so? The answer is surely that the inadequacy of the Law is seen in the fact that one who was *condemned by the Law* has been *pronounced righteous by God*. Christ has been declared righteous, not only *apart from the Law*, but *in spite of the Law*. In the resurrection, the Law's verdict has been overthrown. This is why the righteousness of the Law is not an alternative route to salvation but a blind alley. The death and resurrection of Christ are therefore a demonstration of the fact that the Law is powerless to save.

The features in Paul's thought which Sanders has investigated, and the surprising rarity with which he employs Moses typology, are surely explained by this fact: that Paul sees the Mosaic Law as an interlude, which limited God's mercies to Israel until the time came for all men to be saved. But this does not mean that covenantal nomism is totally foreign to Paul's approach: only that, for him, there is a different covenant and a very different kind of law. The key figures in Paul's plan of salvation are therefore Adam–Abraham–Christ, and Moses is only a subsidiary figure. It is this which leads Professor Barrett to ask the apparently strange question: 'Why does [Moses] appear in Paul's story?'[13] Strictly, Moses does not belong to Paul's scheme. He appears, of course, because he is the mediator of the Jewish Law and cannot be ignored, but it is well to remember that he is, for Paul, primarily a negative figure. To that extent, Sanders is right to stress the difference between Paul and Judaism. But as far as Paul's basic understanding of religion is concerned, Paul is surely right when he claims to be a Hebrew of the Hebrews, and a true interpreter of the Law itself.

[13] C. K. Barrett, *From First Adam to Last* (London, 1962), p. 46.

14

Πίστις Χριστοῦ

Modern translations of the New Testament are united in understanding the phrase πίστις Χριστοῦ to mean 'faith in Christ'. In recent years, however, an increasing number of scholars have been advocating the interpretation of πίστις Χριστοῦ which takes it as a subjective rather than an objective genitive, and understands the phrase as a reference to Christ's own faith or faithfulness. Indeed, there has been so much support for this view in North America, that one recent exponent wrote: 'The correctness of the translation of πίστις Ἰησοῦ Χριστοῦ as the "faith or faithfulness *of* Jesus Christ" has by now been too well established to need any further support.'[1] If he is right, then there is little need for this paper. But I suspect that there is still a large body of opinion, especially on this side of the Atlantic, which holds to the more traditional interpretation. Indeed, those commentators who mention the suggestion tend to dismiss it in a footnote. Thus it would be fairer to say that if any kind of conclusion has been reached, it is that the question is one which cannot be settled on the basis of appeals to grammatical construction alone.[2] This issue can be settled only by exegesis, and because New Testament scholars approach the texts with widely differing presuppositions, they are likely to interpret the phrase in very different ways.[3]

What we are calling the traditional view has not necessarily always been the common interpretation. The Vulgate translates the phrase literally, as *fides Jesu Christi*, the faith of Jesus Christ; so, too, does

Presidential Address, delivered at the 43rd General Meeting of SNTS, held in Cambridge, England, August 1989.

[1] L. Gaston, *Paul and the Torah* (Vancouver, 1987), p. 12.

[2] An attempt to settle the matter on the basis of grammatical arguments was made by A. J. Hultgren, 'The *Pistis Christou* formulation in Paul', *NT*, 22 (1980), 248–63, who argued for the traditional interpretation. Other scholars, however, have not been persuaded; see, e.g., L. T. Johnson, 'Rom. 3.21–26 and the faith of Jesus', *CBQ*, 44 (1982), 77–90; S. K. Williams, 'Again *Pistis Christou*', *CBQ*, 49 (1987), 431–7.

[3] One of the most notable expositions of the 'subjective-genitive' interpretation and one which is based on exegesis of the text, is that by Pierre Vallotton, in *Le Christ et la Foi* (Geneva, 1960). His analysis has been strangely ignored in recent discussions of the issue.

Erasmus: unfortunately this is as ambiguous as the Greek.[4] Nor are the early commentators clear; Luther, however, certainly interpreted the phrase as an objective genitive,[5] and in doing so gave his support to an understanding which was almost unchallenged for 400 years. Clearly the interpretation of the phrase which takes it to mean 'our faith in Christ' was in keeping with Luther's insistence on *sola fide*. Indeed one of the reasons why the suggestion that πίστις Χριστοῦ should be translated 'Christ's faith' has met with such opposition appears to be a concern lest this translation undermines the basic Reformation emphasis on faith. Thus commentators frequently dismiss the meaning, 'Christ's faith', on the grounds that the phrase commonly occurs in juxtaposition with a statement that Christians have believed in Christ, and that the phrase must therefore be interpreted in the same way, and mean 'faith in Christ'.[6] But this is strange logic! For if the sentence *already* contains an expression of the believer's response to God's action, do we need another? The usual translation results in a certain redundancy of expression: to take one example, it leads in Rom. 3.22 to the statement that the righteousness of God is revealed to all who believe, on the basis of their faith in Christ. If we do not take it in this way, it is suggested, we might reduce emphasis on human response to God's action in Christ.[7] But to take πίστις Χριστοῦ as a reference to Christ's own faith/faithfulness is in fact in no way to neglect the faith of the believer; and to take it of the believer's faith in Christ may emphasize that faith at the expense of stating what *Christ* has done.

A second reason why some commentators feel uneasy with the suggestion that Paul is writing about Christ's faith is essentially christological. The objection arises from the assumption that faith is an appropriate action for the believer, but is inappropriate for Christ himself. But why is it considered inappropriate? Is it perhaps because faith is sometimes given somewhat negative overtones, so that it appears to be inferior to knowledge? If so, then we have certainly failed to grasp the meaning of faith for Paul! Or is it that centuries of stress on the otherness of Christ have elbowed out the notion that he himself was dependent on God? Yet if recent christological studies have taught us

---

[4] G. Howard, 'The "Faith of Christ"', *Exp. Tim*, 85 (1974), 213, argues that the Vulgate, Syriac and Sahidic Coptic all support the interpretation which takes the phrase to mean 'Christ's faith', but their evidence appears to be inconclusive.

[5] G. Howard, 'On the "Faith of Christ"', *HTR*, 60 (1967), 459–65.

[6] H. D. Betz, *Galatians* (Hermeneia; Philadelphia, 1979), pp. 117f.

[7] C. F. D. Moule, 'The biblical conception of "Faith"', *Exp. Tim*, 68 (1957), 157; see also 222. It is only fair to point out that this argument is backed up by others regarding Paul's use of πίστις and πιστεύειν εἰς elsewhere.

anything, it is that this is a fundamental misunderstanding of Paul's christology. The term 'Son of God', for example, needs to be interpreted in terms of Christ's oneness with the Father and obedience to his will, rather than in terms of divinity. The later doctrinal formulations of the Church must not be imposed on Paul's thought. If he presents Christ as the Second Adam, the true representative of our humanity, then we can expect him to present him as possessing all those qualities which men and women ought to have: as righteous, obedient and faithful. If we have difficulties with the last of these ideas and not with the first two, it is presumably because Christ is himself so often the object of faith – and indeed, as we have already seen, he is the implied object of faith in the passages under scrutiny.[8]

The third reason why this interpretation has met with resistance is linked to the other two: it is the dislike of the principle of *imitatio Christi*. Paul's emphasis on God's saving action in Christ has often been held to exclude the idea that Christian discipleship can be described in terms of imitation of the earthly Jesus. The most notable example of this position is Käsemann's interpretation of Phil. 2.[9] Insistence on the significance of what God has done, and on the believer's response to that action – in faith – has led to the denial of any other response: imitation has been ruled out because it appeared to place too much emphasis both on the earthly Jesus, and on the ability of believers to follow his example. Paradoxically, however, this interpretation has diminished the close relationship of the Christian to Christ: the believing response of the Christian to the gospel involves not only faith in the resurrection, and confession of Christ's lordship, but conformity to the death and resurrection of Christ, and obedience to his rule. If Christian life is properly seen in terms of participation, then is it participation only in his resurrection, his vindication, his righteousness? Or is it participation also in the death that leads to resurrection, in the obedience that leads to vindication, and in the faithfulness which is acknowledged as righteousness? To be sure, participation is a much better word than imitation. But this being so, should we not *expect* there to be a logical link between Christ's faith and ours, just as there is between his death and ours, and between his obedience and ours?

Perhaps we have said enough to enable us to understand why there

---

[8] See *ibid.*, were Moule argues from the fact that the verb πιστεύειν is used with Christ as object, that the same must be true of the noun also.

[9] E. Käsemann, 'Kritische Analyse von Phil. 2.5–11', *ZThK*, 47 (1950), 313–60 (= *Exegetische Versuche und Besinnungen*, 5th edn (Göttingen, 1967), pp. 51–95); *ET*, *JThCh* (1968), 45–88.

has been considerable opposition in the past to the interpretation of πίστις Χριστοῦ as a subjective genitive, and why, with new developments in Pauline theology, the view that Paul is thinking of Christ's own faith when he uses this phrase has been gaining in popularity. Indeed, from one point of view, one can almost say that if Paul does not use this idea, then he ought to! For he presents Christ as one who reverses Adam's sin, and who sums up all that man ought to be: if Adam is disobedient, then Christ is obedient (Rom. 5); if man fails to give glory to God (Rom. 1), Christ is the one who does not fall short of God's glory (Rom. 3.23); if men and women are faithless, we may expect Christ to be faithful.[10] Paul does in fact refer to ἀπιστία in his catalogue of mankind's sins, in Rom. 3.3, where it refers to the Jews' faithlessness in regard to the covenant; interestingly, it is there contrasted to the faithfulness of God himself.[11] Man's unfaithfulness in no way destroys the faithfulness of God – but the faithfulness of God should have been answered by the faithfulness of man. A priori, we may expect the Second Adam to be obedient, to give glory to God, and to be faithful. Moreover, what the Christian becomes depends on what Christ is; if the Christian is a son of God, it is only because Christ is Son of God (Rom. 8; Gal. 4); if righteous, this is dependent on Christ's righteousness (2 Cor. 5.21); our holiness is also dependent on his (1 Cor. 1.30); spiritual gifts – including the gift of faith – depend on life in Christ (Gal. 5.22). If Paul appeals to his converts to be obedient on the basis of Christ's obedience (Phil. 2.8, 12), is it not likely that their faith also will be dependent on his?

But the crucial question is, of course, not what we expect Paul to say but what he actually does say. Does he in fact refer to the faith of Christ? The passages at issue are few in number but highly significant. There are seven occurrences of the phrase: Rom. 3.22 and 26; Gal. 2.16 (twice) and 20; 3.22; and Phil. 3.9.[12] But I intend to begin this examination somewhat obliquely, by reminding you of a passage where Paul is quite clearly *not* making use of this idea: it is Rom. 4. Now in view of what we have said, it is perhaps surprising to find that Paul makes no use of the idea here. For the main argument of the

---

[10] This contrast is in fact clearly set out in the 'faithful saying' of 2 Tim. 2.13.

[11] The adjective ἄπιστος is used in Paul only in the specific sense of those who do not believe in Christ; 1 Cor. 6.6; 7.12–15; 10.27; 14.22–4; 2 Cor. 4.4; 6.14f; 1 Tim. 5.8; Tit. 1.15. Ἀπιστία occurs in Rom. 3.3 and 11.20, where it refers to the Jews' failure to believe the gospel, and in 4.20, where Abraham is the model of faith. The verb is found in Rom. 3.3 and 2 Tim. 2.13.

[12] An eighth passage may be added to our list if we accept the reading of 𝔓 46 in Gal. 3.26, which concludes: διὰ πίστεως Χριστοῦ.

epistle to the Romans presents us with a clear contrast between Adam on the one hand and Christ on the other. Chapters 1–3 have set out what we may call life in Adam; Rom. 5 sums up the contrast between the two figures, and subsequent chapters go on to explore the meaning of life in Christ. The chapter on Abraham seems something of an intrusion, but it is made necessary because Paul has to show that God's covenant with Israel was based on the principle of faith from the very beginning. This is why the model for faith is here Abraham, not Christ.

Paul's key text is Gen. 15.6: Abraham believed God, and it was reckoned to him for righteousness. Paul spends the first part of chapter 4 exploring the meaning of the verb ἐλογίσθη. First, he establishes that because righteousness is reckoned to one who believes, rather than one who works, it is a matter of grace and not of reward (vv. 3–4): there is no question of Abraham deserving to be considered righteous. Secondly, he spells out the complement to this: Abraham trusts in one who justifies the ungodly, and this trust is reckoned for righteousness; this is backed up by a quotation from Ps. 32 which makes it clear that this means that sin is *not* reckoned – that it is left out of account (vv. 5–8). Thirdly, in answer to the question, '*How* was it reckoned?', he answers 'in uncircumcision, not in circumcision' (vv. 9–12). The first point and the third are of obvious immediate relevance to Paul's argument: he needs them in order to establish that righteousness is dependent on faith, not works, and that it is in no way dependent on circumcision. The conclusion Paul wishes to establish is that neither the works of the Law nor circumcision have anything to do with the fact that Abraham was reckoned as righteous. The second point came in almost incidentally: of course Abraham's trust was in someone who justified the ungodly, since he was not himself righteous, but reckoned as righteous.

It is now obvious why Paul has taken Abraham as the model for Christian faith here – obvious, too, why in this context Christ would be a totally inappropriate model. Paul *cannot* say of Christ that 'he believed God, and it was reckoned to him for righteousness'; he cannot say it, not because Christ did not believe God, but because in his case it was not necessary to *reckon* faith as righteousness, since he *was* righteous. It is therefore Abraham who is the model for our faith: the promise was made to Abraham and to his seed, i.e. whoever shares the faith of Abraham (vv. 13–16): the phrase is τῷ ἐκ πίστεως Αβρααμ, exactly parallel to one of the phrases at issue: τὸν ἐκ πίστεως Ἰησοῦ in 3.26. The analogy of Abraham's faith with ours is then drawn out in the statement that he believed in God, who was able to give life to the dead; without wavering in faith, he gave glory to God – in other words, he did precisely what mankind failed to do in Rom. 1.[13] The text in Gen. 15 was written not only for his sake, but for the sake of Christian believers, who believe in him who raised Jesus from the dead (v. 24).

The case of Abraham is an intriguing one, because there is a sense in which he upsets Paul's argument in Romans. Paul has presented the whole of mankind as totally failing to live as they ought; in contrast to this gloomy picture he is about to turn to Christ, and to draw the contrast between him and Adam. By bringing Abraham into the argument, he has to some extent interrupted his own logic, since he presents him as one who did what was required of him. Abraham believed God, and was reckoned as righteous; he gave God the glory (v. 20): why, then, was this not enough? Why did his obedient faith not undo Adam's disobedience and lead to the restoration of mankind? The answer must be that in his case faith was only 'reckoned' as righteousness: in spite of his faith, Abraham was 'ungodly' – part of fallen mankind. It was necessary for Christ to come in the likeness of sinful man – to share our humanity – in order to reverse the sin of Adam, and enable men and women to share his righteousness.

It is hardly surprising in Rom. 4 to find 'the seed of Abraham' identified as those who share his faith: he is the father of many nations precisely because all who share his faith are reckoned as his seed.

Let us turn now to Gal. 3, and see how the matter is handled there. Paul begins here in a very different way – not with the description of man's predicament found in Romans, but with an appeal to Christian experience: the Galatians have received the Spirit; did this come about through the works of the Law, or through the proclamation of faith?[14] The question is rhetorical, the answer obvious: the Spirit was given on the basis of faith, not works. In verses 6–9 Paul shows how this accords with God's dealing with Israel from the beginning: he quotes again from Gen. 15.6, but on this occasion he does not expound the word ἐλογίσθη. Instead, he goes straight to the point which formed the conclusion of his argument in Rom. 4: it is those who share Abraham's faith who are his children; moreover, scripture foresaw that God would justify the Gentiles ἐκ πίστεως, just as he had justified Abraham ἐκ πίστεως, for it announced the gospel beforehand to him in the promise

---

[13] 'Faith, Abraham's faith, may thus be thought of as rebellion and disobedience, Adam's rebellion and disobedience, in reverse': C. K. Barrett, *From First Adam to Last* (London, 1962), p. 36.

[14] The precise meaning of the phrase ἐξ ἀκοῆς πίστεως is extremely problematical. See R. B. Hays, *The Faith of Christ* (Chico, 1983), pp. 143–9.

that 'in you shall all the nations be blessed' (Gen. 12.3). It becomes apparent later that this promise is fulfilled through the Gentiles becoming Abraham's seed, which is why it is necessary to translate ἐν σοὶ as 'in you' rather than as 'by you'. Thus it is those who are ἐκ πίστεως who are blessed with faithful Abraham. We notice that the blessing is here identified with justification. The relevance of this paragraph to the argument in verses 1–5 becomes clear later when we discover that Paul links the gift of the Spirit with the promise made to Abraham.

So far the argument is similar to that used in Rom. 4: Abraham is described as πιστός, so presumably he is seen as the model of Christian faith; those who are ἐκ πίστεως are his descendants and share his blessing. However, the rest of the chapter concentrates on the significance of the promise given to Abraham in Gen. 12.3. The reason is that in Galatians, Paul's concern is to show that the blessing came to the Gentiles by their incorporation into Christ.

In contrast to the blessing, Paul now introduces the curse. In verse 10 he turns to those who are ἐξ ἔργων νόμου, since it is important for him to demonstrate that the blessing did *not* come through the Law, and that Law and faith are therefore opposed. Those who rely on the works of the Law are under a curse – the curse that rests on those who do not keep the Law (Deut. 27.26).[15] The principle that justification rests on faith is also set out in scripture, where we read: ὁ δίκαιος ἐκ πίστεως ζήσεται (Hab. 2.4). These words from Habakkuk echo Paul's earlier interpretation of the blessing promised to Abraham, that God would justify the Gentiles ἐκ πίστεως. The promise is thus reaffirmed – a promise which operates in a different realm altogether from that of the Law; this is demonstrated by a quotation from Leviticus which sets out the principle underlying the Law, namely, 'whoever *does* these things shall live by them' (Lev. 18.5). In other words, righteousness is a question of faith, not of works of the Law. Paul has established (to his own satisfaction, at least!) that scripture itself affirms that faith leads to life, while the Law (in spite of its apparent promises) brings men and women under the curse. Law is thus an irrelevance to the promise. Now comes the startling statement that Christ has redeemed us from

---

[15] The problems of interpreting this verse are well known, since the quotation pronounces a curse only on those who fail to keep the Law. Could the words ὑπὸ κατάραν perhaps mean 'under the threat of a curse'? I owe this suggestion to Chris Stanley, a graduate student at Duke University, who points out that Paul apparently deliberately avoids applying the term ἐπικατάρατος to those who rely on the Law. See also M.-J. Lagrange, *Saint Paul: Epître aux Galates*, 2nd edn (Paris, 1925), p. 69.

the curse of the Law by becoming a curse for us – a statement which Paul again backs up with scripture; this took place in order that the blessing of Abraham might come to the Gentiles in Christ Jesus, and in order that we might receive the promised Spirit through faith.

Paul here picks up the reference to the blessing promised to Abraham, and shows how the promise made to him was fulfilled. The promise concerning the Gentiles is now specifically said to come to them in Christ: those who were not Abraham's natural descendants are now numbered among his descendants by being in Christ. If special mention is made of the Gentiles, this is because special provision had to be made to include them in the promise. This promise comes through the annulment of the curse of the Law; and it is linked – perhaps identified – with the promised gift of the Spirit, which is received by faith: this is significant, in view of the fact that Paul's argument began from an appeal to the Galatians to remember that they received the Spirit through faith. Paul has demonstrated (a) that the original promise of blessing for the Gentiles was made to Abraham on the basis of faith; (b) that the Law brought not blessing but a curse; (c) that the curse having been dealt with, the blessing has now come to the Gentiles in Christ, and (d) that confirmation of this blessing has been received in the gift of the Spirit.

But why should the blessing come to them *in Christ*? There now follows an argument (vv. 15–16) which establishes that the promises were made to Abraham and his seed, and that since σπέρμα is singular, this seed must be Christ. Paul makes no use of this point in Rom. 4, where it is not necessary to his argument; there, σπέρμα is used in its proper sense of 'descendants', but here he insists that *Christ* is the only true descendant of Abraham, and since in verse 7 the one thing that we were told about Abraham's sons was that they had faith, it seems logically necessary to affirm that Christ also had faith. The Law, given 430 years after the covenant with Abraham, could not make the promise to him void: inheritance depends on promise, not on Law. The Law was thus an interim arrangement, added because of sin, in force only until the seed came to whom the promise was made; it was not contrary to the promises, but because it was incapable of giving life, it was also incapable of giving righteousness (v. 21). Since the Law could not give life, it clearly stands in contrast to faith, which we already know to be the basis of both life and righteousness – a principle that was set out in the quotation from Habakkuk: ὁ δίκαιος ἐκ πίστεως ζήσεται.[16] In verse 22, Paul concludes that scripture shut up everything

---

[16] Since the Law fails to provide either righteousness or life, Paul's argument does nothing to solve the ambiguity in this sentence; perhaps it is intentional.

under sin, in order that ἡ ἐπαγγελία ἐκ πίστεως Ἰησοῦ Χριστοῦ δοθῇ τοῖς πιστεύουσιν.

We have come at last to our crucial phrase: how are we to understand it? Does it refer to the faith/faithfulness of Christ himself, or to the faith of believers? One thing can be said with certainty: the RSV is badly mistaken in translating the phrase as 'what was promised *to* faith in Jesus Christ'. By no stretch of imagination can ἐκ be translated as 'to', and something is badly wrong with interpretation when translators resort to such devices. Clearly ἐκ πίστεως Ἰησοῦ Χριστοῦ refers to the grounds on which the promise stands – but what is not clear is whose faith it is. One argument brought in favour of it being Christ's faith is that another reference to the faith of believers would be redundant in a sentence which already refers to those who believe: but Paul is perfectly capable of using redundant phrases, so that this argument is only significant because the same phenomenon occurs almost every time the phrase is used: this fact does give some support to the subjective genitive interpretation.

I said 'Clearly ἐκ πίστεως Ἰησοῦ Χριστοῦ refers to the grounds on which the promise stands': but does this mean the grounds on which the promise was originally made, or the grounds on which that promise is now ratified? Should we take ἐκ πίστεως Ἰησοῦ Χριστοῦ here with ἡ ἐπαγγελία (understood as the original promise) or with δοθῇ (understanding ἐπαγγελία as 'that which was promised')? If the phrase is understood to signify 'faith *in* Christ', the former interpretation is impossible. But if it is understood as a subjective genitive, either interpretation is possible. It could mean that what was promised on the basis of Christ's faith might be given to those who believe; or that what was promised might be given, on the basis of Christ's faith, to those who believe. Now the promise was made to Abraham *and his seed* (v. 16), but it was made on the basis of *Abraham's* faith; it is fulfilled in Christ, who is Abraham's seed and therefore shares his faith. If the phrase does refer to Christ's faith, then, it seems that it is more likely that Paul is saying that the promise is now ratified on the basis of Christ's faith.

How is the promise in fact fulfilled? The answer to this question is spelt out in the rest of chapter 3 and in the opening verses of chapter 4. First, Paul contrasts the time *before faith came*, when we were confined under the Law, with the situation now that faith *has been revealed* (vv. 23–5). The statement that 'faith came' is somewhat surprising – one expects 'Christ came'; presumably Paul wishes to emphasize the fact that faith is a new element in the situation. The time has come for faith to 'be revealed'; thus we are no longer thinking only of Abraham's faith, but of faith made possible in and through Christ. Secondly, Paul declares that in Christ Jesus those whom he addresses are all sons of God through faith. Immediately he goes on to explain that those who are baptized into Christ have put on Christ; the old divisions which had once been significant in determining who was a son of Abraham have been abolished, and all are one in Christ Jesus: Jew and Greek, slave and free, male and female are all Abraham's seed, and heirs according to the promise. Paul has now completed the argument concerning Abraham's offspring: the one seed, Christ, is an inclusive figure, and the blessing is received in him. Finally, Paul picks up the reference to our status as sons of God: because God sent his Son to be born under the Law, those under the Law are redeemed from its power and become sons of God: and because they are sons, they receive the Spirit of sonship and address God as 'Abba'. The questions raised in 3.1–5 are now answered. Paul has shown that the Spirit was received by faith, not works, and that the blessing promised to Abraham has come to those who are in Christ, the seed of Abraham.

Paul has used the figure of Abraham quite differently in Romans and Galatians, and we must be careful not to confuse the two arguments. In Romans, he is anxious to argue that Abraham's faith is reckoned for righteousness: Abraham is the model for Christian faith, and Christians are his descendants ($\sigma\pi\acute{\epsilon}\rho\mu\alpha$), to whom faith is also reckoned for righteousness. In Galatians, the significance of Abraham is that he is the one to whom, because of his faith, the promise was made concerning future blessing: those who inherit the blessing are his children, and they too are characterized by faith. But they are descendants of Abraham only through their incorporation into Christ, who is the one true seed of Abraham. The key phrase through the argument is $\grave{\epsilon}\kappa$ $\pi\acute{\iota}\sigma\tau\epsilon\omega\varsigma$. The promise was made to Abraham and his seed (v. 16), and it was made on the basis of faith. Now the promise is fulfilled – for Abraham's seed, and for those in him – on the basis of faith. Logic suggests that in verse 22 Paul is referring to the faith of Christ himself.

But how do we know that Christ himself had faith in God? We need to go back to verses 13–14, where we discover Paul's justification for saying that the blessing came to the Gentiles *in Christ Jesus*: it is because 'he became a curse for us' – in other words, because of his obedient acceptance of death on a cross. Already in Galatians we have had brief summaries of the fact that Christ gave himself up for our sins (1.4; cf. 2.20). Now we discover that it was by giving himself up that he annulled the curse of the Law and enabled Gentiles to share in the blessing. Professor Barrett sums it up well: 'Jesus . . . acting in obedient trust in God, qualifies at the moment of crucifixion as the one seed.'[17] The logic of this is that even the faith of believers is discovered not to be their own; in so far as they have faith, it is a sharing in Christ's faith: he is the one true seed. Thus even the faith that they have is *reckoned* to them.

Let us now turn to another occurrence of the phrase πίστις Χριστοῦ which has received less attention than some of the others: it is found in Phil. 3. As in Gal. 3, Paul is concerned with the theme of righteousness, with the contrast between Law and faith, and with the notion of being in Christ.

The argument begins with Paul listing his privileges as a Jew: he had been circumcised on the eighth day, was an Israelite, of the tribe of Benjamin, a Hebrew of Hebrews, a Pharisee in his observance of the Law, and his zeal had been displayed in his persecution of the Christian Church; as for righteousness by the Law, he had been blameless. All these privileges he counted loss for the sake of Christ. To make sure that his readers get his point, Paul spells it out three times, each time using the verb ἡγέομαι, each time using either the noun ζημία or the verb ζημιόω and each time using the phrase διὰ τὸν Χριστὸν or the equivalent:

Whatever was gain to me, I *considered* loss for the sake of Christ;
Indeed, I *considered* everything to be loss for the sake of the surpassing value of the knowledge of Christ Jesus my Lord,
For the sake of whom I lost everything, and *considered* it rubbish . . .

The threefold use of ἡγέομαι in verses 7–8 reminds us of the previous chapter, where the verb is used twice, once in an appeal to the Philippians to *consider* others better than themselves, and then in the statement that Christ did not *consider* equality with God to be ἁρπαγμός. This verbal echo of the previous section is significant, for there is clearly a parallel between Christ's attitude in the so-called christological hymn of Phil. 2 and Paul's attitude here: Christ did not consider the highest privileges possible as something to be clung to/grasped, but emptied himself, taking the form of a servant. Paul now considers the highest privileges a man could enjoy – 'whatever was gain', κέρδη – to be worth nothing. Why? The purpose is introduced with the word ἵνα. It was so that he might gain (κερδήσω) Christ, and be found in him, not having his own righteousness – the righteousness

¹⁷ C. K. Barrett, *Freedom and Obligation* (London, 1985), p. 27.

which comes from the Law – but the righteousness which is διὰ πίστεως Ἰησοῦ Χριστοῦ, the righteousness of God (v. 9). Not only is there an echo of Phil. 2, there is also an echo, in the construction of the sentence, of those passages where Paul speaks of an 'interchange' between Christ and the believer, which often comes to a climax in a ἵνα clause. The closest parallels are in 2 Cor., where in 5.21 we read that Christ was made sin in order that we might become the righteousness of God in him, and in 8.9 we are told that Christ became poor in order to make many rich. Here it is Paul himself who becomes poor, who gives up all he had, in imitation of Christ's *kenosis*; the purpose was that he might be found in Christ; abandoning his own righteousness, the righteousness which came from the works of the Law, he looked for another – the righteousness of God which came διὰ πίστεως Ἰησοῦ Χριστοῦ, and which depends ἐπὶ τῇ πίστει. The echo of Phil. 2 suggests that this phrase ought to refer to the obedient self-surrender of Christ, that is, to his faithfulness. Paul goes on to spell out what 'being in Christ' involves: it means knowing him and the power of his resurrection and the fellowship of his suffering; it means being conformed to his death, in hope of attaining to the resurrection from the dead (vv. 10–11). We have already been given some indication of what Paul means by 'conformity to Christ's death': it means abandoning everything, considering everything loss, in order to win the prize. In other words, 'conformity to Christ's death' means conformity to those attitudes which led Christ to submit to death. And what it leads to is knowledge of the power of Christ's resurrection working in the present and the hope of resurrection from the dead in the future. The 'interchange' of experience works out in the life of the believer. Paul expresses the notion here, not in terms of 'Christ died, in order that we might live' but in terms of 'I died, in conformity to his death, so that I might live, in conformity to his resurrection'.

But this interchange of experience is firmly dependent on what Christ himself has done, and Paul does not allow us to forget this. It is perhaps significant that this passage is sandwiched between two others which together present us with the pattern of interchange between Christ and the believer. For if we read 2.5–11 with 3.20–21, we find that believers will exchange the humiliation which Christ shared with them when he took the fashion of a man for the glory of Christ the Lord to which they are to be conformed. The interchange in Paul's own experience is as it were a plugging-in to this pattern. In the rest of Phil. 3 Paul explains that the second part of the pattern is not yet fully worked out in his life: it is not that he has already obtained the gain which is in store for him; he endeavours to grasp it, but that endeavour is dependent on the fact that Christ has already grasped him (vv. 12–13a). The goal lies ahead – the prize of our high calling is 'in Christ'. Now comes an exhortation which echoes the exhortation which introduced the 'hymn' in 2.6 – τοῦτο φρονῶμεν (v. 15) – and an appeal to be συμμιμηταί μου (v. 17); this is normally understood to mean 'fellow-imitators with other people of me', but has Paul perhaps used the συν- to suggest that they should be fellow-imitators *with him*?[18] At any rate, the pattern is clear, and it is the pattern of Christ himself, for the opposite is the life lived by those who are enemies of the Cross of Christ. Our goal (v. 21) is conformity to what Christ is – a sharing in the glory which was given to him as a result of his self-humiliation. In language reminiscent of the hymn of Phil. 2, Paul brings to a close the pattern of interchange between Christ and the believer which provided the model for Paul's own interchange of experience.

We have now examined two of the seven occurrences of the phrase πίστις Ἰησοῦ Χριστοῦ. In order to explore this topic thoroughly, we clearly ought to consider the other five, but time is insufficient to allow us to examine them, even though they all occur in two short passages, in Rom. 3 and Gal. 2. However, these other passages have been examined in some depth by scholars who have argued for the meaning 'Christ's faith', and this is perhaps sufficient for our purpose. For we have to admit that though a case *can* be made out for the subjective genitive in all these passages, the evidence is no more *conclusive* than in those we have examined. In looking at Gal. 3 and Phil. 3, however, we have several times argued that logic suggests that the subjective genitive is intended. But is logic enough?

Let us turn our attention to two other passages which may throw some light on the problem: they are both in 2 Corinthians. The first comes in 2 Cor. 1.17–22. Paul has been accused of vacillating – of changing his plans. He rejects the charge indignantly: God is faithful, and linked with the fact goes another – that Paul's own word is not

---

[18] Commentators tend to take the μου as an objective genitive on the basis that 'there is no reference to Christ in the context' (M. R. Vincent, *ICC*, Edinburgh, 1897, p. 116; similar views are expressed in many more recent commentaries), but this is to ignore the wider context of the passage. In a short note in *Exp. Tim.*, 5 (1894), 287, W. F. M'Michael argued for the meaning 'fellow imitators with me . . of Christ' on the basis that similar compounds of σύν are never used in the New Testament with an objective genitive denoting a person. See also J. A. Bengel, *Gnomon Novi Testamenti*, 3rd edn (London, 1862), *in loc.*; G. Friedrich, *Der Brief an die Philipper*, *NTD*, (Tübingen and Göttingen, 1962), *in loc.*; T.R. Glover, *Paul of Tarsus* (London, 1925), p. 179.

fickle – is not a matter of 'yes and no'. In some way Paul's behaviour is dependent on God's faithfulness.[19] The next stage in the argument is to appeal to Christ: for the Son of God (i.e. the one who shares the characteristics of God), Jesus Christ, whom Paul preached to the Corinthians – that is, his 'word' to the Corinthians – was not 'yes and no': on the contrary, in him is the final 'yes'.[20] For all the promises of God have their 'yes' in him: in other words, they find their fulfilment – their confirmation – in him. One might say that he was the embodiment of God's faithfulness. And indeed, Paul goes on to say that it is through him, too, that we answer God with the 'Amen' which is to his glory: not only is this 'Amen' to God's faithfulness – the answering confirmation to what he is – embodied in Christ, but the 'Amen' is now affirmed by believers as well, affirmed both through Christ and through us. We now discover how it is that God's faithfulness is relevant to the way in which Paul makes his plans: through Christ he himself shares in that faithfulness. The initiative is with God: it is he who establishes us with you into Christ, and with the words σὺν ὑμῖν Paul inserts a typically neat reminder that the Corinthians are involved too. The verb βεβαιόω means 'to make firm', 'to confirm'. The fact that it is used with εἰς Χριστὸν suggests that Paul means that Christians are 'made firm' by coming into Christ. God also anoints us. Remarkably, this is the only place where Paul uses the verb χρίω: it picks up the use of Χριστός immediately before, and reminds us that Paul is seeing the process he is describing in term of Christians becoming like Christ. But what is this process? The climax of the sentence comes with the words: 'who also sealed us and gave us the ἀρραβὼν of the Spirit in our hearts.' Paul is clearly thinking of baptism into Christ, and also of participation in Christ. The logic of Paul's argument is clear; he is not guilty of vacillating – of faithlessness – because he shares in the faithfulness of God himself; and he shares in that faithfulness by his incorporation into Christ, who is the embodiment of God's faithfulness, the 'Amen' to all the promises of God.

The second passage comes in 4.13. Paul has been describing his ministry as an apostle of Christ: he is commissioned to preach 'Jesus Christ as Lord, and ourselves as your servants for Jesus' sake' (v. 5). His

---

[19] In spite of the criticisms of James Barr, *The Semantics of Biblical Language* (Oxford, 1961), pp. 167ff, the links traced by W. C. van Unnik, 'Reisepläne und Amen-Sagen in J. N. Sevenster and W. C. van Unnik (ed.), *Studia Paulina in honorem J. de Zwann*, (Haarlem, 1953), pp. 25–32, are persuasive. See also F. Young, 'Note on 2 Corinthians 1:17b' in *JTS*, NS 37 (1986), 404–15. Her suggested translation of v. 17*b* runs: 'Or do I make plans at the human level so that yes being yes and no being no rests in my hands?'   [20] Paul uses the perfect, γέγονεν.

Πίστις Χριστοῦ

commission involves sharing in the dying and rising of Jesus, in tribulation and persecution; but the same process of interchange works in him as in his Lord: death is at work in us, but life in you. Then comes verse 13: 'Having the same spirit of faith, even as it is written, "I believed, therefore I spoke", we too have believed, and therefore we speak.' The crucial question here is 'the same spirit as whom?' There is a tendency to assume that Paul means 'the same spirit as the psalmist' – to such an extent that the RSV even paraphrases the verse as 'the same spirit of faith as he had who wrote . . .' But Paul introduces the scriptural quotation with a normal κατὰ τὸ γεγραμμένον, and more than this is eisegesis. The most natural interpretation, in the context, is the same spirit as Jesus, for Paul has been describing his own experience in terms of 'bearing about in the body the dying of Jesus'; he is surely referring to the spirit of faith which enabled Jesus to be given up to death, for the sake of the life which would be manifested in him and in others. This has been argued by A. T. Hanson, who holds that Paul interprets Ps. 116 as a messianic psalm.[21] We are inclined to think that in fact Paul does not interpret the psalm as primarily messianic because the two key words are 'believed' and 'spoke', both of which apply to Paul, who is commissioned to preach Jesus Christ as Lord, but only the first (at least in this context) to Christ. It is enough for Paul's purpose that his experience corresponds both with that of Christ ('having the same spirit of faith as Jesus') and with that of the psalmist (as it is written); there is thus a three-cornered relationship as far as belief is concerned. The passage continues: 'We too have believed, and therefore we speak, knowing that he who raised the Lord Jesus will raise us with Jesus and present us with you.' Paul's faith is in the one who raises us from the dead with Jesus.

These two passages strengthen the case for saying that Paul sees Christian faith/faithfulness as a sharing in the faith/faithfulness of Christ, even though neither of them uses the phrase πίστις Χριστοῦ. But they cannot be said to be decisive. In the case of 1.20, Paul is clearly describing a quality of Christ which belongs to those who live in him: in other words, Paul is thinking of a faithfulness that *issues from* righteousness, rather than of a faith that *leads to* righteousness.[22] But faith in 4.13 is certainly parallel to the faith of believers, for it is faith in God who brings life out of death (cf. Rom. 4.17, 24).

[21] A. T. Hanson, *Jesus Christ and the Old Testament* (London, 1965), pp. 145–7.
[22] The Greek word πίστις has a wide range of meaning which certainly includes both 'faith' and 'faithfulness'. This is in no way denied by Barr (*Biblical Language*, p. 202), whose devastating attack (pp. 161–205) on the linguistic arguments of Hebert and Torrance played an important part in the reaction against their interpretation of πίστις Χριστοῦ. See below, p. 184.

Let us now sum up the evidence from all the passages where the phrase πίστις Χριστοῦ is used:

1 All the passages contain a reference to Jesus, either in the phrase itself or in the context, suggesting that Paul is concerned not simply with 'life in Christ', but with the activity of the earthly Jesus.

2 All the passages refer to πίστις Χριστοῦ *as the ground of the believer's existence*. In three of them, the phrase used is διὰ πίστεως (᾿Ιησοῦ) Χριστοῦ:[23] in three more, we find ἐκ πίστεως (᾿Ιησοῦ) (Χριστοῦ). The seventh passage, Gal. 2.20, describes the life which Paul now lives as being lived ἐν πίστει . . . τοῦ υἱοῦ τοῦ Θεοῦ.[24] There is thus total agreement that the phrase is appropriate in passages which speak of faith as the basis of Christian life.

3 All the passages (with the possible exception of Gal. 2.20) refer quite clearly to the faith of the believer, so that they fall into the pattern: ἐκ πίστεως εἰς πίστιν. Is that phrase in Rom. 1.17 a mere rhetorical flourish? Or does it in fact point to something very profound? If πίστις Χριστοῦ is interpreted as faith *in* Christ, then there is a certain redundancy of expression in all our passages; if, on the other hand, it refers to Christ's own faith, we have a reference both to his faith and to our own.

4 All the passages have to do with righteousness, and all of them contrast the righteousness which is based on Law with that which comes through πίστις ᾿Ιησοῦ Χριστοῦ. It is possible that Paul wishes to contrast the righteousness which rests on our works with that which rests on our faith; but he does not normally speak of *our* works, but of the works of *the Law* in us; the logical antithesis to this is not *our* faith but *the faith of Christ*.

5 All of the passages are about being in Christ.

6 All of them are concerned with the death of Christ.

Let us repeat what we said at the beginning of this study. There is no doubt that Paul is dealing with the question of a righteousness that is received by faith; however we interpret the phrase πίστις Χριστοῦ, we shall in no way undermine the believer's answering response to the

---

[23] So, too, Gal. 3.26, according to the reading of 𝔓46.

[24] 𝔓46 B D* G it^d g Marius Victorinus Pelagius here read ἐν πίστει . . τοῦ θεοῦ καὶ Χριστοῦ. This is rejected as the original reading by Bruce M. Metzger, *A Textual Commentary on the Greek New Testament* (London and New York, 1975), p. 593, on the basis that 'Paul nowhere else speaks of God as the object of a Christian's faith'. But if the genitives are subjective, this objection does not apply. Paul's life is then said to be based on the faithfulness of God and Christ.

activity of God. The crucial question is: how is that righteousness received, and how is the answering response made? As far as righteousness is concerned, the answer is clear: it is by being in Christ. We become the righteousness of God in him, 2 Cor. 5.21; he became for us righteousness from God, 1 Cor. 1.30. In other words, we share his righteousness. But what of the belief that *leads* to righteousness? Is it a case of believing in him, and so entering into Christ? Or is it rather that, because we are in him, we share his faith? The former interpretation, which understands the phrase πίστις Χριστοῦ as an objective genitive, throws all the emphasis on the believer's faith. The second interpretation throws the emphasis on the role of Christ: it is his obedience and trust in God which are crucial, though of course the response of the believer is necessary; the faith which leads to righteousness is a shared faith. Now it may well be objected that we cannot share in what Christ *is* until we enter him, and that we enter him by believing in him, so that our faith must come first. But there is an interesting parallel in Rom. 5.19, where we are told that just as through the disobedience of one man, many were made sinners, so through the obedience of one man, many are made righteous. What we are is established by the work of Christ and, in fact, there is no reference to the faith of the believer, either in Rom. 5.19 or in the parallel in verse 18.[25] Yet just as the many share in Adam's transgression and condemnation, so they now share in Christ's righteousness and acquittal; his obedience is sufficient to establish them all as righteous. But how do they claim this righteousness as their own? If men and women share in Adam's disobedience – and so in his condemnation – do they not also share in Christ's obedience?

In Paul's view, Christians owe everything to the fact that they are in Christ: they are nothing and they have nothing, except by virtue of being in him. Christian faith is always the response to what God has done in Christ and to what Christ is. It seems, then, that they need the faithfulness of Christ, for how are they to have even faith, except by sharing in his? We have remarked several times that logic suggests that the phrase πίστις Χριστοῦ must refer to Christ's own faith, but it seems now that logic *demands* this interpretation. For obviously Christ *is*

---

[25] Nor, of course is there any reference here to the faith of Christ, a fact which C. H. Cosgrove regards as decisive evidence against the 'subjective' interpretation, since 'in the one context where the apostle does focus specifically on Jesus' death as righteousness-producing obedience, he speaks of Jesus' *hypakoē*, not his *pistis*' ('Justification in Paul: a linguistic and theological reflection', *JBL*, 106 (1987), 665, n. 32). But the use of ὑπακοή here is explained by the context, which demands a reference to obedience, in contrast to Adam's disobedience.

faithful: as Son of God, he expresses what God is and shares in the attributes of God; therefore he assuredly shares the πίστις Θεοῦ. But as Son of God he also expresses what man should be, and certainly as examplar of restored mankind he must be faithful. And mankind's faithfulness must depend on his, for how else can one have faith at all?

Paul presents redemption in Christ as a radical restructuring of human nature: it is in effect a new creation (2 Cor. 5.17). Christ became what we are in order that we might become what he is. Throughout this investigation, we have made reference from time to time to the notion of interchange: in the past, we have found this a helpful way of understanding several aspects of Paul's theology,[26] and it is therefore worth asking whether this idea of interchange can help us here.

Now at first sight, the answer is 'no'! 'Interchange' requires the exchange of opposites. What Christ became is almost always expressed in negative terms: he was made sin, became a curse, became poor, was born under the Law; what believers become is expressed in opposite, positive terms. The statement that Christ was faithful/had faith, on the other hand, is certainly positive: it does not belong to the kenotic side of the equation. But here we must remember that 'interchange' is never a matter of straightforward exchange: it is not that Christ and the believer change places, but rather that Christ shares in the human condition in order that we may share in what he is. Christians become, not what he *was*, but what he *is*: it is a matter of participation in Christ. However paradoxical it may seem, Christ does not cease to be righteous in being made sin, nor Son of God when born under the Law. We therefore expect him to display the characteristics of righteousness and sonship in his earthly life: we must expect him to be both faithful and obedient. And indeed, it is because of his obedience that the many will be made righteous (Rom. 5.19). Since faith and obedience are so closely related,[27] should we not expect to discover, also, that it is because of his faithfulness that many are made righteous? If πίστις Χριστοῦ means the faith/faithfulness of Christ, that is precisely what we *do* find.

But even when we put the notion of interchange in terms of Christ sharing our human condition in order that we might share what he *is*, we have not explored the paradox fully. For we discover that 'sharing what he *is*' involves 'sharing in what he *became*'. Participation in Christ

---

[26] See above, chs. 1, 2, 3 and 4.
[27] R. Bultmann, *Theology of the New Testament* (ET, London, 1952), vol. 1, p. 314; 'Paul understands faith primarily as obedience.'

is demanded at every stage: he is the true Adam, who lives our human life as it is meant to be lived. It is not a case of 'Christ died on our behalf; therefore we live', but of 'Christ died and we have died with him; he lives, and therefore we live'. It is no surprise, then, that all our passages contain a reference to the earthly Jesus. Christians must expect, not simply to die with Christ, but to *suffer* with him (Rom. 8.17; 2 Cor. 1.5; 4.10f; Col. 1.24); Paul appeals to his converts to follow the example of Christ: in becoming poor for the sake of others (2 Cor. 8.9, cf. 6.10); in considering others, and accepting them (Rom. 15.1–7), in being obedient to God's commands (Phil. 2.8, 12). As always, these appeals are based on the assumption that Christians live in Christ: it is thus a question of sharing in what Christ is, not a question of imitation. It seems logical to suggest that faith should be seen as a sharing in the faith of Christ, who trusted in the one who was able to give life to the dead. It is hardly surprising, then, that πίστις Χριστοῦ is the ground of the Christian's existence. If the only way in which Christians can be obedient is by sharing in the obedience of Christ, must we not conclude that the only way in which they can believe is by sharing in his faith?[28]

If so, then it is no accident that all the πίστις Χριστοῦ passages refer also to the faith of the believer; they echo the statement Paul makes in Rom. 1.17 that the righteousness of God is revealed from faith to faith. Believing faith depends on the faith/faithfulness of Christ: it is the response to Christ's faith, and claims it as one's own.

Nor is it an accident that all the examples of this phrase occur in passages which are concerned to contrast the righteousness based on the Law with that based on faith. It is precisely this contrast which necessitates an emphasis on the work of Christ, for the alternative to the works of the Law is faith *in Christ*: in other words, the context requires a reference to *what Christ has done*. The believer's status of righteousness depends not on obedience to the Law, but on Christ's obedience to death, and on the fact that the believer is in Christ; that status depends on faith – a faith which one has only because one is in

[28] A further interesting parallel to this notion of sharing in what Christ is may perhaps be seen in the use of the word ὑπομονή. In 2 Thess. 3.5, we find a reference to the 'steadfastness of Christ'; Paul's prayer for the Thessalonians suggests that this steadfastness is to be imparted to them. In Rom. 15.4, the steadfastness which the Romans are to display derives from God, and their lives are to be lived κατὰ Χριστόν. The reference to ὑπομονή and the encouragement of the scriptures in v.4 appears to refer back to the example of Christ himself (v.3), which was in accordance with the scriptures; cf. O. Michel, *Der Brief an die Römer*, 3rd edn (Göttingen, 1966), *in loc.* Finally, in 2 Cor. 1.6, Paul speaks about the steadfastness with which the Corinthians endure sufferings – the sufferings which he has just explained (vv. 5–6) are the sufferings of Christ himself.

Christ. The contrast is between the righteousness promised by the Law and the righteousness given in Christ, on the basis of his saving death.

It is no accident, finally, that all the passages are concerned with the death of Christ, and speak about life in Christ. The believer's status of righteousness, as Rom. 5 reminds us, depends on the grace and the free gift of God; but it also depends on the act of righteousness and obedience of Christ. It is the faith/faithfulness of Christ which lead to the Cross; and it is by *their* faith that believers share his death and risen life.

In an early contribution to this debate in the 1950s, Professor Torrance described the phrase as a 'polarized expression' which referred both to Christ's faith and that of the believer, but argued that the emphasis was on *Christ's* faith;[29] Professor Moule, though agreeing that it *might* refer to Christ's faith, insisted that the emphasis was on the faith of the believer.[30] In the past thirty years, arguments on either side have tended to harden, but recently Sam K. Williams has argued once again that the phrase must include both meanings.[31] He suggests that the phrase should be translated as 'Christ-faith', to make plain that 'the faith of Christ' does not refer exclusively to Christ's own faith, but includes that of the believer. I am intrigued to find that the equivalent German term – *Christusglauben* – was used at the beginning of this century by Adolf Deissmann in his study of Paul, though his translators abandoned hope of finding an acceptable English translation.[32] Deissmann gave up attempts to classify the phrase as a 'subjective' or 'objective genitive', and described it as 'the "genitive of fellowship" or the "mystical genitive", because it indicates mystical fellowship with Christ'. However out of fashion Deissmann's views may be today, he has certainly put his finger on the crucial point. Our study has driven us to the conclusion that the phrase πίστις Χριστοῦ must contain *some* reference to the faith of Christ himself. I suggest that we should think of it not as a polarized expression, which suggests antithesis, but as a *concentric* expression, which begins, always, from the faith of Christ

[29] 'One aspect of the biblical conception of faith', *Exp. Tim.* 68 (1957), 111–4; see also 221f. The issue had been raised two years earlier in an article by A. G. Hebert entitled '"Faithfulness" and "Faith"', *Theology*, 58 (1955), 373–9, to which Torrance several times refers. Because Hebert correlated the difference between these two interpretations of πίστις with a distinction between 'Hebrew' and 'Greek' meanings, he opened himself to a devastating attack on his linguistic approach by Barr, *Biblical Language* pp. 161–205, an attack which stifled discussion of the theological issues for several years. [30] Moule, 'Conception of "Faith"'.

[31] Sam K. Williams, 'Again Pistis Christou', *CBQ*, 49 (1987), 431–47.

[32] Adolf Deissman, *Paulus*, 2nd edn (Tübingen, 1925), p. 127; *Paul*, 2nd edn (London, 1926), p. 163.

himself, but which includes, necessarily, the answering faith of believers, who claim that faith as their own. Moreover, while exegetes have tended to interpret Paul's statements about faith in individualistic terms, Paul was much more likely to have been thinking primarily of the corporate response of the people of God – of the new community of those who are in Christ, who believe in him and trust in what he is.

I suggested earlier that opposition to the idea that πίστις Χριστοῦ refers to the faith of Christ was due at least in part to theological presuppositions. If our conclusions are right, we would expect them to have important theological implications. Such is indeed the case. Firstly, the contrast between the righteousness based on Law and that which is based on faith is far more fundamental than it has often appeared when faith is understood simply as the response of the believer. Faith is certainly not to be understood as a form of human works! Faith derives, *not* from the believer, but from the fact that he or she is already in Christ and identified with him. Those who exchange life under the Law for life in Christ exchange the righteousness which comes from the Law for the righteousness which belongs to those who are in Christ. The true antithesis is not between works and faith, but between the works of the *Law* and the saving work of *Christ*.

This means, secondly, that our interpretation is very much in accord with those interpretations of Paul's theology which stress the importance of participation in Christ. Justification is a matter of participation; so, too, is believing. The Christian moves from the sphere of Adam to the sphere of Christ by accepting all that Christ has done and by becoming one with him: even the believer's initial response – his faith – is a sharing in the obedient, faithful response of Christ himself. This interpretation in no way plays down the importance of the believer's faith; what it does do is to stress the role of Christ.

A third implication is that there is perhaps a greater unity between justification and sanctification than has often been supposed. If believers are baptized into the faith of Christ himself – the faith he displayed in his earthly life – then it is hardly surprising if some of the gifts of the Spirit – patience, self-control, πίστις itself – remind us of his attitudes; after all, life in the Spirit is another way of talking about conformity to Christ. Indeed, as Gal. 3 and 4 remind us, the Spirit is given to those who have justifying faith, and this Spirit is the Spirit of God's Son. Those who share Christ's faith share already in his righteousness; sanctification is indeed a matter of becoming what one is. Christian life is a matter of conformity to Christ from beginning to end, a sharing in what he is: this is the whole matter of justifying faith and sanctifying obedience.

In conclusion, I point to one last passage. In Gal. 4.19, when Paul makes a final appeal to the Galatians to rely on faith alone, he declares that he is in travail with them until Christ is formed in them. What does it mean for Christ to be formed in them? It means that they abandon the works of the Law and rely on faith. But if believing is seen as a matter of Christ being formed in them, then faith itself is understood in terms of conformity to Christ. Here, surely, is confirmation that Paul understands the whole of Christian existence, from the very first response of faith, in terms of participation in Christ: to believe is to share in the faith of Christ himself.

INDEX OF BIBLICAL
AND OTHER REFERENCES

Old Testament

Index

Romans (*cont.*)

		9.3	9, 54
6.3	43	9.4	4, 158
6.4	43–5	10.2	126
6.5	43, 45	10.5ff.	149
6.6	23	10.9	35, 99
6.6–7	44	11	56, 146
6.8	43, 45	11.20	168
6.9	44	11.25–6	3
6.10	44–5	11.27	158
6.10–18	60	12	54–7
6.11	44	12.2	57
6.13	44, 57	12.3–8	58
6.14	44	13.1–7	58
6.16	57	13.4	58
6.19	57	13.5	58
7	19, 23, 39	13.8–10	58, 156
7.1–6	61	13.9	66
7.4	23	13.14	58
7.7	116	14.1–3	58
8	5, 18–19, 31–3,	14.1–23	66
	39, 45, 57–60,	14.5	58
	62–3, 84, 130,	14.5–9	58
	136, 168	14.9	99
8.1	32, 45–6	14.10	58
8.2–3	5	14.10–12	157
8.3	3, 19, 22, 27,	14.12	58
	42, 59, 136	14.13–21	8, 58
8.3ff.	59	14.13–23	66
8.3–4	17, 149	15	8
8.4	60–1	15.1–3	58, 67
8.11	39	15.1–7	91, 183
8.14	42	15.3	9, 183
8.14–15	19	15.4	183
8.14–17	129	15.7–9	67
8.17	33, 36, 45, 51,	15.7–12	58
	183	15.8ff.	61
8.18	23		
8.18–22	129	I Corinthians	
8.20	5, 80	1	37
8.23	129	1–2	104, 108
8.23–5	129	1–3	110, 126
8.29	74	1.12	108
8.29–30	57, 82, 129	1.17	98, 108–9
8.31–9	129	1.18	103
8.32	41	1.18ff.	15
8.33	41	1.18–19	109
8.34	41, 99	1.18–25	64
8.38	116	1.19	108
9–11	3	1.22–31	64

190

Index

INDEX OF AUTHORS